T0248258

TRACING FLORIDA JOURNEYS

UNIVERSITY PRESS OF FLORIDA

Florida A&M University, Tallahassee
Florida Atlantic University, Boca Raton
Florida Gulf Coast University, Ft. Myers
Florida International University, Miami
Florida State University, Tallahassee
New College of Florida, Sarasota
University of Central Florida, Orlando
University of Florida, Gainesville
University of North Florida, Jacksonville
University of South Florida, Tampa
University of West Florida, Pensacola

Tracing Florida Journeys

Explorers, Travelers, and Landscapes Then and Now

Leslie Kemp Poole

Photographs by Bruce Hunt

UNIVERSITY PRESS OF FLORIDA

Gainesville/Tallahassee/Tampa/Boca Raton
Pensacola/Orlando/Miami/Jacksonville/Ft. Myers/Sarasota

Funding for this publication was provided through a grant from Florida Humanities with funds from the National Endowment for the Humanities. Any views, findings, conclusions or recommendations expressed in this publication do not necessarily represent those of Florida Humanities or the National Endowment for the Humanities. As the non-profit, state affiliate of the National Endowment for the Humanities, Florida Humanities supports programs and resources that explore the history and culture of Florida and encourage a lifelong appreciation of literature, literacy, and learning.

Library of Congress Cataloging-in-Publication Data
Names: Poole, Leslie Kemp, author.
Title: Tracing Florida journeys : explorers, travelers, and landscapes then
    and now / Leslie Kemp Poole ; photographs by Bruce Hunt.
Other titles: Explorers, travelers, and landscapes then and now
Description: Gainesville : University Press of Florida, [2024] | Includes
    bibliographical references and index.
Identifiers: LCCN 2023037632 (print) | LCCN 2023037633 (ebook) | ISBN
    9780813080475 (paperback) | ISBN 9780813073248 (ebook)
Subjects: LCSH: Florida—Description and travel. | Explorers—Florida. |
    Landscapes—Florida. | Florida—History. | BISAC: HISTORY / United
    States / State & Local / South (AL, AR, FL, GA, KY, LA, MS, NC, SC, TN,
    VA, WV) | NATURE / Regional
Classification: LCC F311 .P66 2024 (print) | LCC F311 (ebook) | DDC
    975.9—dc23/eng/20230907
LC record available at https://lccn.loc.gov/2023037632
LC ebook record available at https://lccn.loc.gov/2023037633

The University Press of Florida is the scholarly publishing agency for the State University System of Florida, comprising Florida A&M University, Florida Atlantic University, Florida Gulf Coast University, Florida International University, Florida State University, New College of Florida, University of Central Florida, University of Florida, University of North Florida, University of South Florida, and University of West Florida.

University Press of Florida
2046 NE Waldo Road
Suite 2100
Gainesville, FL 32609
http://upress.ufl.edu

To my sons, Blake and Preston, who have listened to the stories and followed many of these trails with me. May your lives be full of adventure.

I am now in the hot gardens of the sun, where the palm meets the pine, longed and prayed for and often visited in dreams, and, though lonely to-night amid this multitude of strangers, strange plants, strange winds blowing gently, whispering, cooing, in a language I never learned, and strange birds also, everything solid or spiritual full of influences that I never before felt, yet I thank the Lord with all my heart for this goodness in granting me admission to this magnificent realm.

John Muir
A Thousand-Mile Walk to the Gulf

It is not to be denied that full half of the tourists and travellers that come to Florida return intensely disappointed, and even disgusted. Why? Evidently because Florida, like a piece of embroidery, has two sides to it,—one side all tag-rag and thrums, without order or position; and the other side showing flowers and arabesques and brilliant coloring. Both these sides exist.

Harriet Beecher Stowe
Palmetto Leaves

Contents

Introduction

Travelers in Time and Place

As the dark waters of the St. Johns River slowly flow by, I scan closely for a rise of sandy ground, cloaked by a dense growth of palms and moss-draped trees. It is a subtle spot, located on a wide stretch of water across from Lake Dexter, an expansion of a river called Welaka—river of lakes—by the Seminole people.

This small point of land, perhaps 6 or 7 feet above a wave-lapped shore, has witnessed much of Florida's history, from Indigenous people in dugout canoes to early European explorers in small skiffs to modern travelers in crafts propelled by outboard motors. On this overcast spring morning, the river rippling with a chilly breeze, it is easy to slip into a reverie about how visitors during past centuries viewed this place, their spirits still hovering much like the osprey that is circling overhead in search of fish.

A few miles to the south, the area's Indigenous inhabitants erected at least three totems, perhaps to denote territory where they lived, fished, and hunted along the river's shores for thousands of years. The wooden carvings may have mystical or religious meanings—nobody is sure. One depicted a pelican, another an owl, and a third was an otter. The only totems discovered outside the Pacific Northwest, they inspire imagination, debate, and conjecture about these early people and Florida's original landscape. Perhaps many more totems are buried in the muck of the river's bottom, waiting to be found and their secrets unlocked.

William Bartram, traveling on the river in 1774 in search of botanical specimens, fished and camped alone at this site, noted on modern maps as Idlewilde Point. He was happy to find dry land to set up his tent and start a cookfire. His ensuing experiences, however, led him to call the waters here "Battle Lagoon" for the aggressive alligator activity he witnessed, likely sparked by plenteous fish and reptilian appetites. No alligators are visible today, but I know they are submerged in the tea-colored waters. A clearing with ashes is an echo of Bartram's presence.

Six decades later, John James Audubon likely picnicked here on a bright spring day, the air intoxicatingly fragrant with orange blossoms. He no doubt lifted a few glasses of wine, provided by his host, a local plantation owner who announced the site would forever be known as "Audubon's Isle," although that name didn't survive. Audubon saw plenty of alligators and shot a few birds for his collections during his day trip, probably not realizing that he was on Bartram's trail.

Harriet Beecher Stowe twice passed this low promontory during a round-trip excursion aboard the steamship *Darlington* between Palatka and Enterprise on Lake Monroe. From the deck of the boat, tourists could "penetrate into the mysteries and wonders of unbroken tropical forests," she recalled in 1873. Stowe also saw alligators but was more alarmed by male tourists who shot at the animals for sport and then watched in amusement their "dying agonies." Her words signaled a rising consciousness of the value of Florida's wild animals and of their potential decline. And her concern had merit: less than a century later the reptiles were hunted to the brink of extinction while their habitats were drained for agriculture and development.

By the time writer Marjorie Kinnan Rawlings and her friend Dessie Smith motored by in 1931, much had changed. Loggers had removed enormous virgin cypress that once dotted the river's shoreline, sending them off to profitable sawmills. Residents had built some nearby homes and cabins. Still, today it is easy to imagine the women's wooden johnboat putt-putt-putting by as they aimed northward toward home. Rawlings had read Bartram's account and shared his affinity for Florida's beauty; perhaps her soul felt his essence here along with the "silent pulsing" of life she often felt in the heart of nature.

Whatever these travelers' impressions and experiences, this lone shore silently holds its memories of them, a cosmic crossroads of Florida's history. That it still exists, undeveloped, is a bit of a miracle in today's state and a gift to those who reach it.

As are the tales told by this book's many travelers, who rarely found the Florida they expected.

They are a varied lot—from Spanish conquistadores in search of glory and gold to botanists marveling at uncatalogued species to writers seeking inspiration. Snippets of views from West Florida offer insight into that long expanse and its changing political history. Accounts of an expedition into the Everglades show the hardships of ill-prepared outings. Author Zora

Idlewilde Point on the St. Johns River is a beautiful spot likely viewed by four of this book's subjects: William Bartram, who fended off aggressive alligators; John James Audubon, who picnicked with a friend; Harriet Beecher Stowe enjoying a steamboat ride to see Florida's natural beauty; and Marjorie Kinnan Rawlings, who motored by while exploring the river and its people. Courtesy of Bruce Hunt.

Neale Hurston's folktale-collecting trips to lumber and turpentine operations reveal a world of bone-wearying labor leavened by uproarious stories and parties.

This volume offers their accounts chronologically and then retraces their footsteps to see what remains. Although Florida drew many renowned people—from nineteenth-century writer Ralph Waldo Emerson seeking a cure for his tuberculosis in St. Augustine to Hollywood stars basking on the sands of Miami Beach to Ernest Hemingway fishing and writing in Key West—the focus here is on visitors who took long excursions through different parts of the peninsula and then chronicled them in journals, letters, or books. Each chapter represents a different historical aspect of the state, allowing a glimpse into Florida's vibrant past. The travelers' words reflect a changing landscape and shifting attitudes from the 1500s to the twentieth century, with the state's paradisical nature feared, appreciated, and then exploited to an alarming degree. Some accounts offer valuable glimpses of early Indigenous cultures that were on the land ahead of these travelers, dispelling notions that they were discovering a "New World." It was new only to the Europeans, whose colonialism, settlement, and development led to the diminishment or demise of many of Florida's original inhabitants.

Through these trekkers' lenses, tinted by their backgrounds, society, and encounters, Florida's history comes alive, not as the prettied-up versions found too often in old textbooks and promotional materials, but as real-life dramas revealing what early visitors saw and felt while moving through different areas of La Florida—the "land of flowers," as the Spanish explorer Juan Ponce de León named it in 1513. It was Easter season, known in Spanish as Pascua Florida—the Feast of Flowers. Whether Ponce saw the state's riotous wildflowers is doubtful given his travels along sandy coasts, but the name stuck, creating an illusion that lingers today despite disappearing natural areas.

Reading these writers and retracing their paths in the modern world offers important insights into the many changes in the peninsula's terrain and society. While many share an Edenic vision of nature, their reputations merit reevaluation in light of contemporary attitudes about racism. De Soto willingly enslaved and killed many Natives, leaving tragedy in his aftermath. Dickinson, Bartram, and Audubon, three elite White men, enslaved people of African descent. During his lifetime, Muir made some derogatory observations of Blacks and Natives, and Rawlings used offensive, condescending terms for some Black members of her community while praising others and befriending Hurston, an esteemed African American author. Their words are complicated and dismaying and should be read in consideration of the culture of their eras, which accepted actions, views, and language abhorred today.

Treasure instead their written recollections of the Florida landscape. Audubon's travels and travails to find birds offer insight into the lives of everyday people. Hurston saw nature in each of her journeys and observed how it shaped the people she encountered—and in turn how they changed the land. And, after visiting Florida and luxuriating in its palm trees and tropical birds, Muir proposed a new way of looking at the human place in the world—a belief that all of God's creations had value. Even the alligators that Bartram feared.

Open this book with eyes wide open. These famous travelers have much to teach us, and we have much to learn about lovely, complex Florida and how it has transformed in the past five hundred years. Find inspiration in these chapters, close this book, and plan your next trip. You don't have to journey all the way across the state or sail down a river to find adventure—although, happily, that still is a possibility. Perhaps you will find yourself on the same spot that beheld Bartram, Audubon, Stowe, and Rawlings. Breathe it all in and imagine.

1

Hernando de Soto

Travels and Travails in Search of Treasure, 1539–1540

Despite the heat and oppressive humidity, Hernando de Soto must have felt a chill of excitement at the sight before him—the great Bahia Honda (deep bay) on the west coast of La Florida, the starting point for what he anticipated would be a glorious path to fame and fortune. More than 600 others and perhaps as many as 725 people—a mix of Spanish clergy, tradespeople, and some slaves—were part of the 1539 expedition into the interior of the peninsula and northward into unknown territory. They had sailed from Cuba a week earlier; many had invested their own funds into the journey and were now eagerly awaiting the beckoning shore, hoping that the journey might yield the riches previously claimed by Spanish conquests in Mexico and South America.

None could foresee what lay ahead: a lack of food, deep rivers, mucky swamps, vast pine forests, cunning Natives, and, most disappointingly, no precious metals or gemstones. Instead, the expedition spent a miserable ten months in Florida seizing the crops of Indigenous people before heading northward. They took a meandering path during the course of three years into what is now Georgia, South Carolina, North Carolina, Tennessee, Alabama, Mississippi, Louisiana, Texas, and Arkansas before de Soto died near the banks of the Mississippi River and the remaining crew built boats to traverse the Gulf of Mexico, reaching Mexico in 1543.

In the eyes of his Spanish peers, de Soto's Florida venture was a failure. But to today's historians, information gleaned from the expedition is priceless. Four accounts of the trip—three by actual members of the de Soto party—provide detailed descriptions of the landscape and Natives they encountered. Modern readers abhor the violence and brutality of his expedition, which helped unleash European diseases that decimated Indigenous populations. But in an ironic twist, de Soto has become a mythical figure

Hernando de Soto had participated in several Spanish conquests in the Americas before leading the 1539 expedition to Florida in hopes of glory and riches. Courtesy of the State Archives of Florida.

in local popular culture as part of a gallant saga, his travels celebrated with annual fetes.

All agree, however, that Florida would never be the same in his wake.

"It's a story of hardship. But it is also the story of an invasion. A well-supplied invasion," said Jerald T. Milanich, who studies de Soto and Florida's Indigenous people. "But they had no idea where they were going. When they got to Arkansas, they spent a year looking for the wealth they sought. On the one side, they were horrible, bloodthirsty people. On the other side, they were heroic. Can you imagine doing what they did to survive?"[1]

De Soto was not the first Spaniard to visit Florida. Juan Ponce de León led the first force to the peninsula in 1513, arriving on the eastern Atlantic coast during the celebration of Pascua Florida—the Feast of Flowers—which led to the moniker La Florida. Ponce had been granted a charter by the king of Spain to explore the area and make claims, a lure and promise offered to subsequent explorers. From there Ponce and company headed south to Miami, around the Florida Keys into the Gulf of Mexico, and then northward to the main town of the Calusa Indians on Mound Key near Fort Myers Beach. Ponce's voyage was the first documented Spanish encounter with Indigenous people, and it may have ultimately proved fatal for him: during a second trip in 1521 to establish a settlement, the Florida Natives chased the Spanish away and Ponce suffered an arrow wound from which he later died in Cuba. Despite the claims of several modern tourist traps,

Ponce visited Florida for personal gain—not to find the mythical Fountain of Youth. He never went far enough inland to see the bubbling springs about which this fantasy has since been created.[2]

Natives aggressively defending their territory were not enough to stop Spanish explorers eager for riches, land, and glory. The Spanish colonial mentality in the Americas had little use for Indigenous peoples, beyond exploiting them for labor and taking their food stores. When the Natives became hostile, force and intimidation through slavery, weaponry, and attack dogs were readily used. Several previous expeditions had traveled the Florida coasts, yielding early maps of the peninsula and its harbors, as well as tales of conflicts with Natives. Although no one had found the longed-for riches, myths of treasure persisted, and that was enough to fuel the desire for conquest.

De Soto's dreams took precedence over the cold, hard facts gleaned from prior trips. A four-hundred-man trip led by Pánfilo de Narváez that began near Tampa in 1528 ended with disaster when the group made it north, probably to the St. Marks River, and opted to build boats to travel by water to Mexico. Only four survivors who made their way west along the Gulf of Mexico shore for eight years reached that destination. One of the lucky four, Álvar Núñez Cabeza de Vaca, spun tales in the Spanish court later that year that didn't truly convey his experiences. "He gave them to understand that it was the richest land in the world," wrote the Gentleman of Elvas, a de Soto expedition member who used that name when he wrote a firsthand account of it in 1557. After making these claims, Cabeza de Vaca declined to return to the area with an inspired de Soto; Elvas said it was because de Soto wouldn't give Cabeza de Vaca money for a ship, and Cabeza de Vaca apparently had his own plans for future land claims. When approached by relatives about whether going with de Soto was prudent, Cabeza de Vaca "advised them to sell their estates and go with him, for in so doing they would act wisely." Others also took the gamble.[3]

"But, as in all great undertakings, the men, we are told, longed for the hour of departure and thought they would never get to the fabulously rich land of Florida," wrote James Alexander Robertson in a 1933 translation of the Gentleman of Elvas's account. "Lured on by their love of adventure and the hope of achieving great wealth, they expected to find another Mexico or another Peru and their imaginations ran riot with the glories they were to achieve. . . . Never were men more grievously fooled."[4]

Banking on hopes and his prior successes in the New World, which included wealth from brutal campaigns in Panama, Nicaragua, and Peru, de

Soto assembled his force. He was described by expedition chronicler Garcilaso de la Vega as "of more than medium stature, of good presence, and appeared well both on foot and on horseback. His face was animated and of dark complexion." However, de Soto was "severe in punishing military derelictions; the rest he pardoned readily," and he "honored greatly the soldiers who were virtuous and brave." De Soto had demonstrated his own bravery in more than one battle, and his aura of success and confidence encouraged those headed to La Florida.[5]

De Soto's crown charter, granted in 1537, gave him the titles of governor of Cuba and *adelantado* of Florida. It required him to "conquer, pacify, and settle 200 leagues" of the Florida coast during an eighteen-month sojourn, write historians Jerald T. Milanich and Charles Hudson. The charter also demanded that de Soto finance the building of as many as three forts in coastal harbors for protection and "pacification" of the area. His reward for success would be receipt of "titles, lands, and a share of the colony's profits"; he had his choice of land totaling about 54,000 square miles. De Soto also was required to take along Catholic priests to convert the Natives.[6]

All Spanish expeditions were under orders to convert Natives to Catholicism, and clergy were to report any violations of Indigenous rights. In addition, expeditions had to read a *requerimiento* statement to Natives announcing that Spain now controlled their lands and they should "pledge allegiance to the crown" and be converted. Although it was to be read up to three times, with any necessary interpreters, it was unlikely that Natives could grasp the ideology and demands placed on them. And those who didn't bend to the Spanish will could be forced into slavery and find themselves at war, as Florida Natives quickly discovered. This was no anthropological study—this was brute force justified by colonial attitudes that many abhor in today's world.[7]

It must have been quite a scene May 30, when the expedition anchored and began to unload its nine ships in what likely is today's southeastern Tampa Bay. The humans were a varied group: soldiers, noblemen (and their servants), as well as tradesmen such as tailors and farriers, at least two women, and a dozen priests. They wore bright, colorful clothing with short breeches and stockings that were fashionable for court but ill-suited for a Florida trek. They wore armor suited to their roles: a horseback soldier might wear thirty-pound chain mail while carrying a lance and leather-covered shield, whereas foot soldiers had lighter garb.[8]

It was a difficult landing in an unwelcoming environment. For the most part, the bay was lined with dense mangrove trees with jumbles of

This shore on southeastern Tampa Bay is the likely landing site for Hernando de Soto's massive party, which included soldiers, horses, craftsmen, and pigs. Author photo.

aboveground roots in muddy areas that were great obstacles to the men and horses. The crew probably found a small, sandy beach to unload, a process that took two to three days and included winching more than two hundred horses onto the ship decks and swimming them ashore. Barrels, casks, baskets, and earthenware containers with food, clothing, and supplies also were unloaded. "To native people who observed the Spaniards unloading their ships and boats, it must have been an amazing spectacle," notes Hudson.[9]

A scouting group encountered six Natives who fought the intruders by shooting arrows. The Spanish killed two, and the others escaped through land "obstructed by woods and swamps" that caused the voyage-weakened horses to be mired, falling with their riders.[10]

Welcome to Florida.

The next night, the scouts discovered an abandoned town—the Natives left when they espied the Spaniards—and saw smoke from fires used as warning signals along the coast. Three squadrons headed out the following day, marching around bayfront mudflats and eventually arriving at the town of Ucita on June 1. The Gentleman of Elvas wrote that the town had seven or eight houses made of wood and palm leaves. In addition, "the chief's house stood near the beach on a very high hill which had been artificially built as a fortress. At the other side of the town was the temple and on top of it a wooden bird with its eyes gilded. Some pearls, spoiled by fire and of little value, were found there. The Indians bore them through in order to string them for beads, which are worn around the neck or arm, and they esteem them greatly."[11]

De Soto and some of his leaders took over a few houses, where they stored ship provisions and set up their base camp. The temple and other houses were burned. Since there was a "vast and lofty forest" around the area, de Soto ordered that it be cut "for the space of a crossbow shot about the town, in order that the horses might run and the Christians have the advantage of the Indians if the latter should by chance try to attack them by night." This Florida wilderness did not inspire wonder and awe—it was a fearsome place of daunting swamps and unnamed rivers that would have to be crossed. Nature was a hazard and an obstacle.[12]

Of immediate importance was capturing Indigenous people to be interpreters. The soldiers, some armed with swords and shields, others with guns and crossbows, traveled through dense swamps to a river where they spotted Natives escaping into the water. The Spanish managed to capture four women and battled with twenty warriors before retreating. The Gentleman of Elvas admired the Natives as being "so skillful with their weapons. Those people are so warlike and so quick that they make no account of foot soldiers; for if these go for them, they flee, and when their adversaries turn their backs, they are immediately on them. . . . They are never quiet but always running and crossing from one side to the other." A Native man could shoot three or four arrows before a crossbowman could fire, and "very seldom does he miss what he shoots at." Some of the arrows were strong enough to pierce a shield, and the arrow points were made of sharpened fish bone or stone. Cane arrows could split and travel through links in Spanish chain mail, causing injury. Importantly, the Natives made it clear that the Spanish had opposition.[13]

About the same time, another group of scouts made an incredibly valuable discovery: a Spaniard from an earlier expedition who had lived among the Natives for twelve years and could serve as a translator.

The tale of Juan Ortiz is almost mythic. He had been part of a search party sent to look for the ill-fated Narváez expedition and had been taken prisoner. De Soto's forces didn't recognize him as a Spaniard—he was naked, sunburned, and tattooed in the Indigenous style. But when they set up to charge Ortiz with their horses, he cried out, "Sirs, I am a Christian; do not kill me. Do not kill these Indians, for they have given me my life." Ortiz called the Natives out of the woods, and they all entered de Soto's camp at nightfall, where they were "received with the same rejoicing."[14]

Ortiz offered a colorful tale: after being seized, he was led to their chief, Ucita. According to the Gentleman of Elvas:

> Ucita ordered Juan Ortiz to be bound hand and foot on a grill laid on top of four stakes. He ordered a fire to be kindled under him in order to burn him there. The chief's daughter asked him not to kill him, saying that a single Christian could not do him any ill or good, and that it would be more to his honor to hold him captive. Ucita granted this and ordered him to be taken care of; and as soon as he was well, gave him charge of the guarding of the temple, for at night wolves would carry off the corpses from inside it.[15]

Later, Ortiz won Ucita's goodwill and lived peaceably with the group.

An Indian princess saves a man by pleading with her father, the chief. It's an incredible story and one that would be repeated decades later by Jamestown colonist John Smith, who claimed to have been similarly saved by a chief's daughter, Pocahontas. An English translation of the Gentleman of Elvas's account was printed in 1610, a decade before Smith's account. Some scholars speculate that Smith may have invented his version after learning of Ortiz's fate.[16]

Ortiz ended up living with a second group of Natives "with little expectation of seeing Christians." When news came of de Soto's arrival, Ortiz was permitted to join them. De Soto gave Ortiz clothes and grilled him about whether "he had heard of any land where there was gold or silver." Ortiz had not, since he had not traveled far, but said that he had heard of a chief 30 leagues away to whom others paid tribute—perhaps he might have information about the area and land "more fertile and abounding in maize."[17]

Ortiz was invaluable to de Soto—he spoke two Native languages and could translate them into Spanish. He negotiated with Native people as the expedition moved north. "The pleasure that the Christians felt was very great, in that God gave them an interpreter and guide at such a time, of which they had great necessity," wrote Rodrigo Rangel, another expedition member, who served as de Soto's private secretary. Ortiz later would save the expedition from a surprise attack after learning about the plan from a Native, proving his great worth. The ensuing fight resulted in the deaths and enslavement of many Natives. Ortiz, however, never realized his dream of returning home, dying during the expedition in the winter of 1541–42.[18]

After several weeks and multiple reconnaissance missions, de Soto took the bulk of his crew and headed north, using foot trails and setting his sights on a series of villages where they could raid food stocks and secure slaves and hostages. The Spanish needed large stores of food before winter set in, and the bayside Natives didn't cultivate extensive agriculture since the soil was poor and there was an abundance of shellfish, fish, and game. In the meantime, expedition ships returned to Cuba to get additional provisions, and a group of men and horses were left at the port with two years' worth of provisions.[19]

The going was difficult. De Soto had his mounted military entourage but also had to manage hundreds of others on foot, as well as horses, war dogs, pigs (the first in North America), weaponry, and provisions as they traveled through tangled swamps and thick vegetation. They were hungry and tired and traveling armored during the height of summer (interesting that the Gentleman of Elvas doesn't complain about Florida's abundant insect life), averaging about 12 to 17 miles a day, an estimate since the different chroniclers sometimes offered conflicting distances. In late July the company crossed a "river with a swift current," making a footbridge for the humans but losing a horse that drowned while attempting to swim across it. The town, to their dismay, was abandoned with no food. While they awaited Spanish provisions and reinforcements, the travelers "were experiencing great hardship from hunger and bad roads, as the land was very poor in maize, low, and very wet, swampy, and covered with dense forests, and the provisions brought from the port were finished." They were reduced to boiling greens with salt for food or eating young maize (Indian corn) stalks. They must have rejoiced upon reaching the town of Cale, where they took three months' supply of maize from the fields. It was a great find for the Spanish but a hardship for the Natives, who attacked, killing three expedition members.[20]

Two captured Natives told de Soto that abundant agricultural fields could be found farther north in a province called Apalachee. And so the expedition slogged onward, raiding small villages, seizing Natives and maize, and crossing rivers. The Spanish arrival was anticipated by most Indigenous people, who often abandoned or burned their villages or led random attacks on the entourage. Some chiefs offered peace and friendship as well as gifts and guides to protect their people. Others were taken as hostages to ensure the cooperation of their subjects. Natives who attacked or were captured might be publicly executed, enslaved in chains, raped, tortured, maimed, or attacked by de Soto's fearsome dogs. It is horrible to imagine today, but de Soto followed procedures used by many New World conquistadores to subdue Natives and protect soldiers.

Rangel wrote that de Soto "was very given to hunting and killing Indians," dating from his prior experiences in the New World, and these practices extended to his subordinates on the Florida trip. To the Spaniards, the Natives weren't human. In one village incident, a Spanish captain, seemingly furious that the town had been burned, set dogs on his Native interpreter: "The reader must understand that to set the dogs on [an Indian] is to make the dogs eat them or kill them, tearing the Indian to pieces. The conquistadors in the Indies have always used greyhounds or fierce and valiant dogs in war; and this is why hunting Indians was mentioned above. Therefore, that guide was killed in that way, because he lied and guided poorly."[21]

"His method was a copy of the Central American one of seizing leaders so that one could extract food and services and, importantly, guides to the next major chiefdom and (perhaps) gold in the mountains once it was clear they were at hand," according to historian Paul E. Hoffman. "Was he worse than some? No, there were a few sociopaths who killed and tortured for sport, but he did have that on his early record. . . . Hard to say he was better or worse; certainly he belonged to a generation of hard men shaped by the brutality of the early years on Hispaniola and Central America and by the strangeness (and numbers) of the peoples they encountered. There were voices, and not just from friars, that denounced the way the Spaniards treated Natives."[22]

On October 26, the expedition reached Anahica, the main town in Apalachee, where agriculture was abundant; the Gentleman of Elvas reported finding maize, pumpkins, beans, and dried plums "better than those of Spain." Rangel wrote that the province was "very fertile and very abundant in supplies with much corn and beans [*fesoles*] and squash [*calabazas*], and diverse fruits, and many deer and many varieties of birds, and near the sea there are many and good fish, and it is a pleasant land although there are swamps."[23]

But the riches and gold they sought were missing, and neither had much to say about the five months they spent in the area.

Upon learning that the Gulf of Mexico was nearby, de Soto dispatched a scouting party that discovered the site where Narváez and company had built boats in a largely unsuccessful effort to reach Mexico. De Soto also sent a group back to the original Tampa Bay encampment with orders for everyone to head north by land and water to Apalachee; one boat with twenty captive women was sent to Cuba to de Soto's wife, Isabel de Bobadilla, who acted as the island's governor in his absence.[24]

Having secured ample food, the expedition reassembled and spent the winter in Apalachee (today's Tallahassee) in North Florida. De la Vega wrote that the residents at the Spanish camp (including army members and captive servants) may have numbered more than 1,500 people, in addition to "more than three hundred horses." While there, scouting parties roamed along the northwest coast looking for ports, reaching as far west as present-day Pensacola, while others explored the uplands and skirmished with combative Natives. Back at the encampment, the Apalachees fought aggressively against the Spanish intruders, ambushing and killing soldiers and setting fire to buildings.[25]

During the layover, priests may have celebrated the first Christmas in what became the United States, and, importantly, de Soto learned from a captive hailing from "the direction of the sunrise" that there was a woman ruler who collected tribute from neighboring chiefs, "some of whom gave her clothing and others gold in abundance," the Gentleman of Elvas wrote. "He told how it was taken from the mines, melted, and refined, just as if he had seen it done, or else the devil taught him; so that all who knew anything of this said it was impossible to give so good an account of it unless one had seen it; and all when they saw the signs he made believed whatever he said to be true."[26]

It *was* too good to be true, but it was what the Spanish wanted to believe.

On March 3, 1540, de Soto resumed his travels, having ordered his men to pack up food stores for a long trip through "uninhabited land." They could not rely on captured slaves to serve, the Gentleman of Elvas wrote, because most "being naked and in chains, died because of the hard life they suffered during that winter." The Spanish moved north into what is now Georgia (where they missed gold in the north) and continued on a meandering path until May 21, 1542, when de Soto died of a fever on the western bank of the Mississippi River. The men tried to hide de Soto's death from the local Indigenous people and buried him quietly. Concerned that his body might be found, they later disinterred and sank his weighted body into the middle of the river. The local chief was told that de Soto "was not dead but had gone to the sky."[27]

The weary survivors, led by Luis de Moscoso, tried to find an overland route, trekking into Texas before turning back to the river. They spent several months building boats and in July 1543 headed south on the waterway, then west along the coast until 311 of the original party reached safety in Mexico in September. They had been gone more than four years, logging some 3,700 miles with little but misery to show for it.[28]

"The Hernando de Soto expedition was a failure," write Milanich and Hudson. "Its leader and half the participants had died, and not a single one of its chartered goals was accomplished. On the other hand, the expedition did provide Spain with a great deal of information on the interior of La Florida and its people. Had gold or silver been found, no doubt Spanish colonists would have been brought in to establish interior settlements and create overland links to Mexico."[29]

Still, the Spanish would not be deterred in their plans for Florida, valuable because of its proximity to the Gulf Stream—an ocean current used by sailing vessels loaded with agricultural and mineral wealth taken from the Americas to navigate back to Spain. In coming decades, settlements were established in what is now Pensacola and St. Augustine as well as a series of missions and forts to facilitate commerce and conversion through North Florida and along the Georgia coast. The mission system, beset by uprisings and diseases that diminished Native numbers, ended by the early eighteenth century in large part because of attacks by English settlers and their Indigenous allies living north of Florida. The English wanted control of the eastern coastline and were trading in deerskins and enslaved Natives, creating a problem for the Spanish in Florida.[30]

St. Augustine, founded in 1565, became a major holding for the Spanish and today is recognized as the oldest continuous European settlement in the United States. Pedro Menéndez de Avilés founded the city in order to secure the Atlantic coast and drive off other European settlements. It became the capital of Spanish Florida and remained important as the capital of East Florida when the colony was ceded to Great Britain in 1763. Twenty years later, the Spanish once again owned Florida, only to lose it to the United States in 1821.

While the European powers wrangled over control of Florida, its aboriginal population declined, the victims of European diseases, battles, and enslavement. As historian Michael Gannon noted:

The most significant practical result of what may be called that extended armed raid was the damage inflicted on the southeastern native populations. Dozens of chiefdoms, overstressed and humiliated by de Soto, went into decline or collapsed. And in the wake of the *entrada* thousands of native people lay dead and dying, not from the sword but from the introduction of Old World pathogens against which the aborigines had no acquired immunities—smallpox, measles, and typhoid fever, among others. That "microbial invasion" had begun many years before with the first slavers or with the crews of Juan Ponce, but de Soto's men unwittingly reinforced it on their long, doubly tragic death march through the interior of La Florida.[31]

"The descendants of the indigenous Florida native groups—the Uzita, Ocale, Potano, Aguacaleyquen, and others who are described in the narratives of the Hernando de Soto expedition—did not survive," write Milanich and Hudson. "It is ironic that those very colonial powers—England, France, and Spain—that provided the modern world with our only firsthand descriptions of those native peoples, also led to their demise." Into the lands came other Natives, importantly of the Creek tradition, who moved south into Florida to flee colonial conflicts. The survivors of Indigenous groups likely were absorbed into these groups, now recognized as the Seminole and Miccosukee Tribes.[32]

The true riches of the de Soto expedition, then, are the descriptions of the Indigenous cultures that the Spanish encountered, along with accounts that offer tribal and place-names, and a description of Florida's landscape. Much of this is now lost—Native communities were mobile and relocated when necessary, and many perished. And the Spanish accounts aren't thorough or unbiased. Even the site of de Soto's landing is disputed, which makes following his expedition's trail puzzling, frustrating, and tantalizing.

Where exactly did de Soto travel in Florida? Milanich and Hudson's 1993 book, *Hernando de Soto and the Indians of Florida,* is the outcome of a ten-year project to map the De Soto Trail. It is the most definitive work, painstakingly triangulating the expedition's chronicles with ancient texts and correspondence, previous research, data from Native archaeological sites, and geography to determine the probable route. The authors offer their best informed opinion about where the Spanish traveled, admitting that the only definitive site is the winter encampment in today's Tallahassee. As with previous histories that attempted the same feat, they expected to be disputed, adding that "for every author's published ideas about de Soto's route in Florida, there are perhaps a hundred people who expound their own theories in letters."[33]

Identifying De Soto's landing spot has long been a guessing game, pitting different Florida cities against each other for a high-stakes claim on tourism treasure: visitors, publicity, historical markers, and annual celebrations. Some have righteously declared that Charlotte Harbor south of Sarasota was the right spot—Milanich was one of this view's early supporters—whereas others, including Hudson, championed Tampa Bay. After extensive research, Milanich conceded, and "now, like a reformed smoker," he "strongly advocates Tampa Bay as the landing site," they write. "Like religion and politics, Hernando de Soto engenders passion."[34]

Their detailed work determined that the probable landing site was near today's Piney Point on the bay's southeastern shore. It is a lonely site, hardly befitting what once was a grand entrance. Located at the end of a paved road off US 41, the sandy shoreline is located between the busy Manatee Port Authority and tall levees that surround a 77-acre holding pond atop gypsum stacks, the by-products of phosphate mining. This site gained national attention in 2021, when the gypsum reservoir began leaking, threatening to flood the local community. Florida officials declared an emergency, evacuating residents and draining wastewater from the site into the bay, creating instead a possible natural disaster.

On a gusty January day, I stood at the site and looked across the choppy water to the mouth of Tampa Bay, where the expedition likely entered. To the right were the unmistakable skylines of St. Petersburg and Tampa, urban landmarks for today's mariners. The bay reaches 9 feet in depth just offshore, making it a good place to anchor de Soto's large boats before unloading crew and equipment.

A few minutes north of Piney Point is the probable location of Ucita, the village where the Spanish set up their base camp. De Soto stayed here six weeks until he headed north, leaving behind about one hundred soldiers, who regrouped several months later in Apalachee. The Ucita area is now known as Shell Point, although the numerous shell mounds once there are long gone, replaced by a marina and waterfront housing. Back on US 41 are modern-day provisioners that include gas stations, food marts, and even a roadside stand selling fishing poles. There are no historical markers or any mention of de Soto. Certainly, he would be bewildered by the route today, but happy for the wide, paved path. There are no archaeological artifacts to support these two sites, but they best fit the Spanish descriptions. And that is the case with most of the expedition's path.

Twenty miles southwest in the city of Bradenton, the National Park Service (NPS) operates the 25-acre De Soto National Memorial Park to commemorate the landing. Rangers offer a variety of programs, including demonstrations at "Camp Uzita" and an annual event reenacting the Spanish coming onshore. It's a lovely site, where the Manatee River meets the Gulf of Mexico, but even the NPS admits it isn't the actual site, chosen instead to appease feverish boosterism.

As early as 1919, different Tampa Bay communities vied to establish an NPS site in anticipation of the four-hundredth anniversary of the landing in 1939. "To American Indians he is not very popular, and you can understand that," said Milanich. "But in Florida we didn't have Washington sleeping here, but we had de Soto. People wanted to use what they thought of de Soto to push their towns and businesses."[35]

The NPS authorized creation of a de Soto memorial in 1930, but with economic downturns and military conflict it wasn't realized for two decades. In the meantime, Bradenton-area advocates, including the Chamber of Commerce, the Optimist Club, and the Colonial Dames of America, proclaimed the waterfront at Shaw's Point to be the true landing site, securing a land donation there and celebrating in 1939 with a parade and the unveiling of a marker on an Indian shell mound. Write NPS historians David E. Whisnant and Anne Mitchell Whisnant:

> It was a moment of public consensus—at least in Bradenton, if not in Tampa. From the outset, however, the commemorative remarks of the assembled dignitaries foreshadowed the ambivalence with which De Soto would increasingly be viewed in subsequent years. In his speech accepting the monument on behalf of Bradenton, the Florida Historical Society's Herbert Lamson was careful to characterize De Soto positively as "the leader of a splendid force" who had "iron resolve . . . [and] indomitable will." Lamson reassured his audience that "in an age of cruelty," De Soto was "distinguished for his moderation . . . [and] his faith in God." Even if his expedition did in fact end in "disappointment, disaster, and death," Lamson said, "so long as the doings of mankind are recorded, his name will be honored as typifying the best of the many fine qualities of the Spanish Cavalier."[36]

By 1949, land was acquired for the site; the visitor center opened two decades later. And Bradenton claimed de Soto as its reason to party. In 2021, after taking a year off because of COVID-19 concerns, the De Soto Heritage Festival Grand Parade returned to entertain an estimated thousands of people along its route. Marching bands, floats, and community groups, including "pirates," celebrated along the route, tossing beads in a Mardi Gras–like fashion. At a fancy ball, a local man was named the new "Hernando de Soto" and "will spend the next year representing Manatee County across the United States" as well as traveling to Spain.[37]

Farther to the south, the city of Punta Gorda, located on Charlotte Harbor, also claims de Soto. A colorful mural on the exterior of a city restaurant depicts an armored de Soto on horseback, accompanied by a large dog. Another mural shows mounted, armored troops heading into the countryside. According to the Punta Gorda Historic Mural Society's website, the 2008 depictions (which include an image of Ponce de León) are of "conquistadors who founded and colonized the Charlotte Harbor area."[38]

That these claims may be historically inaccurate is of little consequence to boosters as long as they attract tourists. Ask Tampa leaders, who annually celebrate a fictional pirate, José Gaspar, with a "Gasparilla" parade, road race, art show, and an "invasion" of fake pirates by water. There is even a "Children's Gasparilla" so that tykes can dress up as marauders and celebrate. The city's professional football team has bought into the same mirage, naming its team the Tampa Bay Buccaneers and celebrating its 2021 Superbowl victory with a boat parade in the bay's waters.

Whatever mythology has arisen, there was a real de Soto who did, indeed, land on Florida's west coast and camp at Ucita. But the route north from that remains uncertain. He crossed rivers whose banks may have changed, trudged through wetlands that may have been drained, and certainly hit areas of sandhills and thick pine forests. Not everyone went in the same direction. Scouting parties often followed different routes, looking for Native villages and crops. Some of de Soto's party traveled by horse, certainly covering more mileage daily than the foot soldiers.

One area that was probably on the route is the lake-dotted region near today's Floral City in Citrus County on US 41. If so, a lake described in later accounts likely is Lake Tsala Apopka, actually a sprawling chain of lakes fed by the Withlacoochee River. Near the Duval Island boat ramp off Orange Avenue stands an easily overlooked kiosk that declares this to be part of the De Soto Trail and the location of the village of Tocaste described by expedition members. Archaeological evidence collected from a nearby site includes a metal axe head, providing a possible connection to the Spanish.

De Soto was looking in the area for the village of Cale, where natives indicated the Spanish would find gold and silver. To reach it meant negotiating the wetlands now known as the Cove of the Withlacoochee. Cale was on the other side of the 24-mile cove. It was in this area that the Gentleman of Elvas reported the hungry men eating unripe maize and boiling greens. After following a "broad" road, probably near the city of Inverness, the party then arrived at a major obstacle: the Withlacoochee River.[39]

There are a few options for the route, but they probably traveled east

De Soto's expedition may have crossed the Withlacoochee River here, now a boat ramp for modern kayakers. Courtesy of Bruce Hunt.

along what today is Turner Camp Road, a winding paved motorway that ends at a riverfront boat ramp and dock. There is no historical marker there, just a warning sign about alligators and snakes, and a big view of the broad, tannic-brown river. Except for flecks of red from maples, most of the trees were bare on the January day I visited, but it must have been lush when the Spanish crossed in midsummer, having to build a footbridge and swimming horses across by using a tackle after the first horse in the river died. I certainly wouldn't want to swim across it, although I did feel a pang of jealousy watching three truckloads of kayakers busily unload their gear on this glorious day under a cerulean sky.[40]

There is little today in the area that de Soto would recognize. Lakeshore and riverbanks are dotted with houses and trailer homes, and the only visible mounds are elevated septic fields. The river's once-enormous cypress trees were logged out in the early twentieth century; those remaining hardly reach the same size and heights. Visitors can eat at Inverness's quaint downtown restaurants or trek along the nearby 46-mile Withlacoochee State Trail, a popular bike path. But these came centuries later, long after the land became more prized for citrus crops and phosphate mining—the former now fading and the latter gone after World War I.

Although some have mistaken it for today's Ocala, the site of the community of Cale (or Ocale) has never been officially located. However, there is compelling archaeological evidence that de Soto traveled through the Cove of the Withlacoochee area. The Spanish army spent weeks in Ocale on the east side of the river before heading north to Apalachee, so there was plenty of time to interact with the Natives in trade and terror. Experts have found valuable evidence in two Cove-area mounds: the Ruth Smith Mound, located along Turner Camp Road, and Tatham Mound, on a small rise west of the river. At Ruth Smith, collectors (who eventually destroyed the mound) found Native artifacts and European-made glass beads from the early 1500s, possibly traded by the expedition. They also examined gold and silver beads, brass rings that might have come from chain mail, pottery, and a chisel, some of which may have come from subsequent Spanish trips.[41]

At Tatham Mound, discovered in 1984, there was even more evidence, including 153 glass beads, iron rings, and chisels, making it one of the "best-documented collections of de Soto expedition-related artifacts from anywhere on the entire route." Importantly, the mound also contained the remains of Native people who appeared to have been injured, "probably by a sword cut," write Milanich and Hudson, noting that de Soto's troops passed through the area three times. "The injuries to the Natives, whose remains were placed in the mound, may have been a result of battles fought with members of de Soto's army on any of these trips." Burial evidence of seventy people interred in the mound indicates a "probable epidemic" near the same time, showing that European diseases already were taking a toll.[42]

The one thing researchers agree upon is the site where the expedition wintered. That was discovered in 1987 by state archaeologist B. Calvin Jones, who found a treasure trove less than a mile from downtown Tallahassee. The location was a construction dig near the Governor John W. Martin site, named for a governor who built a home there in the 1930s. After getting permission from the developer, Jones pulled out a shovel and conducted a series of excavations, looking for a possible mission site, but instead found definitive remains from the de Soto encampment, including pottery, nails, coins, beads, the tip of a crossbow bolt, and chain-mail links. One artifact—a pig jawbone—initially was thought to be strong evidence of de Soto's presence, but carbon testing later proved it to be from the 1800s, probably from early area settlers.[43]

There is little to see now at the 5-acre state-owned site, located in a shady parking lot of an office building complex just off the broad Apalachee Parkway. A lonely lichen-riddled historical marker and an interpretive kiosk with a yellowed photograph of Jones are all that is left to pronounce its importance. The day I arrived, two women were standing outside a nearby building taking a cigarette break, but I was the sole visitor. I closed my eyes and ignored the nearby roar of traffic to imagine what the hilltop looked like almost five hundred years ago, when de Soto's troops took over the Native village and set up camp—an event Jones once compared to a circus. Blissfully unaware of impending hardship, the entourage spent the winter restless with hope for the certain glory and treasure that lay ahead.

Sites that pertain to Hernando de Soto's expedition that you can visit:

De Soto National Memorial Park
8300 De Soto Memorial Highway
Bradenton, Florida 34209
(941) 792-0458 ext. 105
nps.gov/deso/index.htm

At De Soto National Memorial Park visitors can learn about Hernando de Soto through living history programs (Thursday through Sunday), reenactments, and demonstrations. In addition, the park's indoor visitor center features displays of de Soto–era armor, helmets, and weapons.

The park's nature trail winds along a scenic mangrove shoreline that still looks much as it did when de Soto's expedition explored this region. This is also a prime bird-watching and kayaking location and is easily accessible from Bradenton.

Piney Point
Directions: From the intersection of US 41 and I-275 in Bradenton, travel north on US 41 for 3.5 miles; then turn west on Piney Point Road and drive 0.5 mile to the road's end at Tampa Bay.

De Soto Trail Kiosk, Floral City
Duval Island Boat Ramp
7790 South Duval Island Drive
Floral City, Florida 34436
Directions: From Floral City (7 miles south of Inverness on US 41), travel east on Orange Avenue for 0.8 mile. There is a De Soto Trail information sign at the boat parking lot on the right side of the road. The boat ramp

is 0.2 mile farther up on the left, where Orange Avenue becomes Duval Island Drive.

De Soto Winter Encampment Site State Park
1001 Desoto Park Drive
Tallahassee, Florida 32301
(850) 245-6444
exploresouthernhistory.com/fldesoto1.html

Although there are no remaining structures here, this is the site where de Soto's expedition camped in the winter of 1539. Archaeologists found artifacts here in 1987 that verified this as the site. Today the 5-acre park centers around the home of Florida's twenty-fourth governor, John W. Martin (1925–29). The home has been turned into a museum with displays covering four centuries of Florida history.

2

Jonathan Dickinson

A Shipwreck Survivor's Story, 1696

It was a harrowing night of darkness and terror. A violent September storm, possibly a hurricane, had driven the wooden barkentine *Reformation* away from its northward course to Philadelphia and onto shoals of the southeast coast of Florida. As waves slammed over the vessel, the commander, eight crew members, and fifteen passengers desperately hoped the boat, despite its cracking timbers, would hold until daylight, when they might find shore and safety.

At dawn the damage was evident.

By great fortune or—as the survivors would come to believe—by divine intervention, the boat was grounded on a seemingly endless stretch of beach. Seabirds took refuge in the wreckage, and one hog was still on board; the rest of the boat's swine and sheep had washed away. For a moment, the passengers breathed a sigh of relief: they were alive.

"We rejoiced at this our preservation from the raging seas; but at the same instant feared the sad consequences that followed: yet having hopes still we got our sick and lame on shore, also our provisions, with spars and sails to make a tent," wrote Jonathan Dickinson. The "wilderness country looked very dismal, having no trees, but only sand hills covered with shrubby palmetto, the stalks of which were prickly, that there was no walking among them." Nevertheless, they created a shelter under some bushes, lit a fire, and managed to get some provisions ashore.[1]

It was a dismal scene, but what Dickinson could not foresee was the ordeal he was about to encounter as an English Quaker cast ashore in a Spanish colony dominated in 1696 by seemingly hostile Native people allied to the Spanish—England's longtime enemy.

In the ensuing two months the shipwreck survivors endured hunger, bad weather (five eventually died of exposure), and frequent threats by different tribes as they made their way more than 200 miles up the coast to the Spanish city of St. Augustine. But they also received many kindnesses: food, however sparse and foreign to their palates; clothing; and even the willingness of Native women to suckle Dickinson's six-month-old son. Most importantly, they gained safe passage at a time when many shipwreck survivors were quickly killed by Indigenous people.

Dickinson, a thirty-three-year-old merchant, published a journal of the trip three years later called *God's Protecting Providence*—the guiding force, he believed, for his survival. Its popularity led to multiple printings, and today it is widely known as *Jonathan Dickinson's Journal*. The book is an important chronicle of captivity and survival while also shedding valuable if complicated light on an era, place, and Native people that no longer exist—albeit through the eyes of a White, upper-class colonist who had little understanding of the people and terrain he encountered.

The *Reformation* sailed from Port Royal, Jamaica, on August 23, 1696, in a convoy of a dozen ships protected by the frigate *Hampshire*. By traveling together, the crews hoped for safe passage around Cuba, through the Florida Straits, and east into the Atlantic Ocean—the route used by most ships heading to Europe from the Caribbean. The greatest menaces: pirates, shallow waters, and unexpected storms that from 1521 to 1696 claimed fifty-two ships along the treacherous Florida coast. Along the western shore of Cuba, the three-masted *Reformation* hit calm seas, and eventually the crew lost sight of the other ships. Sailing alone when winds returned, the crew continued along the original route, hoping to catch the northerly flowing Gulf Stream current to expedite the northward sea journey.

Planning to open a new family office in Philadelphia, Dickinson chartered the *Reformation* to carry goods and people to the thriving colonial English city. Aboard were Commander Joseph Kirle, who broke his leg during an accident off Cuba, and mariners Richard Limpeney, Solomon Cresson, Joseph Buckley, Thomas Fownes, Thomas Jemmet, Nathaniel Randall, John Hilliard (listed as the "Master's Boy"), and Ben, described as the "Master's Negro." Passengers included Robert Barrow, a sickly Quaker missionary, as well as Dickinson, his wife, Mary, their six-month-old son, Jonathan, and Benjamin Allen, described as a relative of Dickinson's. Also on the boat were eleven enslaved people owned by Dickinson; one of them, Venus, "an Indian Girl," died shortly after they set sail. The remaining enslaved five men and five women of African heritage were Peter, London, Jack, Cesar (also spelled Caesar), Cajoe (a child), Hagar, Sarah, Bella, Susanna, and Quensa (also spelled Quenza).[2]

Even though his family held more than 10,000 acres of land in Jamaica, Dickinson was ready to leave. Four years earlier, a massive earthquake and subsequent tsunami destroyed much of Port Royal, diminishing the family's finances, and British-held Jamaica was a seething bastion of unrest.[3]

During the 1690s, "slave revolts, inconsistent labor supplies, foreign invasions, disease, internal political squabbles, religious persecution, lack of support and supply from the mother country, and the resulting destruction of natural disaster combined in pushing the colony to the brink of collapse," writes historian Jason Daniels. "Accordingly, Dickinson decided to leave the struggling island for the bourgeoning mercantile port and Quaker haven, Philadelphia."[4]

It was a great dream that would be delayed—and almost destroyed—by a storm with northeasterly winds that wrecked the *Reformation* on September 24. While the cold and wet survivors pondered their next steps, a few hours later two Indian men dressed in woven straw loincloths came running up the beach and grabbed two men who were carrying corn from the wreck, Dickinson wrote:

> Their countenance was very furious and bloody. They had their hair tied in a roll behind in which stuck two bones shaped one like a broad arrow, the other a spearhead. The rest of our men followed from the vessel, asking me what they should do whether they should get their guns to kill these two; but I persuaded them otherwise desiring them to be quiet, showing their inability to defend us from what would follow; but to put our trust in the Lord who was able to defend to the uttermost. I walked towards the place where our sick and lame were, the two Indian men following me. I told them the Indians were come and coming upon us. And while these two (letting the men loose) stood with a wild, furious countenance, looking upon us I bethought myself to give them some tobacco and pipes, which they greedily snatched from me, making a snuffing noise like a wild beast, turned their backs upon us and run away.[5]

The travelers avoided injury in this confrontation but realized more clashes were likely to occur. They needed a strategy to survive. "We communed together and considered our condition, being amongst a barbarous people such as were generally accounted man-eaters, believing those two were gone to alarm their people," Dickinson wrote. In a flash of cleverness, the castaways, understanding that Spain controlled Florida, decided to claim to be Spanish. Fortunately, crewman Solomon Cresson could speak

Spanish well. "It was hoped this might be means for our delivery, to which most of the company assented." This proved to be correct.[6]

Two or three hours later, as the storm ended, a large number of Indians arrived "running and shouting," and scouring the wreck for goods. The group of thirty Natives carried Spanish knives and the chief (cacique), called "Casseekey" by Dickinson, held a baganet (bayonet) from the *Reformation*. "They rushed in upon us and cried *Nickaleer, Nickaleer*," Dickinson recounted. "We understood them not at first: they were repeating it over unto us often. At last they cried *Epainia* or *Spaniard*, by which we understood them that at first they meant *English*; but they were answered to the latter in Spanish yea." Thus, the group presented itself as Spanish, with Cresson carrying the burden of communication. Historians have since discounted claims of Native cannibalism, but the survivors, who had no understanding of the local culture or language, believed it to be true. And their concerns about being identified were well-founded: "Nickaleer" may have been the Native pronunciation for "Inglaterra" or "Angleterre"—English.[7]

It was a frightening moment that likely decided the survivors' fates. The Native men waved knives and made threatening gestures while the group sat passively on recovered chests. Eventually the Natives took booty from the chests and trunks and stripped clothes off most of the castaways; the cacique took the ship's money, which was "privately hiding in the bushes." When they were finished, "they asked us again, *Nickaleer, Nickaleer?* But we answered by saying *Pennsylvania*" and asking about St. Augustine, the Spanish colonial city in Northeast Florida, Dickinson recalled.[8]

Although the Natives indicated that the city was to the south, the survivors persevered, knowing it was in the opposite direction. By the end of the day, the chief's "heart was tendered toward us," and he salvaged three coats for the survivors and spent the night in a tent with them. The next day the group endured more questioning about whether each was a Nickaleer; when one person said yes, the Natives stripped clothing from everyone, cut the tents in pieces, and forced them to walk south to the cacique's village, carrying goods. Mary Dickinson carried the baby, and Kirle, limping from his broken leg, was helped by Ben. As they departed, Limpeney used his navigation quadrant to determine their latitude—a measurement that provided accurate mapping of much of Dickinson's path and indicated they wrecked north of today's Jupiter Inlet.[9] "But if any of us offered to lay down our burden," Dickinson wrote, "we were threatened to be shot. Thus were we forced along the beach bare-footed."[10]

After 5 miles they reached an inlet and canoed across to a town that

A Native shell midden, now the site of a county park and pioneer homestead near Jupiter, marks the Hobe village visited by Jonathan Dickinson's shipwrecked party in 1696. Author photo.

Dickinson described as "being little wigwams made of small poles stuck in the ground, which they bended on to another, making an arch, and covered them with thatch of small palmetto-leaves." Dickinson, his wife and child, and Barrow were taken to the cacique's hut, where his wife and some "old women" sat; unexpectedly, the chief's wife handed her suckling child to another woman and took Dickinson's baby to her breast, "feeling it from top to toe." It was an act of great kindness to the family that would be repeated at different villages as Mary became unable to feed the child. They offered the castaways fish, but "our exercise was too great for us to have any inclination to receive food," he wrote. That evening the group stayed under a palmetto shelter next to the cacique's wigwam, but there was little sleeping once a Native ceremony commenced. "Night came on; the moon being up, an Indian, who performeth their ceremonies stood out, looking full at the moon, making a hideous noise, and crying out acting like a mad man for the space of half an hour." When he finished, the others joined in, making a "terrible" noise that lasted until midnight.[11]

Dickinson called the village "Hoe-Bay," at the south side of the inlet. Modern anthropologists identify the Natives in the area as the Hobe, Jobe, or Jove. While the wreck survivors thought them to be "bloodthirsty, pagan cannibals," the Hobe, "who consistently sought to intimidate the colonists and, thus, to control them, seem mainly to have been interested in salvaging what they could from the shipwreck and then sending the passengers away," writes anthropologist/historian Jerald T. Milanich. The Hobe were one of many Indigenous groups that lived along Florida's southeastern coast, and Dickinson and the crew would meet several on their trek. The behavior of the Hobe may have reflected their relationship with the Spanish military government, which "had made it clear to the native groups that the survivors of wrecks were to be protected and turned over to Spanish authorities," Milanich writes, adding:

> They also required the native people to report the presence of non-Spaniards. The native people received payment from the military government for rendering these services. These interactions with Spaniards provided an opportunity for the native people to trade ambergris. Highly valued in Europe as an ingredient in perfumes, ambergris was collected by Florida Indians from the beaches, where it washed ashore after being deposited in the Atlantic by whales. On his trek northward, Dickinson observed such a trade: five pounds of ambergris for a mirror, ax, a knife or two, and tobacco.[12]

Despite the cacique's warning that traveling north was dangerous, after a few days he allowed the shipwreck party to head in that direction. The survivors were determined to reach sanctuary in St. Augustine, and Barrow, the missionary, offered the group assurances and prayers that the Lord "would preserve and deliver us from among them, that our names might not be buried in oblivion," wrote Dickinson, adding that some of the Hobe had watched Barrow in prayer and during Bible readings. With the publication of Dickinson's *Journal,* the aged Barrow would be seen as "the central hero of the tale" because of the devout faith he exhibited throughout the ordeal.[13]

Using a boat salvaged from the wreck, the survivors left on September 28. Some rowed in the leaky vessel while others walked the shore. Soon they

Dickinson and his party canoed and trekked northward on inhospitable coastal beaches, perhaps encountering sites like Blowing Rocks Preserve on Jupiter Island. Courtesy of Bruce Hunt.

passed the charred remains of the *Reformation,* burned by the Natives on the beach. They found a number of fish onshore, perhaps left by the storm, and fed "heartily" that night, knowing that any future meal was not guaranteed. At night the sand flies and mosquitoes were so bad that some buried themselves in the sand; Dickinson and six others returned to the boat and rowed along the shore. During the day they rowed while watching the rest of the party make its way up the coast. Finally able to negotiate the surf, the boaters made it to shore and joined the rest.[14]

On September 30, the castaways encountered a new group of Natives—possibly the Santaluces—at what is today's St. Lucie Inlet. Once again, they were threatened and accused of being Nickaleers. Cresson spoke Spanish to calm them, but the Natives acted in a "barbarous manner" and tore "the few clothes were had," leaving them "naked as we were born." They finally relented and gave Mary Dickinson a pair of breeches and tore pages out of the Bible for the survivors to cover themselves, Dickinson recalled. At the same time the Natives "would deride and smite us; and instantly another of them would snatch away what the other gave us, smiting and deriding us withal." The survivors were intimidated into submission but then gained reprieves.[15]

Once again, they were protected by the chief, his wife, and some of the leaders, "who were made instruments to intercede for us, and stop the rage of the multitude, who seemed not to be satisfied without our blood." They transported Dickinson's party across the inlet, but the constant harassment continued, including a man who held Mary's hair and a knife to her throat as well as another who filled her infant's mouth with sand. The cacique's wife "pulled the sand out of our child's mouth and kept by my wife until we got to the Casseekey's house," a 40' × 25' structure covered in palmetto leaves.[16]

After a debate among the Native leaders, Cresson was called in to speak Spanish with the cacique "but could not hold a discourse." Perhaps their Spanish was weak, enabling the group to carry on the charade. The Natives gave deerskins to the women and woven loin coverings for the men. The survivors were told to sleep on mats on the building's floor. The next day they witnessed an extraordinary scene. The Natives brewed the leaves of a plant—the Spanish later identified it as cassena (today's yaupon holly)—to make a dark-brown drink. Once cooled, it was scooped into a conch shell and then taken to the cacique, who drank first and threw some on the ground; then the rest of his associates drank. This brew, known as the "black drink," was a common drink among southeastern Natives of different tribes and traditions.[17]

That evening, the Natives beat a skin-covered drum and shook a rattle made of a gourd with small stones inside. Dickinson said they also "set up a most hideous howling, very irksome to us, and some time after came some of their young women, some singing, some dancing. This was continued till midnight, after which they went to sleep."[18]

During their stay at the village, the survivors, who repeatedly claimed to be Spanish, learned that a wrecked ship of seven Nickaleers was farther up the coast; those survivors likely would be put to death. "We were silent, although much concerned to hear that report," Dickinson wrote. "They also told us that a messenger would come for us to direct us to the next town, thence to Augustine."[19]

Why the Indigenous loathing for the English? Likely it was based on prior English raids that forced them into slavery. "Native hatred of the English ran deep, and the Spanish were not behind it. The real cause was that the English treated the wild coast like a labor pool, seizing the natives at will and taking them to distant places where they were forced to labor under dangerous conditions that few would survive," writes historian Amy Turner Bushnell.[20]

For a shipwreck survivor, being Spanish or English meant life or death.

After another night of witnessing celebrations, the castaways were ordered to quickly depart with a guide. They headed north, realizing that three people—including Cresson—were missing. Five miles later, they camped on a bug-riddled beach in bone-shivering cold. At sunrise they spotted the remains of the *Nantwich*, which had been part of their original fleet from Jamaica, a ghostly reminder of their dire situation. Soon they reached another inlet, which they crossed by boat and, several miles later, encountered a new chief. "He was an ancient man, his beard and hair gray," and he embraced Captain Kirle. "This old Caseekey seemed to have compassion on us, and said that those people who had served us thus in stripping of us were rogues. But we were his *comerradoes,* or friends, withal he said in [some] few days, he would carry us to St. Augustine." The *Nantwich* survivors, they were told, would not go to St. Augustine, as they were Nickaleers.[21]

Dickinson learned that the *Nantwich* group at first claimed to be Spanish, but soon admitted to being English, creating tenuous circumstances. Disguising themselves as Spanish seemingly worked for the Dickinson group, which had a much better reception from these new Natives; the cacique even washed Mary's and Barrow's feet, which were bruised and damaged from "traveling barefoot on the hot sand" and stepping on stumps, stones, and prickles.[22]

Dickinson's group reached the town of Jece on October 2, where it would remain for a month in a frustrating, unavoidable delay. They were now in Native Ais territory, which included many communities that stretched from the Fort Pierce inlet north to the southern end of today's Mosquito Lagoon near the Kennedy Space Center. The Ais were "geographically outside the main thrust of Spanish colonial activities" but were known to the Spanish because they controlled an area where ships wrecked. The Ais apparently dominated the Natives to the south, as Dickinson would come to understand.[23]

Upon learning about the cargo carried by the *Reformation*—an account enhanced by Cresson, who arrived that night—the Ais chief "grew covetous" and headed south with ten men to claim riches from the Hobe. He promised to send the group to St. Augustine upon his return. After a week, the cacique was warmly welcomed back, bringing with him Dickinson's chest and Cesar, who had been held by the Hobe. But something had changed—the chief now suspected that the castaways were indeed English. In a few days, the doubtful leader took Cresson and six Natives in a canoe, heading to St. Augustine. In the interim, Dickinson and the others were left with increasingly cold weather and diminishing food.[24]

"These people neither sow nor plant any manner of thing whatsoever," Dickinson wrote, "nor care for anything but what the barren sand produce; fish they have as plenty as they please but sometimes they would make it scarce to us, so that a meal in a week was most commonly our portion, and three meals a rarity."[25]

The survivors hungrily scavenged the remainders of the Ais meals—fish gills and guts. "And thus were we daily exercised in sorrow and grievous troubles," Dickinson lamented. "Sometimes doubts would arise amongst us concerning what would be the end of us, and what manner of death we should pass through. . . . One thing did seem more grievous to me and my wife than any other thing. Which was that if it should so happen that we should be put to death, we feared that our child would be kept alive, and bred up as one of those people; when this thought did arise it wounded us deep."[26]

But things were about to improve: the Spanish were coming.

Cresson and the ancient chief had been gone sixteen days when two men came running into the village announcing their arrival. The Natives "were like a people amazed and overcome with fear," especially after they heard four Spanish muskets discharge. Eleven Spanish soldiers and a Native interpreter disembarked from a boat, embraced the castaways, and "expressed

their being glad to find us alive," Dickinson wrote, adding that his group
had trouble conversing as neither spoke the other's language well. At this,
the Natives realized that the survivors were indeed Nickaleers and "looked
enviously on us, so that, could they have had their wills, we believed they
would not have suffered us to have lived many hours; but the Spaniards
awed them."[27]

Upon receiving a letter assuring protection from the Spanish governor,
the survivors realized they finally were safe. "The Spaniards were extraordinary kind unto us, so that we had occasion to rejoice, and thank the Lord
for this part of our deliverance by this means." On November 2, the Spanish
captain sent a group of thirteen survivors of both wrecks via canoe to St.
Augustine. In the meantime, the soldiers searched and looted Indigenous
houses, possibly retrieving the money that the cacique had taken from the
Hobe. Dickinson wrote that the "Old Casseekey seemed much dejected.
We supposed the Spaniards had taken from him the money and what other
things he had carried with him; or that he was vexed he should be so de-
ceived in taking us for Spaniards." Dickinson and crew gave the soldiers
information about the *Reformation*'s wreck and cargo, adding that one passenger, Ben, was still with the Hobe. The Spanish captain ordered the Natives to fetch Ben; the soldiers also did some trading with the Ais—tobacco,
which the Natives highly valued, for linen or silk.[28]

Three days later the remainder of the castaways, Ben included, rowed
north, eventually meeting up with the previous group. The temperature was
dropping, and they had a small amount of berries for food, but they were
nearing their goal. Their hopefulness was dashed when a storm hit, leaving
them exposed on a beach with no shelter or wood for a fire. The weather
was icy and blustery for the next few days as they passed marshy lands and
Indian towns, portaging their boats when necessary. At times the group was
split up, especially when they had to walk. Ultimately, the conditions became fatal. Five people—Dickinson's kin Benjamin Allen, and Jack, Cesar,
Quensa, and Hagar's child Cajoe—died from exhaustion and exposure on
November 13, likely on the shore south of today's Marineland.[29]

After encountering three Spanish sentinel houses and other Indigenous
groups who were part of the Spanish mission culture, the surviving castaways arrived at St. Augustine on November 15. It had been a harsh, dangerous journey; people had died, and Dickinson's son was "so black with cold
and shaking that it was admirable how it lived." Once in the city, the ragtag
group must have thought it had reached heaven as members were offered
European-style clothes, wine, food, housing, and the warmth of fires. They

had traveled 230 miles and reached safety just in time—the next morning's weather left a half inch of ice on the ground.[30]

The governor examined the group, seeking details about the shipwreck and lost money and goods. A statement documenting the journey was prepared during the next few days, and all the survivors signed it. When Mary ailed with fever, the governor ordered his own doctor to tend to her recovery.

After two weeks of convalescence, most of the survivors headed north, the governor embracing some of them and saying, "We should forget him when we got amongst our own nation" and adding "that if we forgot, God would not forget him." The group followed the Atlantic coast north until arriving in Charles Town (today's Charleston) in the British colony of South Carolina on December 26. Dickinson, along with his wife and child and Barrow, sailed for Philadelphia on March 18, expecting a two-week trip. Unfortunately, Barrow, who was in ill health for most of the last few months, died shortly after reaching the city, his death compared by many to that of a martyr. Dickinson remembered that during "all the times of our greatest troubles" Barrow "was ready to counsel us to patience and to wait what the Lord our God would bring to pass."[31]

While convalescing in Charles Town, Barrow, whose age has been estimated at sixty, wrote a letter to his wife, Margaret, in England, the first in ten months—it would be the last he sent her. He recounted the travails of the trip and shipwreck, including days with no food but "Berrys and Wild Grapes and went naked without hat Cap Shirt or Coate stockings or shoes 7 weeks Time . . . the sun being Hot and scorching in the Dayes, and sometimes Rawe & great dewes fell in the Night, that made Cold mornings; we being soe punished with Muskeato Flyes." He assured her that he was well cared for in Charles Town but had been violently ill for about thirteen weeks. He assured her that he wasn't afraid of death and bid his relatives farewell "in the Lord, whether I have the opportunity to see you again or not."[32]

The Dickinsons thrived in Philadelphia. Dickinson managed a successful mercantile business, importing goods from England and the Caribbean and exporting commodities that included flour, deerskins, and tobacco. It was a business that required additional travels to Jamaica and other colonies in the West Indies. "In time he became one of Philadelphia's most active and prosperous merchants" and was a respected city leader by his death at age fifty-nine in 1722. Dickinson was greatly involved in the city's service and politics, serving in the Pennsylvania Assembly, acting as a commission of streets and watercourses, and then rising from city alderman to mayor from 1717 to 1719. The family also increased with four more children and lived a comfortable life in a fashionable four-story, ten-room home.[33]

It bears noting that the wealthy Dickinson was "Philadelphia's largest single slaveholder and one of the most active slave-traders in Pennsylvania," writes Daniels, adding that "Dickinson was not alone in the extent of his involvement with slavery nor was he singular as a Quaker who owned slaves in Philadelphia. In fact, Quaker slave ownership in Philadelphia peaked during the first two decades of the eighteenth century. During Dickinson's lifetime almost every substantial merchant, Quaker and non-Quaker, in the city owned slaves. Enslaved Africans were ubiquitous in early Philadelphia."[34]

Although Quakers were long associated with America's abolition movement, their participation only became unified by the mid-1700s; at one point Dickinson enslaved thirty African people, possibly making him the largest slaveholder in colonial Pennsylvania, and he participated in the slave trade until his death.[35]

Of the other survivors, Cresson settled in Philadelphia, where he became a Quaker, married, and had nine children. His occupation: a turner and chairmaker at a downtown business. Kirle, the *Reformation*'s captain, continued to command ships and gained much business from Dickinson. He even attested to the validity of Dickinson's *Journal* before its 1699 publication.[36]

The publication of the *Journal* was a sensation, the tale pieced together after the group reached safety. Dickinson likely did not carry a journal with him during the ordeal; his first chance at recording his experiences probably came during his St. Augustine stay and then again during the three-month layover in Charles Town. Quaker leaders supported printing the book, made possible because the city had just gotten its first professional printer and the text's message of faith in God during suffering related to their circumstances. Of the first printing, only six copies are known to exist. Since then, the book was reprinted twenty-two times in English, Dutch, and German before the 1945 edition edited by Charles and Evangeline Andrews, which also has been reprinted.[37]

Although the book today largely is read as one of adventure and history, at its original publication it was considered proof of God's protecting hand and of Barrow's faithful example. "Drawing pointed religious lessons from the experiences of the castaways and dwelling at length on Robert Barrow's edifying life and final hours, this composition's tone of pious moralizing suggests what the chief values were that its sponsors found in Dickinson's manuscript," Leonard Labaree wrote in the 1985 edition. "Some present-day readers may agree with this judgment; others with a more secular approach will find different reasons for their interest. In either case, all should agree that this journal is a memorable account of hardship and suffering bravely borne, and of a stirring episode from America's early years."[38]

And, in what would undoubtedly be a surprise to Dickinson, the book has become invaluable for of its descriptions of the customs and lifestyles of the Indigenous peoples of the Southeast Florida coast, especially the Hobe and Ais.

Dickinson's descriptions of his encounters are framed by his own Anglocentric prejudices; what the Natives thought of the castaways can only be guessed at through his words and speculation. Author Eric Gary Anderson notes that "Native points of view are difficult to locate" in the *Journal*. The "relative absence of Native-authored print texts in the early Southeast has compounded the scholarly difficulty of imagining Native peoples of the region as actors, with complex motives of their own and with cultural histories that are both separate and inseparable from the histories of other peoples in the region. But Native voices and Native-constructed knowledge nevertheless emerge in particularly interesting ways in Dickinson's narrative."[39]

It is evident from the *Journal* that the Natives were aware of the European conflicts between the English and Spanish and had established ties to the latter. They were agents, at least in part, of transatlantic politics and trade that mingled people of European, African, and Native ethnicities along the Florida coast. Their relationships were complex and required adaptation to changing allegiances—a worldview that Dickinson couldn't or didn't imagine possible since he viewed them as bloodthirsty cannibals.

"Native Americans had interacted with Europeans along Florida's east coast for nearly two centuries before Dickinson and company arrived in 1696. The interactions, most often between the Spanish and Native Floridians along the east coast, had a long and often unsavory tenure," writes Daniels. "Native American integration of the European colonial endeavor into their worldview, however, should not be taken for granted. Unlike the sedentary, agricultural people of northern Florida, who in large part rendered obedience to the Spanish king and his colonial representatives and accepted Christianity, the Native Americans of central and south Florida typically maintained their autonomy."[40]

By the time of the *Reformation*'s ruin, the Southeast Florida Indigenous groups competed for shipwreck riches, and, clearly, had agreed to deliver Spanish castaways safely back to the colonial government. Such negotiations required some working knowledge of the Spanish language. Perhaps the Natives also were aware of a 1670 peace treaty between Spain and England that guaranteed, among other actions, that the Spanish would aid English vessels and subjects in distress—a treaty that did not erase animosities that erupted again several years later. The Natives' hostility toward perceived English shipwreck survivors reflected conflicts that occurred an ocean away and their experiences with or knowledge of English slave raids in Florida.

Bushnell sums up the riches found in the *Journal:*

Dickinson's journal is valuable for many reasons. It supplies rare ethnographic information about the Indian groups who inhabited Florida's long Atlantic coast. It reveals late seventeenth-century Quaker beliefs and practices. It is a travel narrative of extraordinary complexity, tracing the interactions of Anglo-Jamaican slave owners, Afro-Jamaican slaves, cosmopolitan mariners, wild Indians, mission Indians, and the Spaniards and creoles of St. Augustine, a 130-year-old presidio. The journal deals with castaway survival stratagems, Indian postures of friendship and ferocity, Spanish relations with mission-resistant and mission-reduced Natives, and the transnational code of elite conduct. It also offers a rare glimpse into Indian perceptions of non-Indians.[41]

The seventeenth-century Atlantic world was shrinking for all the players. And, soon, the Native groups would be largely decimated. Within the next century the Ais and Hobe were gone, likely from a combination of European diseases, raids by English slave traders, and intertribal warfare. The same was true across much of the peninsula. By the mid-eighteenth century, Creek Indians had migrated into Florida from Georgia and Alabama and may have absorbed the few Indigenous survivors; they would come to be identified as Seminole and Miccosukee—tribes that continue today in the state.

The *Journal,* then, is a tale of the much-erased past.

More than two centuries after its publication, Charles Andrews, a retired Yale University history professor, and his wife, Evangeline, became intrigued by the Dickinson narrative after wintering in 1935 at a house built on a shell mound that they later learned was the site of the Hobe village. The couple began researching the shipwreck and worked on a new edition of the

Journal; Charles Andrews died two years before it was published by Yale University Press in 1945, with Evangeline finishing the editing.

One can only wonder what Dickinson—and Charles and Evangeline Andrews—would think of the same areas today that have transformed as Florida's coastal population has boomed, bringing with it vast development on the Atlantic shore now known as the "Treasure Coast" for all the ill-fated Spanish galleons that wrecked there. There are a few wild-ish places left as preserves and parks, but the desolate shore that Dickinson trudged is long gone.

Perhaps the only place that can definitively be attached to Dickinson, besides St. Augustine is the DuBois Pioneer Home located on the south side of Jupiter Inlet, the site of the Andrewses' wintering spot. It once was an ancient shell mound (known as a midden) and the location of the village of Hobe, where the Dickinson party was forced to trek after the shipwreck. The mound, with artifacts dating back thousands of years, once was more than 600 feet long and 20 feet high. It kept Hobe high and dry, safe from large storm surges and tides.

In 1898, Harry and Susan DuBois decided to take advantage of the elevated site, overlooking the inlet, to build a home. It reminded Harry of childhood times at the New Jersey shore. They built a wooden home that gradually expanded to become a two-story shingle Victorian house.

Today, much of the shell midden is gone, sold by the DuBoises for road construction projects in the area, but a few bleached oyster shells peek out from the bottom of the vine-covered rise. It now is a county park that features one of the oldest homes in Palm Beach County and provides much-loved recreation for the locals with a shallow swimming lagoon, a view across the turquoise inlet, and a jetty and fishing area that reaches into the waves where the Loxahatchee River meets the ocean. On an unusually warm November morning a large mix of people enjoyed the waterfront: an elderly couple on a bench enjoying the breeze; a couple filming themselves with a drone; two camouflage-clad people peering through a large scope at shorebirds; a dozen men with buckets and fishing gear hoping to land dinner; and families splashing in the shallows.

Across the inlet to the west looms an important local landmark—the scarlet Jupiter Inlet Lighthouse. Built near another Native shell midden, the lighthouse was part of a series of six nineteenth-century beacons meant to keep sailors safe along Florida's coasts, a danger to which Dickinson could attest. The 105-foot tower was completed in May 1860 and has been operating ever since, earning recognition on the US National Register of Historic Places. From its top, the splendor and layout of the coastal areas are clear—a series of barrier islands separated by inlets now prevented from shifting by rocky armaments that ensure the passes stay navigable.[42]

Five miles to the north the *Reformation* wrecked, but today there is no practical way to find the exact site. Jupiter Island is now a mix of high-rise condominiums and ritzy beachfront estates, many with secluded driveways and thickly vegetated lawns. Dickinson would be astonished, as are others who have tried to follow his path. And his motley group likely would not be welcome in this exclusive enclave.

Steve Mentz, an English professor at St. John's University in New York City, became interested in Dickinson while writing a book about shipwrecks and survivor narratives. Dickinson frames his tale as one of providence—of God preserving a virtuous group from the dangers of the shipwreck and Native people. It is that saga of righteous men—Dickinson and, certainly, Barrow—that gained Quaker support for the book's publication.

During a family vacation, Mentz visited the Jupiter shell mound and coast to "see the physical space and to get a sense of what the material conditions of oceanic travel were in that period." His assessment: "Pretty tough. Pre–air conditioning Florida is a pretty tough place to be."[43]

"We think of this land- and sea-scape as beautiful and relaxing, but for Dickinson's party it was barren and inhospitable," he wrote in a blog. "It's an empty, inhuman space, now occupied by mansions, air conditioning, and power boats. Hard to imagine a party of Quakers on that beach today."[44]

Indeed, most of the island is inaccessible to regular folk. A stop at Hobe Sound Beach to the north offers rare public access to enjoy the coastline. An unseasonable November tropical storm prior to my visit left in its wake enormous waves that a few hardy surfers attempted to ride. The vast majority of visitors watched the pounding surf from beach chairs, enjoying the strong breeze under the watchful eye of a vigilant lifeguard. Several others fished along the foam-strewn shore, but nothing was biting. As lovely as a walk along the water seemed, the reality was harsh. The sand was thick and sloped, and a short jaunt was more of a slog, only offering a hint as to how harsh the Dickinson party's ordeal was.

The shipwrecked sailor is better known in these parts as the namesake of Jonathan Dickinson State Park, a 10,500-acre preserve that bears his name but that he never visited. Located inland of the coast, the park is a popular recreational venue that also protects a variety of habitats, including sand hills and scrub forests along the Loxahatchee River. The site has its own intriguing history—it was a former top-secret radar training camp during World War II and, later, was the homestead of an eccentric fur trapper. Ironically, it was named for a man who never stepped foot inside it.

George Blythe, however, is working to keep the "real" Dickinson's memory alive. At eighty-two he still dresses in period clothes to impersonate Dickinson and delight history buffs. In reimagining the Quaker's travails, Blythe emphasizes "brotherhood" in his performances before school and community groups. Blythe says the tale affords him the opportunity to talk about how the Quakers, Natives, and Spanish interacted and how Dickinson's fears of cannibalism were unfounded. Instead, the Natives offered food, shelter, and assistance for the shipwreck survivors to reach St. Augustine—a generosity that still didn't warm Dickinson's heart.[45]

Blythe, of Vero Beach, dons a simple colonial period outfit—now in tatters after much use, resembling clothing that has survived a hurricane, he jokes. He describes Native clothing and "nakedness" to schoolchildren, stressing that "even if someone is dressed different than you, you can still be a friend"—a lesson important in today's world of designer clothing where not every child can compete. "Clothes don't really make the person, I want them to understand."[46]

"I guess I'm trying to teach brotherhood because it's really a brotherhood story," Blythe adds. "I really think everyone was kind to everyone else."[47]

More than three centuries later, Dickinson's ordeal still has much to teach us all.

~~~~~~

To share some of Jonathan Dickinson's experiences, visit these locations:

DuBois Pioneer Home, Palm Beach County Park
19075 DuBois Road
Jupiter, Florida 33477
(561) 966-6600
discover.pbcgov.org/parks/Locations/DuBois.aspx
DuBois Pioneer Home tours: (561) 966-6609

The 1898 Harry and Susan DuBois Pioneer Home, on the south side of Jupiter Inlet, was constructed almost two hundred years after the *Reformation,* carrying Jonathan Dickinson and his family, shipwrecked a few miles north of here. But this is also the site of what was once the Hobe Indian village where Dickinson, his family, and other survivors were taken after being captured. The pioneer house sits atop the remains of a 20-foot-high prehistoric Native Floridian shell midden that likely dates back some six thousand years. The house itself is a museum, displaying what late nine-teenth-century life was like here, on this coast. It was added to the National Register of Historic Places in 1985 and underwent a substantial renovation in 2016. Visitors can take guided tours.

Hours: DuBois Park is open 7 days a week, sunrise to sunset. Docent guided tours of the DuBois Pioneer Home are offered Tuesday, Wednesday, and Thursday, 10:00 a.m.–1:00 p.m.

Admission is free.

Jupiter Inlet Lighthouse & Museum

500 Captain Armour's Way
Jupiter, Florida 33469
(561) 747-8380
jupiterlighthouse.org

Congress had authorized building the Jupiter Inlet Lighthouse, on the north side of the Loxahatchee River, in 1853, but an Atlantic storm that filled the inlet with sand, and then an outbreak of malaria, followed by the Third Seminole War (1855–58) conspired to delay the beginning of construction until 1859. The 108-foot-tall lighthouse finally opened in 1860. However, shortly after that Confederate sympathizers disabled the light. In 1866 it was reactivated, and it has remained in service ever since. Today visitors can climb it provided they meet the 48-inch height requirement.

Hours: Wednesday–Sunday, 10:00 a.m.–2:00 p.m.

Admission: $12 for adults; $10 for veterans and seniors; $6 for children 6–18; children under 6 free.

Jonathan Dickinson State Park

16450 Southeast Federal Highway
Hobe Sound, Florida 33455
(772) 546-2771
floridastateparks.org/parks-and-trails/jonathan-dickinson-state-park

Although Jonathan Dickinson did not actually visit this site, the *Reforma-tion,* carrying him and his family, shipwrecked somewhere on the beach just east of here. No one knows the precise location. Nevertheless, Jona-than Dickinson State Park is a scenic 10,500-acre park worthy of a visit. A good bit of it is scrub pine–covered sand dunes, one of which, Hobe Mountain, rises to an elevation of 86 feet, the highest natural point of land in South Florida. Visitors who walk the boardwalk path to the Hobe Moun-tain observation tower are treated to a spectacular view of the surrounding topography. The park is home to a wide-ranging assortment of wildlife:

deer, foxes, bobcats, and otters. This is also a prime bird-watching location, with some 140 species identified, including the rare and endangered Florida scrub jay. Jonathan Dickinson State Park opened in 1950, but prior to that this was the location of a top-secret World War II Army radar training school, Camp Murphy.

Hours: The park is open 365 days a year, 8:00 a.m. to sunset.

Admission: $6 per vehicle.

Hobe Sound Martin County Beach Park

1 CR 707/Southeast Beach Road
Hobe Sound, FL 33455
(772) 221-1418
discovermartin.com/directory/hobe-sound-beach

Hobe Sound Beach is accessible to the public at Hobe Sound Martin County Beach Park.

Hours: The beach is open 365 days a year, sunrise to sunset.

3

William Bartram

Botanizing in Paradise, 1774

The most famous account of travels in Florida was penned by a man whose life up until that point had been a failure. Reaching Florida's shores in 1774, before the outbreak of the American Revolution, William "Billy" Bartram had no aspirations for literary glory on his expedition into the southeastern British colonies to gather, describe, and draw botanical specimens. He simply wanted to turn his artistic talent and love of nature into a paying career that allowed him to revel in the beauty of wilderness.

Unexpectedly, his collections and observations, the latter published as a book, would excite the English-speaking world and influence writers, scientists, anthropologists, and historians for centuries to come. We are richer for it.

Bartram's *Travels through North and South Carolina, Georgia, East and West Florida, the Cherokee Country, the Extensive Territories of the Muscogulges, or Creek Confederacy, and the Country of the Chactaws*, first published in 1791, today is better known as *Travels*. In the book, which charts his trek from 1773 to 1777, he offered a different way of thinking about the landscape and Native people than was typical of the period. To Bartram, a Philadelphia-area Quaker, nature wasn't a commodity to be consumed or sold—it was a divine creation to be appreciated. Jonathan Dickinson, another Philadelphia Quaker, feared the Indigenous people he encountered after his 1696 Florida shipwreck; Bartram, arriving almost a century later, had a different perspective. Bartram believed the Native people had admirable traits and wondered if his "countrymen who may read these accounts of the Indians, which I have endeavoured to relate according to truth, at least as they appeared to me, will charge me with partiality or prejudice in their favor." It was a decidedly un-Eurocentric view; Thomas Jefferson, in the Declaration of Independence, called them "merciless Indian Savages."[1]

William Bartram, a Philadelphia Quaker, is noted for his travels through the southeastern colonies, where he described a variety of plants and animals. Public domain photo.

The book's introduction proclaims Bartram's love for wild things, particularly plants: "The world, as a glorious apartment of the boundless palace of the sovereign Creator, is furnished with an infinite variety of animated scenes, inexpressibly beautiful and pleasing, equally free to the inspection and enjoyment of all his creatures."[2] And of those scenes, he wrote, none "exhibits a more glorious display of the Almighty hand, than the vegetable world."

Animals also held his sympathy, and Bartram abhorred unnecessary killing, as demonstrated in an early account of watching a hunter kill a bear that had been eating fruit along a shoreline. As they neared the carcass, a young cub approached the dead body, smelled it, and, "appearing in agony, fell to weeping and looking upwards, then towards us, and cried out like a child. . . . The continual cries of this afflicted child, bereft of its parent affected me very sensibly; I was moved with compassion, and charging myself as if accessary [sic] to what now appeared to be a cruel murder, endeavored to prevail on the hunter to save its life, but to no effect!" The hunter shot the cub and "laid it dead on the dam."[3]

Travels, then, was no ordinary natural history book, and Bartram was not a typical explorer. He was "the first native-born American naturalist to devote his entire life to the study of nature," writes historian Thomas P. Slaughter. And Bartram's poetic style, desire for a peaceable kingdom of humans and nature, and scientific descriptions made the book a unique text that raised him to fame in his lifetime, attracting distinguished visitors to his home in search of his advice and knowledge. It was nothing his family ever expected of him.[4]

Historian Thomas Hallock writes that early reviewers "scoffed at Bartram's 'rhapsodical effusions,'" questioned his alligator accounts, and "took umbrage at his sympathetic portrayal of Native Americans." But they couldn't ignore the book. "*Travels*, despite its perceived eccentricities, established a template for natural history in the new nation and a route of discovery for others to follow. In the decades following publication, colleagues wrote to Bartram for clarification about the specimens he described, they tapped into his store of knowledge, and they sought to claim, or take credit for, his principal discoveries." One noted traveler who later would follow Bartram's footsteps was avian artist John James Audubon.[5]

Bartram was born in 1739, in Kingsessing, Pennsylvania, now in the southwest section of Philadelphia. His father, John Bartram, was a celebrated botanist and collector, making forays from his Schuylkill River home, where he maintained a plant nursery, to obtain specimens desired by wealthy European botanical collectors. In 1765 John was appointed royal botanist to King George III of England—a title that brought prestige and a welcome stipend—and was friends with Benjamin Franklin and much of Philadelphia society, affording his son contact with some of the most famous colonists of the day. On a collecting trip for the king to East Florida in 1765–66 (Florida was divided into East and West colonies), John took along twenty-seven-year-old William, who had a talent for drawing. William had accompanied his father on earlier botanizing explorations, his father once referring to him as "my little botanist," but this was their first foray into Florida. They trekked the northeastern part of the peninsula and sought the headwaters of the St. Johns River, then the best pathway into the interior of the state. During that visit, John, sixty-six, suffered a bout of malaria and fatigue, but the pair managed to cover many miles by boat and on horseback, even witnessing a treaty signing with Creek Indians—a group that had moved into Florida areas after the Indigenous people had largely succumbed to disease, war, and enslavement.[6]

William Bartram was entranced by Florida and had no desire to return with his father in 1766 to Philadelphia. He turned down a printing job with Franklin and found little success previously working at his uncle's North Carolina store. He tried running a rice and indigo plantation along the St. Johns north of Picolata, the site of the treaty meeting. Against his father's wishes, he leveraged his inheritance and set up shop; John supplied him with six enslaved people to do the manual labor. It was a disaster. A few months later family friend Henry Laurens visited the plantation, reporting back to John that his son, who has a "tender & delicate frame of Body & intelects" [*sic*], was in a "forlorn state." Laurens wrote that the plantation was at a bad location, 30 miles from any city, and said Bartram's problems and isolation were "discouragements enough to break the spirits of any Modest Young Man & more than any Man should be exposed to without his own free acceptance, unless his crimes had been so great as to merit a state of exile."[7]

A failure once again, William worked for a while as a surveyor's assistant, returning to Philadelphia in 1767, where he tried more jobs and got drawing commissions from some of his father's English contacts. By 1773 Dr. John Fothergill, an English Quaker physician and ardent plant collector, was so taken with the younger Bartram's drawings that he agreed to finance a botanizing trip in Florida. Bartram was to spend two to three years collecting plants and their seeds and make drawings of them at a minimum salary of fifty guineas per year. It was good money and the chance he had longed for—and he turned it into a four-year trip (upon his return Bartram thought he'd only been gone three) that wove throughout the frontiers of Georgia, South Carolina, North Carolina, and East and West Florida.[8]

"It is surprising that a man of slight build, lacking the physical vigor of his father and the aggressive nature needed to be successful in business, would accept and carry out an assignment of such physical and emotional challenge," writes Brad Sanders, who has compiled a comprehensive Bartram guide. Often this meant traveling alone with a horse or small boat while carrying a gun, fishing rod, cooking equipment, camping gear, and collecting essentials through some rough, wild areas.[9]

After leaving Charleston, South Carolina, in April 1774 for Florida, Bartram learned of dangers that lay ahead when his boat encountered a trading schooner whose occupants told him that Natives had plundered a trading store on the St. Johns that Bartram planned to use to resupply goods and send out his collections. Luckily, traders at the store where Bartram had shipped a trunk of supplies were able to secrete it on a river island. Determined to get to it, Bartram exited his boat at Amelia Island and headed up the north-flowing St. Johns (he called it the San Juan) in a canoe with a sail, provisions, a gun, and ammunition. It was mid-April, and he found "fair wind" on his solitary journey, although the size of his boat made it necessary to hug the river's shoreline. Bartram wrote that he was "continually impelled by a restless spirit of curiosity, in pursuit of new productions of nature, my chief happiness consisted in tracing and admiring the infinite power, majesty, and perfection of the great Almighty Creator, and in the contemplation, that through divine aid and permission, I might be instrumental in discovering, and introducing into my native country, some original productions of nature, which might become useful to society."[10]

Bartram's narrative mixed observations of people and place along with in-depth analysis of animals and plants while also providing a very entertaining travelogue. *Travels* purported to include one Florida voyage, but in fact it was woven from two trips up and down the river. His work demonstrated his deep curiosity, with detailed descriptions of all things large and small, often accompanied by acclamations to the Almighty with exclamation points for emphasis. Bartram camped many nights on riverbanks but also welcomed hospitality from plantation owners. He listened to the "roaring of the crocodiles [alligators]," "the croaking of frogs," and often encountered "clouds of musquitoes" along the way. At one stop, a friend told him that the governor of East Florida had met a few days earlier with Lower Creek chiefs to discuss the store raid in an effort to avoid war. The chiefs "promised to indemnify the traders for the loss of their goods, and requested that they might return to their storehouse, with goods as usual, and that they should be safe in their persons and property." Bartram sailed upriver, camping alone and observing what few Europeans had seen. A few days later he retrieved his chest and soon set out on his river journey.[11]

He awoke at his camp one morning to wild turkeys "saluting each other" and observed that the "high forests ring with the noise." Bartram was equally entranced by plant life on the shore—live oaks "of an astonishing magnitude" that reached a girth of 12 to 18 feet at their base. Up the river he spotted a "magnificent grove" that featured palms and 100-foot-magnolias that were "the most beautiful and tall that I have any where seen." The ancient cypresses, logged out in the twentieth century, were "so lofty, as to preclude the sight of the high-land forests beyond them; and these trees, having flat tops, and all of equal height, seemed to be a green plain, lifted up and supported upon columns in the air." Atop the trees he saw nesting eagles, resting storks, and "hovering and fluttering" Carolina parakeets—a colorful species declared extinct in 1939, the victim of habitat loss, hunting, and disease. After observing trees and plants, Bartram carefully detailed their size, color, location, flowers, seeds—even the taste of any fruit.[12]

Native people fascinated him. At one village, probably near today's city of Palatka, Bartram sailed by and observed youths wading and fishing in the river while younger children diverted themselves "in shooting frogs with bows and arrows. On my near approach, the little children took to their heels, and ran to some women who were hoeing corn; but the stouter youth stood their ground, and, smiling, called to me." Older villagers "reclined on skins spread on the ground, under the cool shade of spreading Oaks and Palms," he noted. "They were civil, and appeared happy in their situation." What other White colonists might have disparaged, Bartram painted as an idyllic community.[13]

This stretch of the St. Johns River was territory that Bartram recognized from his previous visit, including an earthen Native mound known as Mount Royal. Bartram described it at length, although the Timucuans who built it and once numbered up to 150,000 strong in North Florida had succumbed by the time of his visit. By 1500 ACE, the site was abandoned, but the area reemerged in the 1590s as a Spanish mission. The mound, which Bartram described as up to 20 feet high, was constructed to bury the dead between 900 and 1300 ACE and was part of a much larger complex that included a 50-yard-wide "noble Indian highway" that led from the mound three-quarters of a mile to an artificial lake on a savanna. In the fifteen years since his first visit, a large orange grove had been cleared and planted with indigo, corn, and cotton "but since deserted." Bartram understood that the site was not a "New World" and had a long history of Native use.[14]

Bartram sailed the next day behind a group of traders and encountered a vast expanse of river dubbed Lake George to honor the ruling British monarch. Its size and the frequency of storms can make it a nightmare for mariners. "I cannot entirely suppress my apprehensions of danger," he wrote of the lake. "My vessel at once diminished to a nut-shell on the swelling sea, and at the distance of a few miles, must appear to the surprised observer as some aquatic animal, at intervals emerging from its surface." A hard wind and gathering thunderstorm forced him to seek cover on an island, probably today's Drayton Island at the lake's northwest. Bartram noticed more Native ruins there, including a "conical pyramid of earth." The fragments of earthenware convinced him that the island was once "well inhabited," and though Bartram saw no people there, he did see much wildlife. "The bears are invited here to partake of the fruit of the orange tree, which they are immoderately fond of; and both they and turkeys are made extremely fat and delicious, from their feeding on the sweet acorns of the live oak." Today the island has homes and a ferry.[15]

The next night Bartram and the traders enjoyed an "enchanting little forest" and a floral scent wafting in the air. While the men set up camp and collected firewood, Bartram took along his flintlock rifle for a walk that led him to some "enchanting" grasslands that "had been lately burnt by Indian hunters, and had just now recovered their vernal verdure and gaiety." He mused about this place and fellow humans: "How happily situated is this retired spot of earth! What an elysium it is! Where the wandering Simi-nole, the naked red warrior, roams at large, and after the vigorous chase retires from the scorching heat of the meridian sun. Here he reclines, and reposes under the odoriferous shades of Zanthoxylon, his verdant couch guarded by the Deity; Liberty, and the Muses, inspiring him with wisdom and valour, whilst the balmy zephyrs fan him to sleep."[16]

Realizing that he had been "seduced by these sublime enchanting scenes of terrestrial happiness" and had ventured too far, Bartram returned to camp where the others were fishing for trout—today's largemouth bass. He observed the traders' fishing methods and later used them.

Just off Lake George, Bartram visited a bubbling "crystal fountain"—to-day known as Salt Springs—populated with various fish of "the most brilliant colors," an alligator, and a stingray; to his Romantic thinking, they were living in harmony. He was enchanted looking into the "abyss," which he likened to art: "This amazing and delightful scene, though real, appears at first but as a piece of excellent painting; there seems no medium; you imagine the picture to be within a few inches of your eyes, and that you may without the least difficulty touch any one of the fish, or put your finger upon the crocodile's eye, when it really is twenty or thirty feet under water."[17]

Bartram reached Spalding's Upper Store, a trading post on the west bank of the river at the present-day town of Astor. It was one of two river trading outposts, the other being Spalding's Lower Store, near Palatka. Natives had looted the Upper Store, an important site where they exchanged goods with merchants and hunters. When Bartram arrived there, a White trader was running the business. Nearby was an encampment of Seminoles, including White Captain, a chief whose "handsome" daughter was the trader's com-panion. "Seminole," which may derive from the name *semanolies,* "which meant 'wild people' or 'runaways,'" was the name used to describe members of the Creek nation and other groups that became the dominant Florida tribe in the 1700s.[18]

After staying several weeks at the post, Bartram set off for the southern reaches of the river. He was accompanied by White Captain's young neph-ew, who needed to travel upriver and agreed to help Bartram. That included rowing the boat "under a fervid sun," which the nephew disliked. He asked to be dropped off on a riverbank. Bartram hoped the young man had simply gone hunting and would return, but he sailed alone the next morning into what was his greatest adventure of the trip—a frightening encounter with alligators.[19]

Bartram had ventured on this part of the river in 1766, recognizing sites and their names. The earlier trip, however, had been in cold months of the winter, when there was frost on the ground and alligators were hidden and dormant. Bartram's second trip came in spring, when alligators amassed to feast on the annual river run of shad and to mate, making them aggressive and noisy in their bellowing.[20]

On a "temperately cool and calm" evening, he made camp on a small 3-acre peninsula on the west bank under a large live oak a few yards from his boat, likely today's Idlewilde Point near the mouth of Stagger Mud Lake. Discovering that he had few supplies, the hungry Bartram set out to fish in a nearby lagoon, noticing flowering plants and birds along the way. And there were alligators:

> Behold him rushing forth from the flags and reeds. His enormous body swells. His plaited tail brandished high, floats upon the lake. The waters like a cataract descend from his opening jaws. Clouds of smoke issue from his dilated nostrils. The earth trembles with thunder. When immediately from the opposite coast of the lagoon, emerges from the deep his rival champion. They suddenly dart upon each other. The boiling surface of the lake marks their rapid course, and a terrific conflict commences. They now sink to the bottom folded together in horrid wreaths. The water becomes thick and discoloured. Again they rise, their jaws clap together, re-echoing through the deep surrounding forests. . . . The proud victor exulting returns to the place of action. The shores and forests resound his dreadful roar, together with the triumphing shouts of the plaited tribes around, witnesses of the horrid combat.[21]

Bartram hurried into his boat to hastily catch some fish and get back to camp, taking a club for defense. It was a prudent move. As he paddled toward what he later called "Battle Lagoon," he was "attacked on all sides, several [alligators] endeavouring to overset the canoe." Two large alligators rushed Bartram, who beat them and headed toward the shore as the reptiles retreated. Determined to get a meal, Bartram resumed fishing but was pursued back to his river camp, "especially by an old daring one, about twelve feet in length, who kept close after me." On land, the alligator "rushed up near my feet, and lay there for some time, looking me in the face, his head and shoulders out of the water." Bartram dashed to camp, grabbed his gun, and fired, ending the encounter. As he cleaned the fish, another alligator

Bartram's drawings of alligators, while not scientifically accurate, demonstrate his interest in the reptiles despite dangerous encounters with them. Courtesy of the State Archives of Florida.

surprised Bartram, who surmised that his last-second glimpse of the reptile was "most providential" since "the monster would probably, in less than a minute have seized and dragged me into the river." He prepared the fish quickly, pulled his boat onto dry land, emptied its contents, and headed back to camp.[22]

Looking back at the river from the camp's promontory, Bartram observed something he could barely believe—a massive gathering of alligators lined up across a narrow pass so that it seemed "that it would have been easy to have walked across on their heads, had the animals been harmless." The reptiles were there to feast on the migration of "I may say hundreds of thousands" of fish that were headed upriver to spawn. It was an easy meal for the alligators, and the scene continued through the night. He hoped it would distract them from him.[23]

But a new danger arose—while Bartram watched the alligators feed, using a method of cooperative feeding that modern scientists have observed in other crocodilian species, the scent of his broiling fish enticed two very large bears to his camp. Bartram grabbed his gun and fired; the bears "galloped off, plunging through the water and swamp, never halting, I suppose, until they reached fast land. . . . They did not presume to return again," he wrote.[24]

After a mostly sleepless night listening to roaring alligators and hooting owls, Bartram awoke to a peaceful morning and once again assumed his naturalist's demeanor. Bartram paddled along the shore, observing young alligators and a nesting site, which he described in detail. Later that day he was fascinated watching anhingas, which he called snake birds, swim and dive in the river.

A remarkable place that Bartram visited was Paynes Prairie, a wide savanna located south of today's Gainesville. He traveled there with a group of traders eager to establish an inland trading post. They planned to meet with Ahaya, a leader among the Alachua Seminoles, who oversaw important cattle-herding and trade on the prairie. The English called Ahaya "Cowkeeper," a term Bartram used in *Travels*.[25]

En route, Bartram observed the sandy scrub landscape and pine forests, studied the fish of inland lakes, and ate a "fat" soft-shelled turtle, which he studied before consuming. Approaching their destination, the group was "cheerfully received" by "various tribes of birds" before finally reaching a mound ahead of Ahaya's town of Cuscowilla near today's Micanopy. "Young men and maidens" welcomed the group and led them to the tall, cheerful chief's house. Rather than shaking hands, Ahaya shook arms, "saying at the same time, 'You are come,'" and they followed him to a reception that included passing a pipe, drinking from a shared bowl, and feasting on stewed venison and corn cakes accompanied by a drink of honey mixed with water.[26]

Ahaya/Cowkeeper was a complicated leader. He hated the Spanish and, from his previous home in Georgia, had aided a 1740 British attack on the Spanish stronghold of St. Augustine. According to Lars Andersen, the ongoing struggle between the British (with colonies to the north) and the Spanish (then holders of Florida) "caused friction among the different Creek factions, who were often on opposing sides." Around 1750 Ahaya moved with his fellow Natives to the prairie near what had been the Spanish ranch of La Chua and managed abandoned cattle that roamed in a free-range style. When the Spanish ceded Florida to Britain in 1763 at the end of the French and Indian War, also known as the Seven Years' War, the resulting peace allowed trading networks to open in Florida's interior.[27]

After the 1774 traders discussed their mission, they told Ahaya about Bartram's work, "and he received me with complaisance, giving me unlimited permission to travel over the country for the purpose of collecting flowers, medicinal plants &c. saluting me by the name of PUC PUGGY, or the Flower hunter, recommending me to the friendship and protection of his people," Bartram wrote. This was a momentous occasion. Bartram had been nicknamed and offered protection by a powerful chief, which may explain his subsequent ability to travel without hindrance or fear of harm from Natives.[28]

After the meal, Bartram and the team camped on the nearby prairie:

> The extensive Alachua savanna is a level green plain, above fifteen miles over, fifty miles in circumference, and scarcely a tree or bush of any kind to be seen on it. It is encircled with high, sloping hills, covered with waving forests and fragrant Orange groves, rising from an exuberantly fertile soil. The towering magnolia grandiflora and transcendent Palm, stand conspicuous amongst them. At the same time are seen innumerable droves of cattle; the lordly bull, lowing cow, and sleek capricious heifer. The hills and groves re-echo their cheerful, social voices. Herds of sprightly deer, squadrons of the beautiful fleet Siminole horse, flocks of turkeys, civilized communities of the sonorous watchful crane, mix together, appearing happy and contented in the enjoyment of peace, till disturbed and affrighted by the warrior man.[29]

Bartram's descriptions of the prairie and the Native town are extensive. He offered details about snakes, trees, and agricultural plantings. Importantly, he described wolves that feasted on a horse carcass, noting they were black, smaller than those in Canada and Pennsylvania, and that they ran away when the men were within gunshot distance. His was the first recorded description of the Florida red wolf, an animal that was once widespread but now is on the brink of extinction.[30]

Importantly, Bartram offered insights into Alachua cattle operations. He wrote that the cattle were as "large and fat" as those grazing back in Pennsylvania and watched as a party rounded up several herds and announced that there would be a feast "in compliment of our arrival, and pacific negotiations." The meal consisted of various cuts of beef—an animal introduced by Europeans—and was intended to impress the traders. "Cattle represented both Ahaya's authority and the source of his autonomy in the region," notes historian Jason Herbert. "Cattle herding became the defining trait of the Alachuas, shaping their decision to occupy the vast prairie expanses in north central Florida." Ultimately it would attract settlers who wanted the Alachua lands.[31]

Many later visitors to the site would recall and confirm Bartram's prairie descriptions.

William Hayne Simmons, traveling across Alachua Savannah in 1823, wrote that Bartram's account was "substantially correct." Observing a vent where water left the prairie and went underground, he asked his guide where the water went and was told it traveled all the way to the Suwannee River: "He said that some years ago, an Indian bathing near the sink drowned and his body afterwards found in the Suwannee. I give this story as I received it." It is a tale that is often repeated but never verified.[32]

After leaving Florida, Bartram wandered through Georgia, South Carolina, North Carolina, and back into territory that would become Alabama and West Florida. He finished his 2,400-mile journey in January 1777 but was not the same man, notes Slaughter: "He had been ill, almost to death; perhaps it was the scarlet fever that had laid him low for over a month in 1775 or poison ivy that infected his eyes, temporarily blinded him, and forever weakened his sight." But he also was "happy," feeling blessed that "Almighty God" had protected him through the long trek that had opened his eyes to the natural world. Bartram, thirty-eight, had survived and thrived through a great adventure. After working on a manuscript for years, he published *Travels* in Philadelphia in 1791 and then in London the next year. It was received carefully, with some readers worried about its poetic descriptions and accuracy. But prominent writers loved it, and today, still in print, it ranks as one of the most important American natural history books ever written.[33]

The book inspired writers such as James Fenimore Cooper and Henry David Thoreau. British poet Samuel Taylor Coleridge used Bartram's descriptions of Florida's crystalline springs as inspiration for passages from "Kubla Khan":

Where Alph, the sacred river, ran
Through caverns measureless to man
Down to a sunless sea.[34]

British poet William Wordsworth also read *Travels,* found inspiration for his work, and carried it with him on a journey. Since then, it has become a text for scientists, anthropologists, land managers, and those seeking to connect with the Florida that existed before wholesale development made much of it disappear. Bartram described more than six hundred species of plants, birds, reptiles, and amphibians new to Europeans and colonists. Some were never again seen where he found them, perhaps a result of changing climate conditions or human actions. His observations included the fact that birds left the cold Northeast for Florida in the winter; others had speculated that they flew to the moon or hid under mud during cold months.[35]

Bartram's influence was much larger than *Travels* and has grown in subsequent centuries. Scholars continue to read his book and visit museums in the United States and England where his drawings and collections are housed. Noted ornithologist Alexander Wilson took drawing lessons from Bartram and "graciously expressed his debt to Bartram," writes historian Charlotte M. Porter, adding that by the time *Travels* was published, "English-speaking travelers had lost easy access to Florida landscapes, now controlled by Spain."[36]

After his father's death, Bartram and his brother John Jr. continued and expanded the family's Philadelphia nursery business, and the garden became a gathering place for scholars and politicians of the era, including President Thomas Jefferson, who corresponded with the botanist. Some proposed that Bartram join subsequent westward exploration journeys, including Jefferson's 1806 Red River expedition, but Bartram's poor eyesight and health—he broke his leg in 1786 falling out of a cypress tree at home while gathering seeds—prevented him from ever venturing far again. His health caused him to decline a lecturer's job at the nearby University of Pennsylvania, but he stayed intellectually busy and consulted with many naturalists who visited his garden.[37]

Bartram died at age eighty-four at the family home and was buried in an unmarked grave, perhaps under a tree that he had planted with a view of the nearby river. Today the 45-acre Bartram's Garden is a National Historic Landmark that attracts up to forty thousand visitors each year. Although it sits amid decaying apartment complexes overlooking the very polluted Schuylkill River, it is possible to imagine it once was a place of peace and harmony.

A multitude of books have been written about Bartram, and many people have retraced his path. To provide modern guidance, large, engraved metal William Bartram Trail markers have been erected throughout the Southeast, noting the dates when he traveled near the spots; as of 2019, there were sixty-four markers, according to the Bartram Trail Conference. The new Bartram Garden at Stetson University is part of that trail. In recent years, a reinvigorated Bartram Trail Society of Florida has held a "St. Johns River Bartram Frolic" to celebrate the author, featuring speakers, music, and Bartram impersonators. Annually, the Bartram Trail Conference meets with representatives of states along his path, with activities ranging from watching documentaries to viewing Bartram-era artifacts to retracing his trails.

"William Bartram was the first great American naturalist and he was the transition between a tentative colonial scientific community dominated by

European minds to an American science characterized by self-confidence, boldness, and a peculiar relationship to the natural world that has produced numerous environmental movements, the world's first national park system, the science of Ecology, and a burgeoning market for outdoor gear," writes Sanders. "The paradox in the *Travels* is that the wilderness as seen and admired by Bartram could not last with the coming of civilization. The historical value of Bartram's work is that he gives us a glimpse of the South as a lost paradise."[38]

"Bartram's ability to marry science with poetry ensured *Travels* a worldwide audience for the last 200 years," writes Dorinda G. Dallmeyer, director of the Environmental Ethics Certificate Program at the University of Georgia. "Paramount among his talents was the power of observation. Through Bartram's words, modern readers can visualize the South of the 1770s, a landscape that resounded with vast roosts of passenger pigeons and the wingbeats of Carolina parakeets, where old-growth hardwoods and millions of acres of longleaf pine forests stood, and in which clear rivers ran free to the sea."[39]

Today an oil portrait of Bartram, a sprig of white flowers jutting from his vest, is displayed in Philadelphia, part of the Portrait Gallery of Independence National Historical Park.

The gentle "Puc Puggy" gazes calmly from the canvas, surrounded by portraits of other prominent Americans—his legacy providing a glimpse into a past that is largely gone today. I've stared into the eyes of Bartram's portrait in wonder and meandered through his family homestead. But it's even more interesting to see the sites he visited in Florida with a view to changes in the past two centuries. My family has endured multiple river trips where I pulled out *Travels* to find the spots he described, and, a few times, they've even matched my enthusiasm.

One largely unvisited spot is Mount Royal, the large Timucuan mound near Welaka, now a state archaeological site listed on the National Register of Historic Places. Two markers declare its importance, but it is difficult to reach because of its location inside a fly-in gated community called Mount Royal Estates that impedes access—a gate code is required to visit. The 1-acre site, shaded by large trees that have sprung up in ensuing years and flanked by posts from a defunct chain-link enclosure, is all that remains. What would have been the "noble highway" now ends at a runway, a blend of old and new that is nothing if not ironic.

Mary Ann Wilcox Anderson's family developed the property in the 1980s and donated the site to the state and maintains a nearby shelter with information to inform curious visitors. She takes great pride in it and keeps materials about its history. On a sweltering July morning I met her there along with Keith H. Ashley, a University of North Florida archaeologist, who brought a collection of artifacts found during excavations at the mound, the last in 1983. Digging in burial mounds is prohibited by law, but earlier excavations established that this was one. Timucuans also built shell mounds around the peninsula that essentially were trash heaps (and evidence today of the richness of marine food resources) but may also have served as territorial markers. Many of Florida's burial mounds were opened in past decades by academics and relic seekers, some following Bartram's route; many others were dug up and used for road building and are now lost to the world, including many mounds that Hernando de Soto passed by.[40]

Remarkably, some of the artifacts found at Mount Royal originated in other places. Ashley explained that copper objects from graves indicate extensive trade connections in North America. Some academics think the Mount Royal community may have been a center for the trade of large shells—possibly exchanged for copper. Ashley held a variety of the thousands of pottery sherds from the site that demonstrated different styles of Native pottery as well as remnants of Spanish olive jars and pieces of china from Spanish and British colonial periods. Residents in the area still periodically find artifacts buried in their yards while gardening.[41]

"Bartram makes a really great, astute description of the site," said Ashley. Bartram recognized it was a burial and ritual place although the Timucuans were deceased by 1774. During that time "no one was writing about mounds or digging them. The fact that he stops and makes this really detailed description is really notable for the time. He recognized it as a really ancient Indian community."[42]

Months later, on a chilly spring day, I boated on the St. Johns River to the site of Bartram's "Battle Lagoon" with my good friend Clay Henderson, an environmental attorney and Bartram aficionado extraordinaire who named his son after the botanist. Along the way, we counted twenty-two species of birds (you can't go out with Henderson and not count birds—he is a former president of the Florida Audubon Society). Henderson, now in his sixties, first read Bartram three decades ago and has made several forays to follow the Quaker's path, as have I. Houses now dot the river's eastern shore, but soon we reached an area where both sides of the river are preserved, giving us a vision of Old Florida.

We disembarked at Idlewilde Point, a 6–7-foot rise on a bank dense with vegetation, and immediately felt Bartram's spirit. Nearby, a lone fisherman cast a line into the lagoon, perhaps looking for bass. There were recent campfires here, maybe on Bartram's old site. Across the river was the expanse of Lake Dexter, its metallic-colored surface rippling with the wind. We spotted alligators all morning and pointed to a myriad of birds along the way.

So, why Bartram? Why are we still talking about him?

"What's not to like?" replied a grinning Henderson. "He sees God in all of nature, treated Natives as real people, and has a spiritual connection to all around him. We're still trying to find that."[43]

Henderson first learned of *Travels* from a developer who wanted to build a housing subdivision centered around an ancient live oak. The proposed name for the project: Bartram Oak. Henderson, who has been engaged in state land preservation efforts for decades, thought to himself, "I don't think so," and quickly joined the effort to save the property, once the site of a plantation that Bartram visited. The land today is part of Blue Spring State Park.[44]

Travels has been used by state land managers as a baseline manual for restoring property to as original a state as is possible in today's Florida, which now holds more than 22 million residents. The big trees, including the enormous cypress that once lined the river, are gone, but it still is possible to find Bartram's world on the river, just an hour away from the urban bustle of Orlando. That is a remarkable gift.

"Through his writing and his natural eye, we have the best description of Florida's natural environment before we messed it up," Henderson said.[45]

Helping others discover Bartram was central to a project that Henderson brought to life during his former work at Stetson University. While helping develop plans for the DeLand school's Sandra Stetson Aquatic Center on the west side of Lake Beresford, Henderson oversaw the planning and installation of the Bartram Gardens & Trail. The site features native vegetation, including species that Bartram observed when traveling nearby. The college obtained digital images of Bartram's journal and drawings and used them in the garden's signage and information kiosks. "It is an opportunity to see his art and embrace his words in a place that contributed to his journey," Henderson said.[46]

Bartram is also the inspiration for the preservation and restoration of Paynes Prairie State Preserve, the Alachua Savannah that he described so eloquently. In 1970, owing to efforts by tireless activists, the preserve was created, protecting 17,346 acres at a cost of $5.1 million. Land managers turned to *Travels* to restore the prairie as closely as possible to that which

Bartram marveled at the beauty of Paynes Prairie, now a state park where wild horses graze near the visitor center. Courtesy of Bruce Hunt.

Bartram encountered. Many of animals he saw are now extinct—the Carolina parakeet, the ivory-billed woodpecker, the passenger pigeon—and others such as the red wolf and Florida panther have disappeared from the area. At the same time, non-native species had invaded, including house sparrows, starlings, and armadillos. Land managers decided to do the best they could and, in keeping with the area's natural history, released bison and Spanish horses to the prairie. Old dikes became hiking paths, and one of the most popular, La Chua Trail, at the prairie's north end, is a favorite for birders and for anyone wanting to view enormous alligators.

Andersen, who penned a history of the prairie, met me on a July day at the preserve's visitor center at the south end of the savanna. It is built on a bluff that affords a long vista of the landscape, made even better by a wooden tower. From there we spotted the horse herd grazing casually, one young foal shadowing its mother. The heat was scorching, but the tanned, relaxed Andersen seemed immune to it, perhaps a result of his regular work guiding canoes and kayaks along the area's rivers. His enthusiasm about Bartram and Paynes Prairie is infectious.

"The Alachua Savannah speaks to me," Andersen said, gazing past the horses to the far side of the prairie. Today, it "looks very much like what Bartram wrote."[47]

Interestingly, the majority of Bartram's plant and animal descriptions were very accurate. But a few he got wrong, like describing alligator jaws as hinged on the top or describing a rattlesnake cleaning plates at a trading post. A flowering plant he described, today known as Bartram's ixia, wasn't found again until 1931, stopping the doubters. "But his accounts of the St. Johns are true," Andersen said, as is the plant information. The prairie was known before Bartram arrived, but "the real connection today is when it came into public hands, the park service decided to model the ecosystem after his writings."[48]

Bartram is also an inspiration for modern artists and activists.

In 2020, a film about Bartram was released throughout the country. *Cultivating the Wild* was directed by Eric Breitenbach, a retired senior professor at the Southeast Center for Photographic Studies at Daytona State College in Daytona Beach, Florida. It was a work of love sparked by Breitenbach's first reading of Bartram back in the 1980s. New to the state, he decided to visit and photograph every county in Florida. First, he was told, he needed to read *Travels*.

"I liked everything about it . . . his poetic descriptions, his obsessiveness about certain things," Breitenbach said. "I glommed onto the book."[49]

For years he kept a file with notes, and in 2016, after collaborating with Dallmeyer, filming began. The hour-long documentary includes observations from the botanist's Florida and Georgia travels along with profiles of six modern-day "Bartrams"—activists and writers who exemplify his love of nature. In hearing their stories, viewers may be inspired to act to preserve the natural world.

"I think *Cultivating the Wild* will be a step in the right direction . . . toward environmental consciousness," Breitenbach said, noting that it has probably been seen by hundreds of thousands of viewers. "Hopefully it moves people forward a little bit."[50]

In one of the most powerful scenes, James Holland, a former activist for Georgia's Altamaha River, treks into an ancient swamp to commune with a massive cypress tree. It's "God's country," he declares. "If Bartram were alive today and I could converse with him after the work that he has done in the wild and nature itself, all I could say is thank you, thank you, thank you, because you made my life better."[51]

Gone more than two centuries, Bartram is still teaching and inspiring people about natural beauty.

To share some of William Bartram's experiences, visit these locations and websites:

Paynes Prairie Preserve State Park
100 Savannah Boulevard
Micanopy, Florida 32667
(352) 466-3397
floridastateparks.org/parks-and-trails/paynes-prairie-preserve-state
-park

One of Florida's most scenic and most accessible nature habitats is Paynes Prairie Preserve State Park, just south of Gainesville. It was Florida's first official state biological preserve, acquired by the state in 1970, and encompasses 21,000 acres that straddle I-75 on its west side, and borders on the southern side of Gainesville to the north and the northern edge of Micanopy to the south. Much of the park is open savanna and marshland, known as the Paynes Prairie Basin. In 1774, when William Bartram visited here, it was just called the Alachua Savannah. A hundred years later a sinkhole in its center filled in and became blocked, turning the savanna into a giant lake. For twenty years it was regularly crossed by paddleboats. But in the summer of 1891, the sink suddenly drained, leaving fish and paddleboats stranded in the mud. In recent years the savanna has begun filling with water once again, and what were once hiking trails are now only navigable by canoe or kayak. When Bartram was here, he observed a wide variety of birds, and today Paynes Prairie is still one of Florida's best and most popular bird-watching locations. An abundance of sandhill cranes, egrets, herons, ibises, anhingas, and hawks call it home and share the space with somewhat rarer limpkins, wood storks, bald eagles, and Harris's sparrows. In addition, wild horses roam the prairie, and in 1975 a small herd of bison were introduced to the park.

The visitor center and main entrance to the park can be reached at the park's south end, down Savannah Boulevard off US 441 just north of Micanopy.

Hours: The park is open from 8:00 a.m. to sundown every day of the year.
Admission: $6 per vehicle with 2-plus occupants; $4 per vehicle with a single occupant; $2 for pedestrians or bicyclists.

Bartram Trail Conference
bartramtrail.org/
Bartram Trail sites and historical markers
bartramtrail.org/page-1647833

The Bartram Trail Conference maintains a website with extensive information, directions, and interactive maps. There are dozens of Bartram sites and historical markers throughout the north and northwestern region of Florida, and the Bartram Trail Conference website pages above are the best source for locating and visiting them.

Bartram's Garden

5400 Lindbergh Boulevard
Philadelphia, Pennsylvania 19143
(215) 729-5281
bartramsgarden.org

Bartram's Garden sits along the west bank of the Schuylkill River in southwest Philadelphia, on the 45-acre property that was once the home and farm of botanist and naturalist John Bartram, William Bartram's father. Several miles of hiking trails meander through a living display of plants and trees, many discovered or at least first described in detail by the Bartrams. In addition to the Bartram home and barn, the grounds include his plant-exchange business greenhouse, built in 1760, where John Bartram collected and nurtured thousands of species of both native and exotic plants.
Hours: Open daily on weekdays, 10:00 a.m.–4:00 p.m.; on weekends, April 1 through the first weekend in December (except Thanksgiving Day and the Friday after Thanksgiving), 10:00 a.m.–6:00 p.m.
Admission is free. Guided tours, conducted Thursdays–Sundays, are free to members; $12 for adults; $10 for seniors; free for children under 2 years old.

4

John James Audubon

Looking for a Paradise of Birds, 1831–1832

Florida was supposed to be Eden, filled with beautiful birds and a lush, idyllic landscape to busy an artist's brush. Instead, John James Audubon found himself in a place where the "stink of the River Water" sickened half the crew of his boat, and all about him was "a *wild* and *dreary* and desolate part of the World." There were "thousands" of alligators, "sand Barrens," and "now and then an *Impenetrable* swamp," he wrote to his wife, Lucy, adding that his "*account* of what I have or shall see of the Floridas will be far, very far from the corroborating of the *flowery sayings* of Mr. Barton [Bartram] the Botanist."[1]

It was February 1832, and Audubon, fresh from his successful publication of *The Birds of America*, was in Florida looking for new additions to the collection. Audubon had spent several years traveling in Europe, selling subscriptions for periodic sets of 2' × 3' life-sized engravings of his avian watercolors and lecturing about wildlife in the United States. Returning triumphantly to the United States, where he previously had received little recognition for his abilities, Audubon was determined to finally achieve fame.

One way to accomplish this was for Audubon to style himself as the "American Woodsman," a persona that biographer Gregory Nobles describes as "a highly masculinized amalgam of art and science, but still a friendly denizen of the frontier." It was brilliant marketing for the era, and Audubon, with his long, shoulder-length hair and hunting prowess, certainly played the role. "The American Woodsman wasn't just a catchy nickname; it was a well-chosen role. Audubon didn't just live his life; he performed it."[2]

In reality, Audubon's early background was far from the frontier. The illegitimate son of a French ship captain and a chambermaid, Audubon was

John James Audubon traveled to Florida in 1831–1832 searching for birds he could include in *The Birds of America* collection. Public domain.

born in 1785 in Les Cayes, Santo Domingo (now Haiti), where his father had a plantation. In 1791, Audubon, whose mother had died a few months after his birth, went to France, where he was raised by his father's wife. To avoid conscription into Napoleon Bonaparte's troops in 1803, Audubon headed across the Atlantic Ocean to his father's Pennsylvania estate, where potentially lucrative lead ore had been discovered on the property. The United States had just announced the Louisiana Purchase, opening the continent to settlement but also to curiosity about what existed there—an attitude that would spark Audubon's life and work. While in Pennsylvania, he met and married Lucy Bakewell, who would be his lifelong correspondent and supporter of his career.[3]

Three decades later, Audubon had reinvented himself as a self-made scientist and artist, with a goal of painting all the birds in the young United States. Audubon, forty-six, energetically headed to Florida, anticipating that the enthusiastic writings of colonial naturalist William Bartram about the peninsula's flora and fauna would be true—that the peninsula was an avian paradise that would inspire and enrich his work.

It was forty years after William Bartram's *Travels* was published when the hopeful Audubon, in August 1831, returned from England and began plotting his Florida venture. He gained permission from the US government to travel on a revenue cutter into Florida waters, first stopping in Charleston, South Carolina, where he met Lutheran minister and naturalist John Bachman, resulting in a lifelong friendship. In November, Audubon landed in St. Augustine, part of the Florida Territory that the United States acquired ten years earlier from Spain.[4]

He was deeply disappointed.

The city "is doubtless the poorest village I have seen in America—The Inhabitants principally poor Fishermen although excellent Fishers—The streets about 10 feet wide and deeply sanded—backed by some thousands of orange Trees," he wrote to Lucy. The Spanish fort, the Castillo de San Marcos, he wrote, was "now decaying fast." And despite "hunting a great deal," he'd only found two birds to draw.[5]

Audubon's entourage included taxidermist Henry Ward, on hand to prepare bird skins that Audubon would gather, and landscape painter George Lehman, in charge of creating illustrations for backgrounds to the images. The men spent their days walking with guns and Plato, Audubon's Newfoundland dog, "uninterruptedly till dusk" when they could find birds. Other times they rowed into marshes, anchored the boat, waded "through mud and water, amid myriads of sand-flies and mosquitoes, shooting here and there a bird or squatting down on our hams for half an hour, to observe the ways of the beautiful beings we are in pursuit of." As evening began, they watched "cranes, herons, pelicans, curlews, and the trains of blackbirds" heading overhead to their roosts. He wrote to a friend: "I know I am engaged in an arduous undertaking; but if I live to complete it, I will offer to my country a beautiful monument of the varied splendour of American nature, and of my devotion to American ornithology."[6]

It was laborious work. Lacking the modern tools of binoculars and photography, Audubon had to rely on his vision, a telescope, and sketches to compose his works. In order to get a close look at birds, he shot them and wired the carcasses to create a pose from which to draw. Each composition attempted to show birds in their natural state, with local landscapes in the background.

As historian Kathryn Hall Proby wrote, the artist created some notable sketches in the area, including a herring gull, with the St. Augustine harbor as a backdrop, and the greenshank, which offered "a sweeping view of Saint Augustine in the distance" that included the Castillo. The male greenshank collected by Audubon in the Florida Keys, notes Proby, caused some consternation as it is a European species "never recorded before or since in North America. It is thought that Audubon probably mistook a Greater Yellowlegs for the Greenshank." However, modern ornithologists have since verified a greenshank in an Ohio collection that was obtained in Tampa in the late 1800s, lending credence to Audubon's work.[7]

Despite the new scenery and bird collections, Proby noted, "Florida at this point had not measured up to the flowery sayings of the naturalist William Bartram, and Audubon and his companions were still months away from the ends they sought."[8]

By mid-December, with hundreds of bird skins and drawings of about a dozen species, it was time to move on, writes biographer William Souder. "Audubon felt he had exhausted the area or soon would. In truth, much of what he saw disappointed him, from the scrubby desolation of the land to the indifferent shooting. If it could be managed, he hoped to travel on foot and by boat all the way down the eastern shore of Florida." It was an area reported to be "an untouched wilderness of waterways and forests that was home to a great many birds."[9]

Audubon's party headed south for 30 miles to the plantation of General Joseph Marian Hernandez, but their relations were difficult. "The dignified Spanish-American general regarded Audubon as a spectacle of the backwoods, a man of unwarranted and unreasonable vocation," wrote Proby. "The two men could not reach a mutual ground of communication, so each went his own way, Hernandez ruling his rich cane fields while Audubon roamed the woods." Audubon did procure an American coot for his collection.[10]

On Christmas, Audubon and company walked 15 miles farther south along the sandy King's Road to "Bulow Ville," the largest plantation in East Florida. It was owned by the welcoming John Bulow, a twenty-five-year-old French-speaking bachelor known for having "one of the best wine cellars in America." He was so well-stocked that he used wine bottles as erosion control in his boat slips on a marshy tidal creek. Lehman drew scenes from the sugarcane plantation, including a "magnificent ground-level view of the primordial salt marsh with the ghostly outlines of palms and moss-craped cypress in the distance that became the background of Audubon's portrait of the tell-tale godwit, or snipe." The background scene in the portrayal of the bird, also known as the greater yellowlegs, shows several buildings, probably a few of the forty-six 12' × 16' wooden cabins where Bulow housed the people he enslaved; an 1830 census showed 197 enslaved people working on the plantation that produced sugarcane, indigo, rice, cotton, and food stores.[11]

Bulow provided a boat and crew of enslaved laborers to help Audubon explore the area, which the artist hoped would provide him with pelicans. On a Halifax River expedition, Audubon managed to shoot two pelicans before his gun jammed. On the return trip, the boat was battered by wind and waves and became stuck in the mud, forcing the group to spend the night dangerously exposed to the elements. Audubon wrote, "Good God, what a night! To sleep was impossible; the cold increased with the breeze, and every moment seemed an hour, from the time we stretched ourselves down until the first glimpse of the morn; but the morn came, clear as ever a morn was, and the north-easter as cold as ever wind blew in this latitude."[12]

The next day, they pushed and pulled the boat through shallow waters and muck at a pace Audubon said felt "as if we had been clogged with heavy chains." After making little progress through the salt marsh, they abandoned the boat, loaded up Audubon's equipment and dead birds, and walked back to the plantation.[13]

In January 1832, while wintering with Bulow, Audubon rode 20 miles southwest on Indian horses with a "Scotch gentleman" through sandy pine barrens, across the three Haw Creeks, and into more rolling lake-dotted terrain toward the plantation home of Colonel Orlando Rees. After breakfast the next day, the hospitable Rees took Audubon to "the celebrated spring" that had inspired the trip. Audubon noted the spring's depth, width, color, and smell—a sulfur emission he found "highly nauseous."[14]

The spring was one of more than a thousand in Florida, with waters flowing upward from underground water deposits fed by percolated rainwater or captured ancient water supplies. The largest are found in North and Central Florida, with varying depths and constant water temperatures of 68 to 76 degrees. Audubon observed that the spring's waters poured into Rees's Lake via Spring Garden Creek and then eventually into the St. Johns River. Rees boated with Audubon along the creek and across two lakes to the river. Along the way Audubon spotted "numerous alligators" as well as waterbirds, including two ibises, which he shot. The latter were on a "small island covered with wild orange trees, the luxuriance and freshness of which were not less pleasing to the sight, than the perfume of their flowers was to the smell," he wrote, adding that while sharing a picnic, Rees "informed me that this charming retreat was one of the numerous *terrae incognitae* of this region of lakes, and that it should henceforth bear the name of 'Audubon's Isle.'"[15]

In February, Audubon sailed 100 miles on the St. Johns River, Bartram's watery avenue through the heart of the peninsula. To Audubon, the St. Johns "did not seem to me equal in beauty to the fair Ohio; the shores were in many places low and swampy, to the great delight of the numberless Herons that moved along in gracefulness, and the grim alligators that swam in sluggish sullenness." He recalled one day of thick fog and "blind musquitoes" that, although they didn't bite, "covered every object, even in the cabin" to the extent that they "more than once fairly extinguished the candles whilst I was writing my journals, which I closed in despair, crushing between the leaves more than a hundred of the little wretches."[16]

He explored the woods along the river and later encountered a Seminole Native in a canoe who approached the boat to trade. Audubon, a lover of wild places and people, felt great sympathy, no doubt because of ongoing efforts by the federal government to remove Native people from Florida.

> The poor, dejected son of the woods, endowed with talents of the highest order, although rarely acknowledged by the proud usurpers of his native soil, has spent the night in fishing, and the morning in procuring the superb-feathered game of the swampy thickets; and with both he comes to offer them for our acceptance. Alas! thou fallen one, descendant of an ancient line of freeborn hunters, would that I could restore to thee thy birthright, thy natural independence, the generous feelings that were once fostered in thy brave bosom. But the irrevocable deed is done, and I can merely admire the perfect symmetry of his frame, as he dexterously throws on our deck the trouts and turkeys which he had captured. He receives a recompense, and without smile or bow, or acknowledgement of any kind, off he starts with the speed of an arrow from his own bow.[17]

The next month, a weary and disappointed Audubon returned to Charleston, South Carolina, hoping a trip to the tip of the peninsula might be richer in bird life. In April he and his party joined the cutter *Marion* for its two-month trip into the waters around southern Florida. After acquiring more than one thousand bird skins, Audubon now turned his attention south in the hope of finding showy waterbirds.[18]

After the months of cold, unpleasant weather in Northeast Florida, Audubon was about to find his avian nirvana. Approaching Indian Key, located in the middle Florida Keys, Audubon's "heart swelled with uncontrollable delight," he recalled. Once on shore:

> With what delightful feelings did we gaze on the objects around us!— the gorgeous flowers, the singular and beautiful plants, the luxuriant trees. The balmy air which we breathed filled us with animation, so pure and salubrious did it seem to be. The birds which we saw were almost all new to us; their lovely forms appeared to be arrayed in more brilliant apparel than I had ever before seen, and as they gambolled in happy playfulness among the bushes, or glided over the light green waters, we longed to form a more intimate acquaintance with them.[19]

But these weren't bird-watchers—these were men with guns on a mission.

Taking a boat to a nearby island, Audubon and his team readied for their work. "Few minutes had elapsed, when shot after shot might be heard, and down came whirling through the air the objects of our desire," he wrote. The boat's Bahamian pilot, James Egan, "besides being a first-rate shot, possessed a most intimate acquaintance with the country," and he shared his knowledge of bird roosting and nesting areas. The group stowed bird bodies under the gunwales, carrying them back at the day's end for Ward to skin; Lehman kept busy sketching the island, and Audubon busied himself writing notes about the birds and events of the day.[20]

One day they rowed 20 miles through Florida Bay to "Sandy Island," within view of the "southernmost cape of the Floridas," Audubon wrote. "The flocks of birds that covered the shelly beaches, and those hovering over head, so astonished us that we could for a while scarcely believe our eyes. The first volley procured a supply of food sufficient for two days' consumption."[21]

Pelicans, cormorants, godwits, curlews, herons, ibis, gallinules—the Florida Keys hosted a bounty of species that brought Audubon's dreams to life. They shot so many at one site that the collected mass "looked not unlike a small haycock." And, yes, they ate many of the birds and their eggs. But the Keys held other challenges as well—bugs, tides, sharks, muddy flats, and unexpected weather. Audubon did spot a prized flock of flamingos during one outing—a view that "agitated my breast!" he wrote, adding that he saw a flock flying in a line. "I thought I had now reached the height of all my expectations, for the voyage to the Floridas was undertaken in a great measure for the purpose of studying these lovely birds in their own beautiful islands." Audubon was unable to shoot any flamingos, and today it is a rarity to spot a wild one in the state.[22]

Returning from the island, today known as Sandy Key in Everglades National Park, Audubon observed an approaching black cloud and felt a light breeze; the crew quickly took down the boat's sail, and Egan warned that "We were 'going to get it'" as they hurried toward shore. It was a "furious cloud" that "approached so swiftly, that one might have deemed it in haste to destroy us." Although Audubon might have called the weather a hurricane, in fact it was one of Florida's famed afternoon thunderstorms, ferocious but brief:[23]

> And now in contemplation of the sublime and awful storm, I gazed around me. The waters drifted like snow; the tough mangroves hid their tops amid their roots, and the loud roaring of the waves driven among them blended with the howl of the tempest. It was not rain that fell; the masses of water flew in a horizontal direction, and where a part of my body was exposed I felt as if a smart blow had been given me on it. But enough!—in half an hour it was over. The pure blue sky once more embellished the heavens, and although it was now quite night, we considered our situation a good one.[24]

Egan stayed with Audubon and company for the next few weeks as they explored islands and searched for much-desired birds. At one point they encountered floating bales of cotton, flotsam from a shipwreck. The disabled ship was surrounded by several schooners—the vessels of "wreckers," local residents who made a living legally scavenging cargo from damaged ships. Ever the student of nature, Audubon later spent time in the company of wreckers, dining and learning about seashells and bird eggs.

Audubon stayed at Indian Key for a week before moving on to other areas, but the island soon earned a notable place in Florida history. The year before the visit, Jacob Housman bought the key to be a base for his wrecking business. Housman had a series of buildings from which to store and sell his salvaged goods, often at odds with wreckers in Key West. In 1836 Indian Key was named the first county seat for Dade County, newly split off from Monroe County; the Dade County seat later relocated to Miami. Noted horticulturalist and physician Dr. Henry Perrine moved to the island with his family in 1838, but two years later he was killed and all buildings on the island were destroyed by Seminoles during the Second Seminole

Booby Gannet

Male

Drawn from Nature by J.J. Audubon, F.R.S. F.L.S.

Lith. Printed & Col.d by J. T. Bowen. Philad.a

Among the waterbirds Audubon drew in Florida was the booby gannet, pictured with an illustration of Indian Key in the background—a site he visited. Author collection.

War. Housman, who had lost his wrecker's license, and Perrine's family fled. Audubon missed all this drama but wrote about the wrecking business in his third volume of *Ornithological Biography*. Indian Key is immortalized as the background of Audubon's booby gannet, which he procured later in the Dry Tortugas.[25]

The next layover for Audubon and the *Marion* was seventeen days in lively Key West, a hub of maritime activity because of its deepwater port and strategic location near extensive reefs and Gulf Stream shipping routes. The city, with a population of 517 in 1830, was a designated federal Port of Entry where salvaged materials from shipwrecks in US waters were to be taken for official claims in this very lucrative business.[26]

While there, Audubon enjoyed the company of Dr. Benjamin Strobel, a physician and amateur collector, and the two hunted together and explored the environs. Strobel, editor-publisher of the *Key West Gazette* and naturalist collector, helped Audubon get a branch of a Geiger tree; the plant is in the background of the later white-crowned pigeon illustration. Strobel wrote in 1833 that Audubon was "frank, free and amiable in his dispositions, and affable and polite in manners. . . . In addition to the possession of these qualities, Mr. Audubon is the most enthusiastic and indefatigable man I ever knew. It is impossible to associate with him without catching some portion of his spirit; he is surrounded with an atmosphere which infects all who come within it, with a mania for bird-killing, and bird stuffing. For my own part, I must confess that I have become an incurable victim to the disease."[27]

The Dry Tortugas, a group of islands 68 miles west of Key West, also held avian delights. The islands initially were named "Tortugas" in 1513 by the Spanish explorer Juan Ponce de León for the sea turtles found there. "Dry" was added later to let mariners know there was no freshwater at the site. In the five centuries since, the islands have changed in shape and number, altered by storms, water flow, and human activity. In 1826 a lighthouse was erected on Garden Key to direct and warn shipping traffic. Audubon wrote that the five or six small isles were mostly populated by wreckers and turtlers—hunters of sea turtles then prized for their eggs and meat.

While in the Tortugas, Audubon drew three birds—the sooty tern, the noddy tern, and the brown booby—before returning to Key West on May 16 for a six-day stay. Traveling north, he stopped again at Indian Key, where he revisited Cape Sable and Sandy Key, and then headed for Savannah and Charleston, satisfied that he had more material for his bird publications. Audubon hoped to revisit the peninsula in 1833 but was waylaid by publishing issues and never returned except for a one-day trip to Pensacola in 1837. The simmering Seminole Wars didn't help, either. His Florida birds—he found fifty-two types of birds new to him—can be found in the four volumes of his 1838 *Birds of America* that contains 435 life-sized bird watercolors. A year later he completed the fourth of his *Ornithological Biography* volumes that would seal his fame as America's beloved avian painter. Despite Audubon's miserable start in the state, Florida had proven to be a treasure trove.[28]

Almost two centuries later, the best way to envision Audubon's world is to gaze at his marvelous birds. At the Museum of Arts & Sciences (MOAS) in Daytona Beach, Zach Zacharias guided me into a large backroom storage area where the museum's sixty-three Audubon prints are stored. They include depictions of the black skimmer, herring gull, great white heron, sooty tern, golden eagle, and, famously, the dramatic scene of four mockingbirds fending off a rattlesnake in their nest; some naturalists denied that rattlesnakes could climb trees, but scientists since have observed them doing so. The art is dramatic and mesmerizing; most of the birds are in motion as if ready to soar away. MOAS has 103 Audubon objects, including prints, letters, and journal entries that were collected by a St. Augustine aficionado. These include an 1824 oil painting on canvas of Townsend's bridled weasel, an art study of the animal that has a curious mistake—the weasel on the left has two tails, as if Audubon was testing to see which was more authentic; in the final product it has one tail.[29]

"To me it is one of the most important artifacts we have in the museum," said Zacharias. But on this day, it was in a darkened, cool storage area. Zacharias, familiar with Audubon's continuing popularity, has led an area bus tour called "Walking in the Steps of Audubon" to transport the curious to sites along the state's east coast.[30]

The first stop is Hernandez's barrier island plantation, Mala Compra, located north of Flagler Beach along the buzzing US A1A highway. Today all that exists of the 30' × 18' wooden home are its coquina-rock foundations in a sheltered state archaeological site. In 1816 Hernandez bought the property (its name means "bad bargain" or "bad purchase"—an ominous beginning) as one of three plantations along the east coast where his slaves grew sea island cotton. There is a view of the intracoastal waterway from the homesite, burned by Natives in 1836 during the Second Seminole War—one year after Hernandez was mustered into the American army to fight the tribe. He scandalously met with Seminole leaders in 1837 for a supposed conference under a white flag of truce but instead captured eighty of them, including the famed leader Osceola. Hernandez was court-marshaled but not convicted and went on to a political career, serving as mayor of St. Augustine and then as the first Hispanic member of the US Congress while Florida was still a territory.[31]

A few minutes north of Mala Compra is the site of another Hernandez plantation, Bella Vista. His daughter married a distant relative of US president George Washington, and the complex today is preserved as Washington Oaks Gardens State Park. It stretches across the barrier island from an undeveloped expansive beach to a manicured botanical garden to a serene site overlooking the Matanzas River.

On an overcast summer morning, Neil Rasnick, fifty-eight, sat on a bench overlooking the saltwater river, enjoying the view of ospreys and herons at the state park he first visited at age fourteen. He didn't appreciate the park then but now visits it weekly, toting a camera with a large telephoto lens in order to "capture" birds in a method unknown to Audubon.

"Birds are my passion," declared Rasnick, a St. Augustine commercial photographer. In his baby-blue shirt, plaid pants, hiking boots, and backward-facing baseball cap, he was dressed for the work and armed with an Audubon level of patience. He proudly showed a photo of bright cardinals atop shiny oranges, captured after five days of waiting to get just the right shot. "I like birds just because. They are just about always pretty, and they are always up to something."[32]

A short drive away onto the mainland is Bulow Plantation Ruins Historic State Park, once the comfortable home of John Bulow and Audubon's base for several weeks. The park, now a shady, forested spot, once was a noisy, bustling site. The large two-story house, measuring 62' × 42', faced a brackish marsh along Bulow Creek where boat slips were located. Slave cabins once lined the shore on either side of the house, and agricultural fields have been reclaimed by nature. I can only imagine the slaves' difficult field work, worsened by Florida's humid heat. A quarter of a mile west of the house was the centerpiece of the plantation—the state's largest sugar mill, where sugarcane was processed into sugar for commercial export. Today only silent remnants of the house's foundations exist, and the towering coquina walls of the sugar mill ruins have a ghostly presence.

But the saltmarsh remains, and a boat ramp provides access into the creek where one can paddle into the brown, tannic water amid gold-and-green banks where Audubon picked his way, looking for birds. During a summer kayaking trip, I was struck by the quiet of the plantation and creek that once would have echoed with noise from the mill and landing. My patience was rewarded with sightings of osprey, cormorants, a group of tri-colored herons, and an alligator that lazily moved across my path and dis-appeared beneath the brown-stained waters. A birder's joy.

Following the old King's Road from Bulow's plantation ruins, I drove southwest and headed down SR 11, a mostly rural road that crosses pastures as well as thickly forested lands and sections of Haw Creek, then flooded from recent rains. Audubon's party easily crossed creek sections with their horses, something better accomplished by car in the twenty-first century. A western turn down Arredondo Grant Road, named for a former land grant from the Spanish government, merging into Spring Garden Ranch Road, led across SR 17 and onto Ponce De Leon Boulevard and the entrance to De Leon Springs State Park.

The park is the modern site of Rees's Spring Garden plantation, featur-ing a large spring that once powered a sugar mill on the site. Today you can make pancakes at the Sugar Mill restaurant, a favorite park-goer activity. On a weekday morning few people were at the park, which centers on the concrete-lined spring that bubbles up 19 million gallons of water daily. A family splashed in the spring waters, and an elderly man swam laps across it, enjoying its constant 72-degree temperature. In the turquoise waters the whitened shells of ancient snails were visible, the remnants of meals from long-ago Native people who visited the same shores. Two dugout canoes found in the spring may be the oldest ever discovered in North America, dating back at least five thousand and six thousand years.[33]

The plantation changed hands several times and ended up as a tourist destination in the 1920s, named after Spanish explorer Ponce de León and the persistent myth that he traveled Florida looking for the Fountain of Youth. "It's a powerful myth with deep roots in our psyches," writes Rick Kilby, noting that many sites in the state also make the same claim. In fact, de León never traveled anywhere close to this site, but the moniker brought in the curious, who may have stayed at the small hotel and dived into the spring waters. When the property was threatened by development decades later, including adjacent high-rise buildings, the community rallied, and it was preserved as a state park in 1982.[34]

The spring still pours into the creek where Audubon and Rees boated to the St. Johns River and picnicked on an island that Rees proclaimed would be named for Audubon. Most of the banks are now part of the Lake Woodruff National Wildlife Refuge, where there is no Audubon Island to-day, leaving the site a mystery. Proby, during research for her 1974 book *Audubon in Florida,* looked for an island high enough to grow oranges and finally surmised, after catching the scent of wild orange trees, that it might have been Idlewilde Point on the St. Johns River. Ironically, that may be the spot where Bartram had his famous alligator encounters in 1774. Audubon surely would have found this amusing—but, then, maybe not, since he was annoyed with Bartram's promises of wildlife riches.[35]

He surely would be pleased, though, with the words "Audubon Lookout" emblazoned on a large wooden tower at the refuge. A view from the top reveals a large marshy expanse that attracts more than 230 species of birds every year, their numbers increasing during the fall and spring migrations.

Along the path I met Carol MacDonald, a seventy-eight-year-old retired English teacher from Satsuma who enjoyed an early-morning hike. McDonald, an avid nature lover whose straw hat sported a large feather, had been studying an aristocratic great blue heron standing along a watery ditch. "I love nature," she proclaimed. "I have since I was a little girl." When she suffered a brain inflammation a few years ago and ended up in a rehabilitation center, she was asked what her goal was for physical abilities. "I told them I wanted to get back to what I love," she said, smiling and gesturing to the broad, sunny preserve around her.[36]

Although Audubon had some success in Northeast Florida, to really understand his heart, one must head to the Florida Keys, to the sites of his most fulfilling moments. In the island town of Tavernier, I joined Jerry Lorenz, state director of research for Audubon Florida, and his wife, Linda Lorenz, for a boat ride into dazzlingly blue waters and a trip back in time. After dropping anchor, we waded ashore at Indian Key to wander amid the ruins that remain of this once-vibrant settlement. Street signs noted the names of sandy paths that led to abandoned cisterns, building foundations, and a wide, empty area that once was the center of town. The island is now Indian Key Historic State Park and is accessible only by water. It has the eerie feel of a ghost town, home only to a nesting pair of ospreys and thorny plants that cling to cloth on passersby. "There is a whole lot of stuff on this island that bites," Jerry Lorenz advised.[37]

When Audubon visited the island, Housman was a relative newcomer, still building up his empire. Now a replica of Housman's gravestone is the strongest reminder of his aspirations, and non-native agave plants that send up 30-foot bloom spikes are what remains of Perrine's plant ambitions. Lorenz, who has lived in the area more than thirty years, often finds old homesteads on keys by looking for exotic plants and trees. Everyone wanted to "improve" the islands to their own aesthetics.

Many of Audubon's most successful bird-hunting expeditions launched into the islands and mangroves in nearby Florida Bay, now Lorenz's realm as he and his team monitor the Everglades ecosystem, which sends freshwater into the bay, making it an important nursery for marine life. And birds.

Specifically, Lorenz, who holds a PhD in marine biology from the University of Miami, looks to the populations of roseate spoonbills as indicators of the system's health. This "beautiful and singular bird," as Audubon described it, lived in groups, stalking "about with graceful steps along the margin" of muddy pools or in shallows "in search of food." Audubon shot them, when possible, and noted that their feathers were "manufactured into fans" as trade items. Lorenz instead studies the birds that state wildlife officials designated as a "threatened" species and that need very specific habitat and food to survive. Their spoon-shaped bills require particular water levels and salinity for feeding, and they need to nest in areas where mammals such as raccoons can't reach their eggs and young. They still nest on Sandy Key, which Audubon visited, but the island is off-limits to visitors during breeding season to protect the species and other wading birds that rely on it. Once hunted for their bright-pink feathers to adorn women's hats, the birds now are in trouble because of water management—or mismanagement—in the Everglades and development in the Keys.[38]

In Florida Bay, spoonbills peaked at 1,260 nests in 1979 but then declined as wetlands were drained for the Keys' development, which removed 80 percent of the bird's feeding areas. Other problems include manipulated water releases into the Everglades, which, if wrongly timed, may inundate nests and chicks and make it impossible for adult birds to forage. Sandy Key spoonbill nests, once the largest colony in Florida Bay, dropped from 250 in the early 1990s to 22 in 2019.[39]

"I'm guardedly optimistic," Lorenz said of efforts (that now include his consultation) to repair the Everglades' water quality and flow, thus helping the spoonbills. "I think the Everglades restoration has true potential. But restoration has to be operated for wildlife restoration." Another unknown is what predicted sea level rise in coming decades will do to the spoonbills' ability to survive.[40]

There is some irony in the fact that Lorenz's agency is named for Audubon, who loved birds but didn't think twice about killing as many as possible to succeed in his mission. When activists created the first Audubon Society in 1886, they did so because they felt he had taught Americans to love birds and they needed to promote public awareness that many of their avian friends were in serious trouble. Their plumes—and heads or whole bodies—were more valued as adornments on ladies' hats than as living species. Millions of birds were killed by plume hunters, whose hardscrabble lives were supplemented by prized income from the slaughter. In the meantime, millinery companies made millions and touted their products as the latest in fashion. To counter this, Audubon societies sprang up around the country to fight for bird protection laws and to change public opinion; Florida's was created in 1900 in Clara and Louis Dommerich's living room in Maitland. Audubon groups hired game wardens to patrol and protect the birds, including Guy Bradley, who was killed by plume hunters in 1905, setting off a firestorm of publicity and making him a national martyr. In another ironic twist, Bradley was murdered as he tried to stop birds from being killed at Sandy Key in Florida Bay—a site Audubon had shot up seventy years earlier.

Audubon may have killed many birds, Lorenz acknowledged, but "what he was doing was nothing compared to what the plume hunters were doing." At Sandy Key, Audubon reported the sky "darkened by whistling wings," but today perhaps only 10 percent of that wondrous population exists. "You have a hard time fathoming that—those kinds of numbers." Lorenz wondered if Audubon would even visit the Keys now. "Today I think he'd just have a heart attack" about the changes in the area, he said. "The overdevelopment of the Keys is distressing."[41]

Indeed, the islands have changed dramatically since Audubon's visit. They have been transformed into a tourism paradise, with cruise ships regularly docking in Key West. The Keys have come under great scrutiny for a lack of planning that has led to a mishmash of building and dwindling species, including the key deer, a species endangered because of road kills.

Key West, once a funky outpost of individuality, is now a bustling city of T-shirt stores, open-air bars, and day visitors seeking tacky trinkets. One refuge in the buzzing tourist district is the Audubon House and Tropical Gardens, an airy wooden home that, despite its name, Audubon never entered. However, a Geiger tree, perhaps the one from which the artist used cuttings as a backdrop for the white-crowned pigeon illustration, still grows in the house's luxuriant gardens. Audubon's spirit pervades the two-story structure, which displays his massive prints on the walls, including that of the roseate spoonbill.

The house originally held a four-volume double-elephant folio of *The Birds of America* (so named because of its massive size—26" × 39")—one of perhaps one hundred known survivors of a printing of probably fewer than two hundred copies. The structure was bought in 1960 by Miami philanthropist Mitchell Wolfson, whose family foundation saved it from de-

The islands of the Dry Tortugas, now part of a national park, remain vibrant nesting sites for a variety of birds, including thousands of sooty terns and brown noddies. Courtesy of Bruce Hunt.

molition in 1958. The volumes were stolen from a glass display in 1977 but recovered three weeks later in New Jersey and North Carolina, leading to eight arrests. The Wolfson family then moved them to the safekeeping of the HistoryMiami Museum. Good idea—one complete folio set sold in 2018 for $9.65 million.[42]

The finest place to feel Audubon's wonderment is Dry Tortugas National Park, a series of islands in 100 square miles of protected waters reached by park service boats or seaplanes. Arising out of sparkling aquamarine waters, the main island, Garden Key, is the site of Fort Jefferson, a hexagonal three-story brick fortress erected to protect US shipping interests. Audubon saw none of this—only a 70-foot-tall lighthouse finished in 1826 to guide mariners. Today the crumbling fort, constructed between 1846 and 1875 but never finished or fully armed, and its adjacent coral reef are what draw visitors to the site, along with its birds.

To the east of the fort, a spit of sand attaches to Bush Key. On a sunny February day, the key was vibrantly alive; until September, the key is home to breeding colonies of up to 80,000 sooty terns and 4,500 brown noddy terns. Thousands of parents flew up and down to nests tucked into bushes of low dunes, their raucous cries filling the air. In an almost eerie counter to that, huge magnificent frigate birds hung silently in the air over the nearby fort, looking toward the sheer chaos of the cordoned-off nesting isle. Farther to the east was Long Key, a frigate bird colony's home.

In the 1960s, Charles Lee, then a Miami sixteen-year-old, became a convert to the Audubon cause when he joined an effort to band these birds for scientific study. When he wasn't casting for grouper and snapper in the channel next to the fort, Lee helped net adult birds and crawled under bushes to catch chicks. When netted birds vomited, it was Lee's job to gather those contents so researchers could understand the birds' diet. It was far from glamorous, but it captured the teenager's heart and mind. "As a boy who came to the Tortugas motivated by fishing, my admiration for birds, and understanding of their role in the ecosystem was crystalized on the sands of Bush Key while looking at these miraculous specimens," recalled Lee. His Tortugas adventure included riding out Hurricane Alma with others inside the fort, near the cell once occupied by Dr. Samuel Mudd, sent to the stronghold in 1865 for four years as punishment for treating the broken leg of John Wilkes Booth, President Abraham Lincoln's assassin.[43]

The research trip inspired Lee's career; he worked for Audubon Florida since 1972, often pacing the halls of the State Capitol in Tallahassee as he works to get legislation passed to protect birds, their habitats, and wild places, particularly the Everglades.

For Audubon, the Tortugas were paradise. Approaching the nesting terns, he saw a "cloud-like mass" rise from the islands. "On landing, I felt for a moment as if the birds would raise me from the ground, so thick were they all round, and so quick the motion of their wings. Their cries were indeed deafening." Of course, he killed birds and ate their eggs. But for a long while, more than 180 years since his visit, I stood quietly, my binoculars aimed at the sky, channeling the enthusiasm Audubon felt upon encountering this enormous show of life.[44]

To share some of John James Audubon's experiences, visit these sites:

Bulow Plantation Ruins Historic State Park
  3501 Old Kings Road
  Flagler Beach, Florida 32136
  (386) 517-2084
  floridastateparks.org/parks-and-trails/bulow-plantation-ruins-historic
  -state-park

Visitors to the Bulow Plantation can tour the ruins of John Bulow's early nineteenth-century sugar mill operation. In addition, the park offers scenic hiking trails and kayak/canoe access to the Halifax River/Bulow Creek.
Hours: Thursday–Monday, 9:00 a.m.–5:00 p.m.
Admission: $4 per vehicle; $2 for pedestrians.

Washington Oaks Gardens State Park

6400 North Oceanshore Boulevard
Palm Coast, Florida 32137
(386) 446-6780
floridastateparks.org/parks-and-trails/washington-oaks-gardens-state
-park

In addition to the park's formal gardens, known for their azaleas, camellias, roses, and other flowers, the park features inland hiking trails ideal for wildlife viewing, plus unusual coquina-rock formations along the park's segment on the Atlantic Ocean.
Hours: 8:00 a.m. to sunset, 365 days a year.
Admission: $5 per vehicle.

Museum of Arts & Sciences

352 South Nova Road
Daytona Beach, Florida 32114

The museum houses a substantial collection of Audubon artifacts including prints and written journal and notes.
Hours: Monday through Saturday, 10:00 a.m.–5:00 p.m.; Sunday, 11:00 a.m.–5:00 p.m. (closed most major holidays).
Admission is free; guided tours $10.

Lake Woodruff National Wildlife Refuge

2045 Mud Lake Road
De Leon Springs, Florida 32130
(386) 985-4673
fws.gov/refuge/lake_woodruff

Lake Woodruff is a 22,000-acre wildlife refuge with hiking trails that follow elevated shoreline embankments and also wind through forested hammocks. Several observation towers along the trails make this a prime bird-watching destination.
Visitor Center **hours:** November–March, 7 days/week, 8:00 a.m.–4:30 p.m.; April–October, Monday through Friday only.
Admission is free.

De Leon Springs State Park

601 Ponce de Leon Boulevard
De Leon Springs, Florida 32130
(386) 985-4212
floridastateparks.org/parks-and-trails/de-leon-springs-state-park

Old Spanish Sugar Mill Restaurant
(386) 985-5644
oldspanishsugarmill.com

Although Juan Ponce de León never actually visited this spring, John James
Audubon did, in 1832. Today visitors are allowed to swim in the spring's
72-degree crystal-clear water. Visitors can take a 50-minute guided trip on a
pontoon boat through the waters of the park and adjacent Lake Woodruff
National Wildlife Refuge. At the Old Spanish Sugar Mill Restaurant, next
to the spring, pancake lovers can make their own at tables with built-in
griddles.
De Leon Springs State Park **hours:** 8:00 a.m. until sunset, 365 days a year.
Admission: $6 per vehicle.
Old Spanish Sugar Mill **hours:** Monday through Friday, 9:00 a.m.–2:00 p.m.;
weekends and holidays, 8:00 a.m.–2:00 p.m.

Indian Key Historic State Park
Islamorada, Florida 33036
(305) 664-2540
floridastateparks.org/IndianKey

Robbie's Marina Kayak Rental
77522 Overseas Hwy
Islamorada 33036
(305) 664-4878
robbies.com/kayak-and-paddleboard-rentals-tours.htm

Indian Key rests about three-quarters of a mile offshore, east of Robbie's
Marina on Lower Matecumbe Key and just southwest of Islamorada. Hiking
trails (some with street signs) crisscross the 11-acre island past the remnants of what was once a tiny but busy community in the early 1800s. For
a short time, Indian Key was the county seat for Dade County. There is a
boat dock on the west side of the island, but check to make sure it is open.
You can also reach the island by kayak, and rentals are available at Robbie's
Marina.
Hours: Indian Key Historic State Park is open 8:00 a.m. until sunset, 365
days a year.
Admission: $2.50 per person; children under 5 free.

Audubon House Museum & Tropical Gardens
205 Whitehead Street
Key West, Florida 33040

(305) 294-2116
audubonhouse.com

Key West wrecker fleet owner and harbor pilot Captain John Geiger began construction on this grand three-story home in 1846, fourteen years after Audubon visited the city. Audubon, however, may have visited the garden of the previous owner. The Geiger family continued to live here until the mid-1950s, but by then it had fallen into dilapidation. In 1958 it was scheduled to be demolished by the city, when Mitchell and Frances Wolfson bought it and restored the house, which they felt was historically significant. Their decision likely initiated the trend here of saving rather than tearing down old houses, which continues today and has helped to preserve much of historic Old Town Key West.

It is called the Audubon House because the Wolfsons collected original and early-edition Audubon prints and lithographs, amassing a substantial enough collection to open the house as a museum in 1960. It is an outstanding collection of Audubon works, and Audubon fans should not miss it.

Hours: Open daily 9:30 a.m.–4:15 p.m.

Admission: $14 for adults; $10 for students; $5 for children 6–12; under 6 free.

Dry Tortugas National Park

(305) 242-7700
nps.gov/drto

Dry Tortugas encompasses a cluster of seven islands (or keys) in the Gulf of Mexico, 70 miles west of Key West. The second-largest of these, Garden Key, is home to the largest brick fortress in the United States. Construction on Fort Jefferson (one of several fortifications built during that time to protect the southern coast) began in 1846, fourteen years after Audubon visited. Today the fort makes the perfect elevated platform from which to observe flocks of nesting birds like those that Audubon observed here.

Other than by private boat, there are two ways to get there: by ferry, a two-hour ride; or by seaplane, a 30-minute flight. Although twice as expensive, the seaplane trip is quite spectacular. Flying low over the clear water, you'll likely see sunken wrecks, sea turtles, and manta rays.

Dry Tortugas Ferry: $180 for adults; $125 for children (up to 16); $170 for students/active military/seniors $170. drytortugas.com/rates-reservations. Seaplane: Key West Seaplane Adventures: $361 half day, $634 full day for adults; $289 half day, $507 full day for children. keywestseaplanecharters .com.

5

John Muir

Finding Florida Beauty on Foot, 1867

As he lay in a darkened room, his pale-blue eyes stripped of sight from an industrial accident, young John Muir worried that his sight would be closed "forever on God's beauty."[1] It was one of the worst things he could imagine, a calamity for a promising inventor whose passion was roaming the countryside admiring the marvelous intricacies of nature.

This near-tragedy became a blessing for Muir, who, once his sight returned, hastened to make good his dream of experiencing the world, embarking on a plant-collecting trip across the American continent. The journey, particularly time spent in the wilds of Florida, where Muir had a brush with death, deeply shaped his ethos about the living world that in coming years would influence the way Americans felt about wilderness, national parks, and nature's beauty. Muir would become a national icon, founding the nation's first environmental activist group and rallying citizens to join in preserving the country's natural splendor. It is a legacy that lives on today.

But in March 1867, the pain and foreboding were agony for Muir, confined for weeks to a bed and dark room in the hope that his eyes would recover. He had been fixing a belt for a circular saw in an Indianapolis factory when a file slipped from his hands. It hit his right eye, just outside the cornea, causing blindness. Soon his left eye darkened from sympathetic shock, creating the possibility that he had lost his vision forever. A local newspaper reported his accident, and friends and family soon learned the news. A close friend wrote, "I have often in my heart wondered what God was training you for. He gave you the eye within the eye to see in all natural objects the realized ideas of His mind."[2]

Vision in his left eye returned soon, and, in answer to Muir's hopes, his right eye eventually healed, evidenced only by a corneal scar. After many weeks of reflection, Muir was determined to head out on a grand adventure, eventually going into the jungles of South America in the steps of one of his botanizing idols, Alexander von Humboldt. The Yosemite Valley of California also was on his growing wish list of places to visit. But going back to his previous occupation was no longer an option.

"The accident awakened him to the potential losses of continuing to pursue a machinist's career or any other career that entailed settling down," writes historian James B. Hunt. "The recovery of his eyesight elevated the importance of botany so that Muir became passionate to see more of 'God's inventions.' Coupled with his desire to do field work and study botany at a deeper level was a desire to see plants of the tropics."[3]

After a quick visit to Wisconsin, where he had lived on a farm for most of his youth since immigrating from Scotland with his stern, religious family, the twenty-nine-year-old Muir made preparations for his first big trip: a 1,000-mile walk from Indiana to Florida. From there he hoped to head south into South America for an indeterminate period. Muir knew it was a risky venture: before leaving he assigned some of his assets to heirs.

"In that darkened room he had glimpsed death," writes biographer Donald Worster. "It was not something he feared, but he wanted to be ready for the possibility that he might never return."[4]

Then he was off, catching a train to southern Indiana; from there a boat took him across the Ohio River. On September 2, 1867, the official journey began as he walked through Louisville, Kentucky, and headed south, hoping his pocket map and compass would guide him through the Appalachian Mountains into the flatlands of Georgia and then into the tropics of Florida. Muir was a hardy man who packed light. Dressed in a single suit with a flat-brimmed hat, Muir, with his Scottish accent, must have seemed a harmless, poor traveler; indeed, he carried very little money, relying on cash telegrams for funds at different stages of the trip. He had a wooden plant press for collecting samples and wrote that his rubbery bag contained a "comb, brush, towel, soap, a change of underclothing, a copy of [Robert] Burns's poems, [John] Milton's Paradise Lost, and a small New Testament." A much larger botany book weighed down the sack, but it was essential for Muir's travels. Importantly, he had pen, ink, and a journal into which he inscribed his identity: "John Muir, Earth-planet, Universe."[5]

It was a declaration from someone with a big picture of life that was about to explode.

The journal, its edited contents published posthumously as *A Thousand-Mile Walk to the Gulf*, would be his greatest companion. He wrote daily, often adding drawings of his discoveries, and edited his words along the way.

And although he was focused on botanizing during the fifty-two-day trip, during which he sent specimens back to his brother, the journal's details offer a wealth of information about the places he visited, many of them suffering the aftermath of the Civil War, for which he had avoided service by going to Canada. Just two years after the conflict's conclusion, which resulted in the deaths of an estimated 750,000 people, the South that he visited was a dangerous, unpredictable place in great disarray. Enslaved people were emancipated but had gloomy employment prospects beyond agriculture, specifically sharecropping; railroads were damaged or destroyed; cities and homes were burned to the ground; and vigilantes and thieves roamed the countryside. Twice Muir was accosted by would-be robbers—one left when Muir intimated that he had a gun, and the other, offering to carry Muir's satchel, took a look at its meager contents and "handed back my bag, and returned down the hill, saying that he had forgotten something," he wrote.[6]

Along the way Muir slept in the woods as well as in plantation homes, when invited, and in sparse camps that he encountered. He dined with the rich and the poor, Black and White, happily partaking of any food he was offered, even just a spare glass of milk. But his real attention was on the flora. The Cumberland Mountains of Kentucky "were the first real mountains that my foot ever touched or eyes beheld," he noted. He appreciated the mountain vistas as well as roadside vines, briars, and flowers: "How little we know as yet of the life of plants—their hopes and fears, pains and enjoyments!" He described mountain streams, leafy valleys, gorgeous sunsets, and vistas "far grander than any I ever before beheld."[7]

One overnight host, a blacksmith, was at a loss to understand why a "strong-minded man" like Muir wasn't employed in something better than to "wander over the country and look at weeds and blossoms. These are hard times, and real work is required of every man that is able. Picking up blossoms doesn't seem to be a man's work at all in any kind of times." Muir summoned up biblical references, noting that the Old Testament's Solomon wrote a book about plants and quoting: "Christ says, 'Consider the lilies.' You say, 'Don't consider them. It isn't worth while for any strong-minded man.'" The blacksmith conceded and then warned Muir about the dangers of traveling, particularly from guerrilla bands wandering the area. Muir, who had just overcome blindness, replied "that I had no fear, that I had but very little to lose, and that nobody was likely to think it worth while to rob me; that anyhow I always had good luck." Nothing was going to stop his "glorious walk." Indeed, shortly after this warning he caught the attention of a ten-man guerrilla group; Muir walked briskly by them, saying "Howdy," saved, he believed, by his probable resemblance to a "poor herb doctor, a common occupation in these mountain regions."[8]

Muir was a man on a mission, whose innate passion for plants swayed others to his thinking. His journal contains observations about culture and landscape valuable to anyone interested in postwar life in the South. It uses racial language common to the era that today is offensive. But the overriding theme of Muir's journey was an evolving philosophy of the human place in the world that would be his lodestar for the remainder of his life. It began to solidify in the final leg of his journey, perhaps spurred by near-starvation while staying in a cemetery, and it hardened with a brush with death on the humid Florida coast.

On October 8, Muir reached the coastal town of Savannah, Georgia, with three dollars in his pocket. Money from his brother had not arrived at the telegraph office, leaving him feeling "dreadfully lonesome and poor." After one night at the "meanest looking lodging-house that I could find, on account of its cheapness," Muir searched for better, cheaper accommodations while awaiting the funds and ended up in Bonaventure Graveyard—a safe haven, he thought, from dangerous humans. He camped the next five days in solitude among tombstones, flowers, and ancient moss-covered live oaks. The site, a former plantation, fronted the Wilmington River, east of Savannah, providing Muir with a new landscape from which to mull the world. It was, he wrote, "so beautiful that almost any sensible person would choose to dwell here with the dead rather than with the lazy, disorderly living." During his time at the wildlife-filled cemetery, Muir mused upon the meaning of death and of the human fear of it. Nature and the cycle of life, he decided, were the antidotes to this phobia: "But let children walk with Nature, let them see the beautiful blendings and communions of death and life, their joyous inseparable unity, as taught in woods and meadows, plains and mountains and streams of our blessed star, and they will learn that death is stingless indeed, and as beautiful as life, and that the grave has no victory, for it never fights. All is divine harmony."[9]

"What Bonaventure revealed to him, in contrast to the old pessimism, was that death is not a form of punishment," writes Worster. "Death and life are forever and inextricably blended together in a positive whole. The animal or plant dies, or the human being dies, and others take their place in the ever-renewing circle of nature. All is 'harmony divine.'"[10]

After five days at Bonaventure and down to his last twenty-five cents, Muir was "becoming dangerously hungry" and anxious for his seventy-five dollars to arrive. Finally, the express office clerk announced that the package was there but demanded identification. After a frustrating and rather humorous encounter with the clerk and his boss, Muir got his money and speedily bought some gingerbread to make a "large regular meal." He quickly booked steamship passage south to Fernandina, in northeastern Florida, seeking the "special home of the tropical plants" he hoped to find.[11]

On October 15, Muir reached Florida, "the so-called 'Land of Flowers,' that I had so long waited for, wondering if after all my longings and prayers would be in vain, and I should die without a glimpse of the flowery Canaan." He disembarked on a rickety wharf, bought some bread, and hurried out of town. Soon he threw down his plant press and bag, admiring the exotic new land, and leaned on his elbow while eating bread.[12]

> While thus engaged I was startled from these gatherings of melancholy by a rustling sound in the rushes behind me. Had my mind been in health, and my body not starved, I should only have turned calmly to the noise. But in this half-starved, unfriended condition I could have no healthy thought, and I at once believed that the sounds came from an alligator. I fancied I could feel the stroke of his long notched tail, and could see his big jaws and rows of teeth, closing with a springy snap on me, as I had seen in pictures.
>
> Well, I don't know the exact measure of my fright either in time or pain, but when I did come to a knowledge of the truth, my man-eating alligator became a tall white crane, handsome as a minister from spirit land—"only that." I was ashamed and tried to excuse myself on account of Bonaventure anxiety and hunger.[13]

Later he drew a journal sketch depicting an alligator sitting on a log while another one held a man between his jaws. As Hunt notes, the man in the drawing doesn't have a beard, as Muir did, "hence it is likely that John Muir did not imagine himself to be food for the alligators—though he felt fear along with his curiosity."[14]

Muir's roaming in other states had taken him along roads, paths, and streams. But now he found Florida to be so "watery and vine-tied" that he decided to cross the state by walking along a raised railway line or its sandy embankment that linked Fernandina on the Atlantic coast with the small community of Cedar Key on the Gulf of Mexico.[15]

His trek was along the Florida Railroad, a 156-mile line that opened in 1860 amid controversy about its costs, construction, and its president, David Levy Yulee, Florida's first US senator and the first Jewish person ever elected to that post. The rail line was ready for the Civil War, which lasted from 1860 to 1865, and "was the first American conflict to involve railroads," writes historian Gregg Turner. Steam engines and rails were the central transportation system of the war. When Confederate General Robert E. Lee came to Florida in 1861, he advised Confederate President Jefferson Davis and Floridians to focus protection on the state's "valuable interior, where cattle and agricultural products were produced in abundance. Most of the provisions were shipped by rail, along with troops, munitions, and wartime supplies."[16]

Yulee's line was a prime target early in the conflict. In January 1862, Union forces burned ships in Cedar Key's harbor and "torched the railroad's depot, freight cars, and warehouses," Turner writes. Fernandina was visited by Union naval forces two months later; a gunship fired at a train crossing the railroad trestle, killing several people. Yulee was on the train and, "according to legend," jumped from it and "escaped to the mainland in a canoe." With the loss of both of its terminals, damage to miles of tracks, and seizures of its locomotives and rail cars, the Florida Railroad was in bad shape at war's end. It was partially repaired and operated while Yulee and other Confederate leaders served prison time, but the company was poor and ultimately sold at auction.[17]

This was the rail line that Muir encountered, its rights-of-way overgrown by native plants and vines, and its traffic light. But it was high and dry (many wetlands had been destroyed or filled to create a passable elevated roadbed) and easily traveled, affording Muir a long view forward and much of interest to the side: "I am now in the hot gardens of the sun, where the palm meets the pine, longed and prayed for and often visited in dreams, and, though lonely to-night amid this multitude of strangers, strange plants, strange winds blowing gently, whispering, cooing, in a language I never learned, and strange birds also, everything solid or spiritual full of influences that I never before felt, yet I thank the Lord with all my heart for his goodness in granting me admission to this magnificent realm."[18]

Muir continued to rely on strangers' provisions and stories. A group of Florida loggers Muir thought were far more barbaric than the "long-haired ex-guerillas of the mountains" may have seemed wild and savage, but "they gave me a portion of their yellow pork and hominy without either apparent hospitality or a grudge, and I was glad to escape to the forest again." Three men, whose dogs attacked Muir, offered him "liver pie, mixed with sweet potatoes and fat duff" and a second helping of potato. He heard stories of alligator attacks, although he only saw one in all his travels. But Muir's musings, perhaps born from the Transcendental movement that advocated finding spirituality in nature, began to develop a new attitude about wild animals:

> Many good people believe that alligators were created by the Devil, thus accounting for their all-consuming appetite and ugliness. But doubtless these creatures are happy and fill the place assigned them by the great Creator of us all. Fierce and cruel they appear to us, but beautiful in the eyes of God. They, also, are his children, for He hears their cries, cares for them tenderly, and provides their daily bread. . . . How narrow we selfish, conceited creatures are in our sympathies! How blind to the rights of all the rest of creation! With what dismal irreverence we speak of our fellow mortals! Though alligators, snakes, etc., naturally repel us, they are not mysterious evils. They dwell happily in these flowery wilds, are part of God's family, unfallen, undepraved, and cared for with the same species of tenderness and love as is bestowed on angels in heaven or saints on earth.[19]

This was uncommon American thinking in the 1860s. Manifest Destiny was the creed of the era—the belief that humans had the right and direction from God to have dominion over creation and to spread civilization across the continent, refashioning the natural world. Pioneers tore up the Great Plains, displacing ancient, complex prairie ecosystems and bison with monoculture crops and domestic cattle. Rivers were dammed to power mills, leaving fish unable to migrate and spawn. Majestic stands of longleaf pine forests were damaged for turpentine and lumber—and to clear land for cotton. Hunters and farmers happily tried to rid the landscape of large predators to make safe their operations. There was little sympathy for the nation's native flora and fauna, much less Muir's growing belief that the world's creatures were as deserving of life as humans. But that is where Muir's thinking was moving as he negotiated his way through Florida—from an anthropocentric "to a bio-centric view."[20]

As he headed southwest, Muir stayed at a "sort of tavern" in Gainesville, slept "in the barrens at the side of a log," and then lodged for a few nights at the home of Captain Simmons, a former Confederate officer. When Simmons brought up slavery "and its concomitants," Muir changed the conversation to that of birds, animals, and the climate. On a deer hunt with Simmons, they startled a deer, but Muir didn't shoot, leaving him pondering why humans killing the Lord's "well-kept beasts, or wild Indians" was proper, but wrong if the creatures hurt humans. "Well I have precious little sympathy for the selfish propriety of civilized man, and if a war of races should occur between the wild beasts and Lord Man, I would be tempted to sympathize with the bears." Muir did exult, however, in a large stand of palm trees stretching "as far as the eyes could see," that Simmons directed him to; Muir referred to it as a "palm congregation" and journaled extensively about them.[21]

While walking west on October 23, Muir was hit with the "scent of the salt breeze" that flooded him with memories of his childhood on the Scottish coast. He emerged from a forest to find the Gulf of Mexico "stretching away unbounded, except by sky. What dreams and speculative matter for thought arose as I stood on the strand, gazing out on the burnished, treeless plain!" He had reached Cedar Key, where he hoped to find a boat to take him south to Tampa or Key West and then off to Cuba and/or South America. At a store that "had a considerable trade in quinine and alligator and rattlesnake skins," Muir learned that a schooner headed to Galveston, Texas, was due to arrive at a sawmill to pick up a load of lumber. He walked the mile to the mill to inquire about passage on the boat.[22]

Cedar Key, officially established in 1843 on Atsena Otie island, had about one hundred residents when the Civil War broke out, most of them living on two of the five keys that made up the community. Its main industry was the railroad line, the boat terminal, and sawmills that handled the area's lumber: pine, cypress, and red cedar, the latter of which was processed and sent north to be turned into pencils.[23]

R. W. B. Hodgson ran one of these sawmills. He agreed that Muir could work at the mill to earn money for the sea passage. Muir quickly made himself valuable, fixing a cover on a pulley; it earned him a bunk in an employee lodging house. It was fortunate that Muir had found shelter and employment—the next day he began to come down with what likely was malaria—possibly contracted from mosquitoes during his stay in the Savannah cemetery. He "felt a strange dullness and headache" and swam in the Gulf but got no relief. He felt "inexorable leaden numbness" but did not "fear any serious illness, for I never was sick before, and was unwilling to pay attention to my feelings," he wrote in his journal. Craving citrus, on the third day, Muir walked into town to buy lemons but on the return was hit by fever that literally knocked him out. He awoke to a starlit night and began staggering and then falling several times before reaching the bunkhouse. The watchman, thinking Muir was drunk, refused to help, and Muir finally crawled into bed.[24]

After several days of delirium, Muir was moved to Hodgson's home, where his wife, Sarah, tended to the young man for about three months and saved his life. "Through quinine and calomel—in sorry abundance—with other milder medicines, my malarial fever became typhoid. I had night sweats, and my legs became like posts of the temper and consistency of clay on account of dropsy." A soon as he could get out of bed, Muir quietly headed into nature, sailing on a small skiff to observe trees on the islands and lying under majestic live oaks "listening to the winds and the birds."[25]

His thoughts turned to the human place in the world, now tempered by his brush with death and disease: "This star, our own good earth, made many a successful journey around the heavens ere man was made, and whole kingdoms of creatures enjoyed existence and returned to dust ere man appeared to claim them. After human beings have also played their part in Creation's plan, they too may disappear without any general burning or extraordinary commotion whatever."[26]

The Galveston boat came and went during Muir's illness, but in January 1868 he found a schooner heading to Cuba with a load of lumber. He booked passage for twenty-five dollars and left when the north wind filled its sails. Thus, Muir ended his 1,000-mile adventure, embarking on a monthlong trip to Cuba. Finding that "my health wasn't improving," he decided to leave the island but, unable to find a boat to South America (where malaria was rampant in some areas), revised his plans and headed north to New York "and thence to the forests and mountains of California. There, I thought, I shall find health and new plants and mountains, and after a year spent in that interesting country I can carry out my Amazon plans."[27]

The rest is history.

Muir's venture into California changed his life and the perspectives of an entire country—and world. He would go on to champion Yosemite National Park and create the Sierra Club, America's first environmental advocacy group. His writings of the West, including adventures in Alaska, would spark the nation's imagination as he advocated for the protection and creation of more national parks in the United States. Muir ferociously fought the damming of the Hetch Hetchy Valley inside Yosemite National Park—a battle he lost. But in doing so, he created a vigorous campaign that forced a national conversation about the future of national parks.

"He changed the perception of nature in the nation which is hotly debated today," said Robert Bendick, director of the Gulf of Mexico Program for the Nature Conservancy. "The national park system and the idea of national parks were unique to the United States, and John Muir had a key role in defining national parks and defending what they were."[28]

In the last 150 years our views about nature have shifted to be closer to

Muir's "very American strand of global environmental thinking. He was a superinfluential figure. He was really, really important in shaping the global conservation movement and the national parks in America," Bendick noted. The Hodgsons, by saving Muir's life, "gave the gift to the country of John Muir and his legacy."[29]

Muir promised Sarah Hodgson that he would return, and he did so in 1898, finding Sarah, a widow, living in nearby Archer, Florida. At first she didn't recognize him, but when he said his name, her reaction was immediate. "'My California John Muir?' she almost screamed," he recounted in a letter to his sister. Sarah Hodgson and her children had kept track of his rising fame, and he had kept his pledge to come back. After a four-hour visit, Muir left, but they stayed in touch by post. In May 1907 Kittie Hodgson wrote to tell Muir of her mother Sarah's death, enclosing a newspaper clipping about it. Kittie said she would have written sooner but had heard "that you were dead and did not know it was a mistake till recently."[30]

At the time of his 1914 death, Muir had written numerous books and was revising his journals for publication. *A Thousand-Mile Walk to the Gulf* was published in 1916 and remains a favorite for those interested in the formation of his life's philosophy and for travelers eager to take up his path. Some do it for adventure, others to immerse themselves in history, and others for healing.

After losing his fifteen-year job at a research station in North Florida, ecologist Bruce Means decided "to put the trauma behind me" and "focus on the new future ahead and quit brooding about the past." Having read many early naturalists, especially those who wrote about the southeastern United States, Means, then forty-three, chose to follow Muir's path in 1984, thinking it might be "very illuminating about both the natural ecology of the route and what has happened to it in the years since Muir's passing." He got a copy of Muir's handwritten journal from the archives at Stanford University and plotted a course, walking on the same days through the same territory.[31]

It had changed greatly.

In his unpublished manuscript about his trip, "Walking Out Loud," Means describes walking along paved highways filled with the "pandemonium" of traffic; staying at local hotels or with friends and sometimes camping; eating at diners; and giving interviews to curious media along the way. He notes acts of kindness by strangers along the way (including a few car rides), blisters the size of "spectacles," and a plethora of roadside litter and roadkill that Muir could never have imagined. Means suffered through fever and a virus while trudging through Georgia and stopped to recuperate, giving himself time to consider how Muir didn't have knowledge of ecology, the science of the interconnectedness of species to each other and their surroundings, to inform his understanding of nature:

> One of the outstanding impressions to be gained from reading Muir's *1,000-Mile Walk* is realizing that he "couldn't see the forest for the trees." This is not intended to be a criticism of Muir's scientific abilities, but rather is a reflection of the state of the discipline of ecology in Muir's day. Botanists and zoologists of that day were busy with discovering and naming the world's many species, the building blocks of natural species assemblages, or communities, and not in recognizing higher levels of order in nature. After all, without a basic understanding of those very building blocks one is severely handicapped in trying to decipher any rhyme or reason at a higher level anyway.[32]

In Florida, Means discovered that much of the rail line Muir walked had been removed or rerouted, forcing him to trek on busy highways in sandspur-filled rights-of-way. The longleaf pine forests were largely gone, and the large stand of cabbage palm trees near Gulf Hammock that Muir visited had since been "blitzkrieged by the timber companies." At the historic Island Hotel in Cedar Key, he wrote, the owner surprised him by stating: "'I know who you are. You're the guy walking the John Muir trail.' I am a little surprised that she knows that. Later I find out that the *Cedar Key Beacon,* a new town weekly, picked up my story from the *Louisville Journal* two months ago, published the story and a picture of me on the front page of their second issue!" On his last day, Means wondered as he walked "how much all the environmental degradation I have seen is worth in human lives. Is a tree equivalent to one person, ½ a person, 1/100th of a person, 1/1000th of a person . . . or none at all? . . . I would argue, as Muir felt, that every living being, plant or animal is equal on a one-to-one basis with every human life. Each organism arrived at the same point in time through the same general processes of reproduction and survival of the fit, through remarkably similar chemistry, and all stemming from the same common ancestor somewhere nearer or farther back in time depending upon which two organisms are being compared."[33]

Back home, Means founded the Coastal Plains Institute and Land Conservancy, a nonprofit organization that focuses on environmental research and education in the biodiverse Florida Panhandle. His forty-nine-page résumé includes numerous books and articles, and he now teaches in the

Merald Clark is such a John Muir fan that he often dresses like Muir to inform groups about the botanist/author's 1867 walk through North Florida. He also has retraced much of Muir's path on foot. Courtesy of Bruce Hunt.

biology department at Florida State University and is considering submitting his journal manuscript for publication.[34]

On a sunny October day, I met up with another Muir aficionado, Merald Clark, who has been tracing the naturalist's Florida path in a piecemeal method for the past decade. Clark holds a master's degree in anthropology and has spent eleven years as an educator and guide at Gainesville's Morningside Nature Center. In researching the area's history, he learned about Muir's trip and now describes it in public talks. It's an interest that has become a mild obsession—Clark has scoured newspapers, railroad schedules, museums, and public documents (and has ventured into some private property) to determine the exact sites Muir visited. Then, when time allows, he and a friend take off to follow the route, with Clark dressed à la Muir and carrying materials similar to that of the great naturalist.[35]

"It's a reason to get out and go walking," he said, noting that Muir would have traveled through the area about the same time of year. A disabled friend keeps tabs from a car, providing water when Clark needs it during long stretches of asphalt. Clark keeps to the left on the highway, and most cars move for him, but he can't replicate Muir's hardiness. "Most of his walk was a marathon every day." In his travels Clark has found plants and flowers that Muir described as well as modern-day loggers still felling Florida's forests.[36]

Clark was a featured speaker at a 2017 Sierra Club conference in Cedar Key that celebrated the 150th anniversary of Muir's walk while also considering the ramifications of impending climate change. An estimated 150 people attended the conference, said Paul Thibault of the Tampa Bay Sierra Club, noting that the group was able to locate several Muir sites, including the oak tree where he convalesced and the site of the sawmill, the latter now part of a gated community.[37]

Why the continuing interest in Muir?

"In Cedar Key during the time of his recovery he came to his conclusion about the environment and man's place in the environment," said Thibault. "That difference carries through the environmental movement now. The snake has a right, the fish has a right. . . . [T]hey are sharing the environment with us."[38]

To my great delight, I was able to spend October 15 in Fernandina, Florida, the same date and place that Muir stepped into the state. And as Clark and Means discovered, there is very little opportunity to walk in Muir's exact path. It is illegal now to walk along the train tracks, which stay busy, and the original train path is now mostly highways. In Yulee, Florida, a small roadside area with prominent public restrooms, proclaims itself the John Muir Ecological Park. A boardwalk leads along a small creek and into a thicket of pines, palmettos, and ferns. Signs tell the story of Muir as well as the history of the local railroad. But the roar of cars and squeals from braking semis spoil any pretense of being in wild Florida.

On another chilly day beneath cerulean skies, a group of friends, including Bob Bendick, joined me to walk 4.5 miles along a section of Muir's journey—a former rail line that has been converted into a paved pedestrian and biking path. With a backdrop of accelerating jet engines, we tried to

An enthusiastic group of friends joined me on a very chilly winter day to hike along Muir's trail into Gainesville, Florida. The rail line he walked is now a well-used recreational path. Author photo.

channel Muir as we trekked south from the Gainesville airport, crossing several large intersections before entering a shady, quiet leg into the city. Our end point was Depot Park, a former railyard contaminated by wastes that was cleaned up and opened in 2016 as a public recreation and historic site, featuring an old wooden train station. Along the way we saw longleaf pines and cabbage palms that fascinated Muir, stopped to examine flowers, tried to explain to a perplexed panhandler what we were doing, and waved to a group of men warming themselves by a fire. But try as we did, we found little of the wild, natural charm he encountered. I longed for a calm, peaceful stretch in which to contemplate his writings.

Muir's route ended in Cedar Key, where the track led to the Gulf of Mexico. One day I retraced the end of his journey in a half-mile jaunt on the Cedar Key Railroad Trestle Nature Trail overseen by Florida's Nature Coast Conservancy. It is a sandy footpath on an elevated berm among trees and mangroves with signs providing information about plants. But once at its end, there was a view of the water and of old railroad bridge pilings. I inhaled the unmistakable scent of saltwater that has harkened me many times to the Gulf Coast. As I watched glittering waves and gulls flying overhead, I realized that this may be as close as anyone can get to Muir's actual experience. Florida's environment may be changing, and not usually for the better, but in this one spot I could feel his love of nature and breathe the intoxicating aroma of plants, water, and air that instills hope for the future.

To share some of John Muir's experiences, visit these locations:

John Muir Ecological Park
463039 State Road 200
Yulee, Florida 32097
nassaucountyfl.com/Facilities/Facility/Details/16
floridahikes.com/john-muir-ecological-park

Shortly after arriving by steamship in Fernandina, Florida, John Muir set out to follow David Yulee's Florida Railroad line south and west. Only a few miles out of town he would have had to cross the railroad trestle bridge at Kingsley Creek, a tributary of the Amelia River. SR 200 parallels the rail line here, and 8 miles west of Kingsley Creek, along SR 200, you will reach the John Muir Ecological Park on the north side of the road. The park features a quarter-mile-long elevated boardwalk that winds through dense pine forest and swamp. Muir walked through this area, or at least very near here, and visitors get a good view of some of the terrain he had to navigate.

Depot Park
874 SE 4th Street
Gainesville, Florida 32601
depotpark.org

Gainesville's original railroad depot was built at this location, circa 1860, and then enlarged in subsequent decades. A Rails-to-Trails pathway passes through here, and John Muir walked this route. Depot Park, a Gainesville city park, opened in 2016 with the restored depot ticket and waiting room building, an old-fashioned general store, a playground, a picnic pavilion, and a venue for concerts.
Hours: Open 7 days a week.

Cedar Key Railroad Trestle Nature Trail
Grove Street, just off SR 24
cedarkeyguide.com/downloads/rrTrestle.pdf

Florida's Nature Coast Conservancy
PO Box 401

Cedar Key, Florida 32625
floridasnaturecoastconservancy.org/projects/rr-trestle-nature-trail

When John Muir finally arrived in Cedar Key, in October 1867, he crossed the marshy tidewater on a railroad trestle that terminated on the other side in the town of Cedar Key. Today the Railroad Trestle Nature Trail, maintained by Florida's Nature Coast Conservancy, can be hiked from its north end (at Grove Street, ¾ mile north of 2nd Street/center of Cedar Key) for about ⅓ mile until it ends at the water, where you can see the remaining trestle pilings from the original railroad bridge. Although a short hike, you might see some of this area's native wildlife: roseate spoonbills, ibises, and ospreys.

Cedar Key Historical Society and Museum
609 2nd Street
Cedar Key, Florida 32625
(352) 543-5549
cedarkeyhistory.org

To learn more about Cedar Key's rich history, visit the Cedar Key Historical Museum in the middle of town at the corner of 2nd Street and D Street (SR 24).
Hours: Sunday–Friday: 1:00 p.m.–4:00 p.m.; Saturday: 11:00 a.m.–4:00 p.m. Admission is free, but donations to tour the museum are welcomed.

6

Harriet Beecher Stowe

A Voyage into "Fairy-Land," 1873

It was a long, nauseating ocean journey on gray, rolling seas. But once she reached Florida in March 1867, Harriet Beecher Stowe found enchantment. The noted author, whose 1852 novel *Uncle Tom's Cabin* had galvanized abolitionist emotions in the years before the Civil War, now looked to escape from cold northern winters of Hartford, Connecticut, while helping her ailing son Frederick in a new farming venture. Perhaps he would leave the drinking behind and find success growing cotton. Stowe also wanted to create a colony of like-minded northerners and help formerly enslaved people exercise their new freedom through education, something she deemed to be "Christ's work on earth."[1]

Leaving the Atlantic Ocean at the mouth of the St. Johns River, her boat now calmed, Stowe, fifty-five, was stunned by the beauty of the river's banks, inhaling the wafting fragrance of blooming orange trees. She wrote to her family that she "went to her room, 'stripped off the woolen garments of my winter captivity put on a thin dress white skirt & white saque & then came & sat down to enjoy the view of the river & the soft summer air,'" writes biographer Joan D. Hedrick. "When she broke a sprig from an orange tree and put a blossom in her hair, 'feeling quite young and frisky,' her rebirth was complete: 'I feel as if I had wings—Every thing is so bright & the air is so soft.'"[2]

In coming years Florida would be the scene of new adventures for Stowe—a place of respite, of fresh experiences, and a new direction in her writing career. Already internationally renowned as a writer and a member of an esteemed religious family, Stowe longed to put her faith to work and find new literary expressions. Her subsequent travel articles extolling Florida's natural beauty were among the state's first promotions, reaching a broad audience of northern readers as they suffered through long wintry

Enchanted by the weather, writer and abolitionist Harriet Beecher Stowe bought a riverfront winter home in Mandarin, Florida, in 1867. Courtesy of the State Archives of Florida.

months and dreamed of warmer climes. Exceptional among her descriptions are those recounting steamboat travel on the Ocklawaha River, a narrow, jungle-like waterway with sights that were marvelously exotic to northern sensibilities. Her experiences highlight the era's booming steamboat travel and offer insights into her early conservationist ethic, born of her aesthetic appreciation for the state's flora and fauna and recognition of its fragility.

During her first Florida stay, Stowe spent three weeks at Frederick's rented farm on the eastern shore of the St. Johns River at the community of

Orange Park, south of Jacksonville. She hoped Frederick, who had suffered a head wound at the bloody Battle of Gettysburg, would run the business. One day the pair traveled east in a rowboat across the river to the community of Mandarin, where mail was delivered; its high banks and stunning western views captured Stowe's attention. She wrote to her brother, Charles Beecher:

> We are now thinking seriously of a place in Mandarin much more beautiful than any other in the vicinity. It has on it five large date palms, an olive tree in full bearing, besides a fine orange grove which this year will yield about seventy-five thousand oranges. If we get that, then I want you to consider the expediency of buying the one next to it. It contains about two hundred acres of land, on which is a fine orange grove, the fruit from which last year brought in two thousand dollars as sold at the wharf.[3]

Mandarin was a Timucuan Indian village in the 1500s, but by the time William Bartram visited in 1774 it was an English colony that centered on agriculture, notably growing indigo. The area's forests of pine, cypress, and oak soon were felled for naval goods and damaged by tar and turpentine production. The name "Mandarin" was first registered in 1830; it was chosen for the mandarin orange by a prosperous local resident.[4]

Soon after deciding to buy the Mandarin property, Stowe asked her brother to consider becoming clergy in the Episcopal Church, possibly taking over a new church she hoped would be built along the riverfront. Charles, however, was not interested in such a position: he had served in Presbyterian and Congregational churches, having been relieved of his latest duties among charges of violating doctrine. Eventually Charles came to Florida, but he bought property in Newport, south of Tallahassee, and served as the state superintendent of public instruction from 1871 to 1873.[5]

Stowe, however, went forth with her plan and for $5,000 bought 30 riverfront acres for herself and her husband, Calvin, that included an "orange grove and comfortable cottage" to be her winter residence. They were joined each season by their twin daughters, Hattie and Eliza. By 1869 she was shipping fresh citrus to northern markets, the crates marked: "Oranges from Harriet Beecher Stowe, Mandarin, Florida." Fame had its commercial advantages, but the real benefit of the Florida setting was its luxuriant loveliness, mild winters, and the writing it inspired. Her son Charles Edward Stowe recalled:

No one who has ever seen it can forget the peaceful beauty of this Florida home and its surroundings. The house, a story and a half cottage of many gables, stands on a bluff overlooking the broad St. John's [*sic*], which is five miles wide at this point. It nestles in the shade of a grove of superb, moss-hung live-oaks, around one of which the front piazza is built. Several fine old orange trees also stand near the cottage, scenting the air with the sweet perfume of their blossoms in the early spring, and offering their golden fruit to whoever may choose to pluck it during the winter months. Back of the house stretches the well-tended orange grove in which Mrs. Stowe took such genuine pride and pleasure. Everywhere about the dwelling and within it were flowers and singing birds, while the rose garden in front, at the foot of the bluff, was the admiration of all who saw it.

Here, on the front piazza, beneath the grand oaks, looking out on the calm sunlit river, Professor Stowe enjoyed that absolute peace and restful quiet for which his scholarly nature had always longed, but which had been forbidden to the greater part of his active life. At almost any hour of the day the well-known figure, with snow-white, patriarchal beard and kindly face, might be seen sitting there, with a basket of books, many of them in dead and nearly forgotten languages, close at hand.[6]

Her son Charles also noted in *The Life of Harriet Beecher Stowe,* his 1889 book that included her journals and letters, that some "Northern visitors" would "land at the wharf, roam about the place, pick flowers, peer into the house through the windows and doors, and act with that disregard of all the proprieties of life which characterizes ill-bred people when on a journey. The professor had been driven well-nigh distracted by these migratory bipeds." In one incident, a wayward sightseer broke off a fruit-laden branch of an orange tree in front of an outraged Calvin Stowe, who "in a voice of thunder" excoriated the "horror-struck culprit."[7]

Such was the price of celebrity for the famous author and her family, in the former Dixie. Passing steamboat captains entertained their passengers by pointing out the couple on the veranda. One travel writer of the era, using the pseudonym Silvia Sunshine (her actual name was Abbie M. Brooks) recalled attending a Southern Methodist church in Jacksonville in the 1870s where Calvin Stowe was to speak. As the couple entered, "a slight rustle was heard in the congregation, and a few persons left the house. Mr. and Mrs. Uncle Tom were more than a Sabbath dose for some of the Jacksonville community." She described Stowe's appearance, stating that the "three snowy curls on each side of her face give her a matronly look, and her stout-built frame, well covered with flesh, a substantial appearance." Snarkily, Sunshine wrote that Stowe dozed off during the sermon: "She looked the picture of content, and was no doubt dreaming of that far-off, beautiful country, where those who create dissensions and stir up strife can never enter."[8]

Relocating the Stowe household was burdensome—books, clothing, and domestic goods had to be loaded up twice a year to accommodate the family's travel to and from their Hartford home, either by steamer or train. Hedrick likens the planning and work such travels entailed to "Grant's army marching to Vicksburg." While in Mandarin, Stowe worked to uplift the community, with a keen interest in improving the lives of freed slaves and their families. She helped build a schoolhouse for White and Black students that doubled as a church where she taught Sunday school and singing classes. Stowe encouraged other like-minded northerners to join in creating a new, progressive postwar colony in the area and promoted creating an Episcopal church in Mandarin. And most local residents appreciated it. Several times the family was heartily greeted upon their arrival in Florida. Stowe wrote in 1876: "We had a triumphal entrance into the St. John's, and a glorious sail up the river. Arriving at Mandarin, at four o'clock, we found all the neighbors, black as well as white, on the wharf to receive us. There was a great waving of handkerchiefs and flags, clapping of hands and cheering, as we drew near. The house was open and all ready for us, and we are delighted to be once more in our beautiful Florida home."[9]

Stowe was entranced by the state's natural beauty, writing about it to her family and friends. She regularly mentioned flowers and plants, particularly those that were blooming, and marveled at the birds that nested on her property. She once described her arrival in Florida as having "stepped from December to June." She tried to depict the verdant environs of her Mandarin home to writer George Eliot (the pen name of Mary Ann Evans), then living in England:

Every tree bursts forth with flower; wild vines and creepers execute delirious gambols, and weave and interweave in interminable labyrinths. Yet here, in the great sandy plains back of our house, there is a constant wondering sense of beauty in the wild, wonderful growth of nature. . . . This wild, wonderful, bright and vivid growth, that is all new, strange, and unknown by name to me, has a charm for me.

It is the place to forget the outside world, and live in one's self. And if you were here, we would go together and gather azaleas, and white lilies, and silver bells, and blue iris. These flowers keep me painting in a sort of madness.[10]

Writing consumed several hours of Stowe's time daily. She worked on the manuscript for what would become *Oldtown Folks,* an 1869 novel about life in Calvin's hometown of Natick, Connecticut. That same year she began writing articles about Florida, an enterprise that expanded when her brother Henry Ward Beecher bought the *Church Union,* a New York newspaper, which he renamed the *Christian Union.* Stowe, listed as a contributor, was delighted that the publication provided the opportunity to "have the pulpit she had always desired," writes Hedrick. Many of her articles, however, served as evangelical calls to the temple of Florida's beauty, making Stowe one of the earliest travel writers beckoning visitors to the state, supporting a fledgling tourism industry. She wrote articles about St. Augustine and Jacksonville; descriptions of magnolias, yellow jessamine, citrus, and swamps; picnicking and sailing trips; and how to buy land in Florida. She made little mention of biting insects, diseases, racism, and other troubles, depicting a fantasy world that was perpetuated well into the next century.[11]

The newspaper claimed 81,000 subscribers in 1872, mostly affluent New Yorkers, write historians John F. Foster Jr. and Sarah Whitmer Foster. "The combination of a famous author, Stowe, and a highly popular platform, the *Christian Union,* lends support to the novelist's observation that Florida tourism tripled between 1872 and 1874. There is creditable evidence that this is true." In 1873 a collection of these articles was published as *Palmetto Leaves,* a volume of almost three hundred pages that included maps and etched illustrations. It was Florida promotion at its finest, and the income helped pay Stowe's debts, helpful since her husband had retired from teaching.[12]

Soon after the book appeared, Stowe published one of her finest Florida essays in the *Christian Union.* Entitled "Up the Okalawaha—A Sail into Fairy-Land," the May 14, 1873, article tells of her journey on a steamboat on the twisting Ocklawaha River. (Spelling of the river's name varies, but the common spelling today is Ocklawaha.) It was a popular tourist pilgrimage that ended at the crystalline waters of Silver Springs—a sight foreign to most travelers—and one that required endurance and patience with a dose of good humor and venturesome spirit.

At the time of her trip, steamboat tourism in Florida was reaching its

Like many other writers and nature lovers in the 1800s, Stowe voyaged on a steamboat much like this one to experience the natural beauty of the serpentine Ocklawaha River. Courtesy of the State Archives of Florida.

peak. Interior travel was miserable and difficult, owing to poor roads. Only two major roads existed, having been built by Spain during its colonization of the state, and the railroads that eventually supplanted the boats in the 1890s were still being constructed. Water was the best route.

The first steamboat to ply state waters arrived in Jacksonville in 1829, bringing winter visitors to the state. Many boats transported tourists to Florida from Savannah and Charleston, but soon the boats were taking tourists from Jacksonville or Palatka up and down the St. Johns and Ocklawaha Rivers. It was a thriving business that transformed river cities like Palatka into tourist-based economies. And it changed the waterways, once filled with pole-propelled commercial barges and logs being floated to market, into sightseeing corridors. The rivers could be difficult to travel, riddled with downed trees and shifting water levels. Night was especially hazardous as crews tried to avoid hitting tree-lined shores and river impediments. Steamboat traffic was substantially easier on the wider, deeper St. Johns River.[13]

Stowe recounted a St. Johns trip in *Palmetto Leaves*, describing it as "the grand water-highway through some of the most beautiful portions of Florida." She detailed the scenery along the shore (she deliberately waited until the early May magnolias were blooming) and the crew of the *Darling-ton*, commanded by a man and by a freed woman known as "Commodore Rose." Rose "knows every inch of the river, every house, every plantation along the shore, its former or present occupants and history; and is always ready with an answer to a question." The two-day trip ran from Palatka south to Enterprise on the river's shore at Lake Monroe and back. Stowe was entranced by the scenery but horrified by male tourists (she called them sons of Nimrod) who fired at birds and alligators from the boat—then considered great sport.[14]

> One annoyance on board the boat was the constant and pertinacious firing kept up by that class of men who think that the chief end of man is to shoot something. Now, we can put up with good earnest hunting or fishing done for the purpose of procuring for man food, or even the fur and feathers that hit his fancy and taste.
>
> But we detest indiscriminate and purposeless maiming and killing of happy animals, who have but one life to live, and for whom the agony of broken bones or torn flesh is a helpless, hopeless pain, unrelieved by any of the resources which enable us to endure. A parcel of hulking fellows sit on the deck of a boat, and pass through the sweetest paradise God ever made, without one idea of its loveliness, one gentle, sympathizing thought of the animal happiness with which the Creator has filled these recesses. All the way along is a constant fusillade upon every living thing that shows itself on the bank. . . . Killing for killing's sake belongs not even to the tiger. The tiger kills for food; man, for amusement.[15]

Random killing of birds and wildlife, which left many riverbanks devoid of fauna, helped fuel the 1890s rise of the Audubon movement across the country two decades after Stowe's lament. The Florida Audubon Society (FAS), founded in 1900 in Maitland, specifically pushed for protective laws for the state's wading birds and songbirds and sought to sway public opinion into a conservation ethic of saving and protecting wildlife. The FAS also tried to end the high fashion of adorning bird plumes in hats—a practice that led to millions of birds being killed for the millinery industry. Stowe's observations about the damage caused by one boat full of sportsmen anticipated the rise of this crusade.

Stowe had avoided the Ocklawaha River trip from Palatka at the St. Johns River down to Silver Springs, after observing the small steamer *Ocklawaha* that plied those waters. She confessed that "we shuddered at the idea of going on a bush-whacking tour through the native swamps of the alligator in such a suspicious looking craft as that." But friends who returned "fairly inebriated with enthusiasm, wild with incoherent raptures" convinced her to make the trip. "It was a spectacle, weird, wondrous, magical—to be remembered as one of the things of a lifetime."[16]

Traveling on the serpentine, tree-lined Ocklawaha River was difficult. "The truth is the boats were not built to travel a river full of stumps, snags, sunken logs, and all manner of other hazards," writes historian Bob Bass. "This river required a different kind of boat from the ones that were common on the St. Johns." The river's path was like "a dark jugular vein. It is weirdly contorted and loops around, doubling distance and then redoubling it until a navigator soon gets lost."[17]

The *James Burt* was the first steamboat to run the river, probably a stern-wheeler less than 60 feet in length. Hubbard Hart bought it in 1860 to be part of what would become a thriving steamboat line. The Civil War sidelined tourist business, but after the war, Hart began anew, adding the *Ocklawaha,* built in 1867 or 1868, which ran twice a week from Palatka to Silver Springs. By 1871 Hart had three boats on the river, but, unlike those on the St. Johns, Ocklawaha boats "were not pretty craft by any means," Bass writes. "They were built to be functional and looked like a not-yet completed houseboat on a rowboat-shaped hull. They usually had two decks, with the lower one for freight and machinery and the upper one for passengers." Boats had to be narrow and low enough to navigate the river's path.[18]

It was a trip fraught with perils. Trained river pilots, usually African Americans, had tough jobs guiding boats that traveled by day and night. They had to avoid or remove fallen trees and snags in the river and tried to keep a safe distance from the overhanging trees that could damage the boat and endanger passengers. At night the crew lit wood fires in braziers atop the pilothouse to help chart the course. Some travelers described a red light flaring from the boat, casting an eerie glow on the water and vegetation on the banks. And it was not uncommon for fires to get out of control, setting some boats on fire. At the same time, the boats made stops at some of the many different landings—there were eighty-seven from Palatka to Silver Springs listed in 1901—where they unloaded supplies and mail for local residents and stocked up on wood and food such as eggs and venison for the guests. And trying to pass an oncoming boat was an exercise in precise maneuvering and sheer luck that often led to boats scraping the shore and crews holding their breaths.[19]

Her nerves stoked and curiosity fueled, Stowe finally took the Ocklawaha trip on Tuesday, March 27, 1873, returning the following Tuesday. She exulted at her experiences on the journey, reporting, "We have done it! Whether in the body or out, we have been to dream-land, to the land of the fays and the elves, the land where reality ceases and romance begins. In the measurement of earth and in the geographic language of reality this was accomplished in a six days' journey, on the little steamer Okalawaha."[20]

She was among twenty passengers who boarded the boat in Palatka, where they were greeted by the crew, assigned cabins, and then provided with a large dinner. "If the proof of the pudding be in the eating, certainly the guests did ample justice to their meals, eating to right and left in a most complimentary manner. In fact, although we started on this expedition feeling rather poorly, and with a very faint appetite, we became uncritical devourers of whatever was set before us, merely from living all day in the fine open air that blew across the boat's deck," she wrote. In the middle of the night she awoke as branches scraped the boat; she looked out the open window to "see that we were gliding through palmetto forests and weird grottos, lit up with blazing pine torches. It seemed part of a fantastic dream as our weary eyes closed and the boat rippled on." Birdsong awoke her the next morning as the boat floated "through the arches of an unbroken forest." She joined others on a platform in front of the pilothouse to watch as they moved "into the very heart of the tropical mysteries."[21]

Stowe described many trees, birds, and alligators encountered along the way—and once again her peace was interrupted by men shooting wildlife from the boat. The boat whistled as it approached landings, a signal to local residents.

> Sometimes a group of two or three smart hunters in high peaked hats, attired in homespun garments with knives in their boots, stood leaning on their guns, waiting the approach of the boat. They seemed a grave, taciturn, unsmiling race, long-haired, bearded, and roughly attired. . . . Occasionally a wild turkey or a saddle of venison, hung in the tree, promised a supply to the provision market of the boat. They brought pailfuls of new-laid eggs and sometimes baskets of great golden oranges, which the captain bought and dispensed liberally among the passengers. The weekly touching of the boats at these lonely landings are the only communication these settlers hold with the outside world. A more solitary life cannot be imagined.[22]

Stowe's river trip flowed south through savanna lands and then into a chain of lakes in what is now Lake County. On the return trip, they sang hymns—it was Sunday, and this was Stowe—and then readied themselves for the main attraction, Silver Springs.

> Sunday night the wonders of our voyage came to a climax. The captain had announced to us that the boat would enter the Silver Spring between one and two o'clock, and advised us to sit up if we wanted to see the very finest part of the route.
> We did sit up, prepared as we were by a night's experience in wild forest traveling. We were taken by surprise by the wonderful scenes through which we passed. . . .
> What a night was that! Everybody watched and wondered, and the most prosaic grew poetic. About one o'clock we glided into the Silver Spring run, and by two, we were all gathered on the lower deck, looking down into transparent depths that gave the impression that our boat was moving through air. Every pebble and aquatic plant we glided over seemed, in the torch-light, invested with prismatic brightness. When the boat at last came to landing in the Silver Spring, we laid us down to sleep, fairly tired out with excitement, to wait for the morning.[23]

At daylight Stowe and others boarded a skiff to float over the springs, observing aquatic plants and fish as well as "various objects" thrown into the spring to observe its clarity and depth. By late morning they reboarded the steamboat and were homeward bound. "As the boat passed from the shadows of the Okalawaha to the broad St. John's, three cheers made the woods ring, and our 'camping in the wilderness' was over."[24]

Stowe was one of many travel writers who raved about their experiences on the Ocklawaha River. In 1875 noted southern poet Sidney Lanier wrote *Florida: Its Scenery, Climate, and History.* Lanier, hampered by bills and tuberculosis, was commissioned to write the guide at $125 per month by the Atlantic Coastline Railroad Company. Lanier capitalized on a growing interest in the subtropical wilderness and the railroad's anticipation of increased tourist traffic.

"For a perfect journey God gave us a perfect day." So begins Lanier's chapter about a May trip on the Ocklawaha River aboard the *Marion.* Lanier described turning off the "garish highway of the St. Johns" and "into the narrow lane of the Ocklawaha, the sweetest water-lane in the world, a lane which runs for more than a hundred and fifty miles of pure delight betwixt hedgerows of oaks and cypresses and palms and bays and magnolias and mosses and manifold vine-growths, a lane clean to travel along for there is

The highlight of Stowe's six-day steamboat journey was Silver Springs, a popular tourist destination for Florida visitors then and now. Courtesy of Bruce Hunt.

never a speck of dust in it save the blue dust and gold dust which the wind blows out of the flags and lilies, a lane which is as if a typical woods-stroll had taken shape and as if God had turned into water and trees the recollection of some meditative ramble through the lonely seclusions of His own soul."[25]

In 1883, Kirk Munroe offered a similar account of the trip, in a news article headlined "A Trip Over 'Crooked' Water" for *Harper's Weekly.* "No visitor to Florida who has any regard for his own peace of mind can leave the State without having made the trip up the Ocklawaha River, at least to Silver Spring. He may have explored every other river in the State from its source to its mouth, but if he has neglected this one river, his friends who have sailed its 'crooked waters' will insist upon it that he has failed to see the chief object of interest, and really knows nothing of Florida." Munroe described a singing crew, the wonder of the spring, and an amusing story of how an overhanging cypress branch broke, forcing an elderly gentleman's silk hat down onto his face to catch on his "rather prominent nose." The hat had to be cut apart to release the man.[26]

Silvia Sunshine told an even funnier story in her 1880 recounting of an Ocklawaha River trip in *Petals Plucked from Sunny Climes.* Aroused from slumbers, a steamboat passenger eager to see the spring opened his window, and "a very fresh morning breeze fanned his brow, causing him to make a most convulsive sneeze," resulting in his false upper teeth being "ejected from his mouth into the water." She continued:

> Soon as day dawned, sympathetic friends gathered around him with words of condolence, while the services of all experts in the art of descending into the watery fluid, without being drowned, were called into requisition. They all went down repeatedly, and returned without the lost treasures. Poles were spliced, armed with instruments of various designs with which they raked and dredged for hours, with toothless success. Large rewards were offered, while hope in the heart of the owner sunk below zero, and expectation stimulated the movements of only one artisan, who finally succeeded in securing the truant grinders by fastening a tin scoop on the end of a forty-foot pole, and bringing them out, amid the congratulations of friends and the great joy of the owner, who gave the persevering negro his proffered reward—ten dollars.[27]

These writers' observations of the river, the springs, and the transportation systems that moved on them provide great insight into early Florida tourism and wildlife. In the 1960s, activists trying to stop the Ocklawaha River from being destroyed for a barge canal project employed Lanier's account of the river and its beauty to make their case.

Marjorie Harris Carr, who helped lead the battle waged by the Florida Defenders of the Environment (FDE) against the Cross Florida Barge Canal project, often quoted Lanier in her speaking engagements and in articles opposing the project. She particularly liked his "sweetest water-lane in the world" description. Carr and FDE vehemently opposed the project, which was spearheaded by the US Army Corps of Engineers. The Corps claimed the state needed a canal from the Gulf of Mexico across the northern part of the peninsula through a large section of the Ocklawaha to the St. Johns River and, finally, the Atlantic Ocean. It was meant to boost business and avoid the dangers of shipping along the state's coast. Carr and FDE argued that the economic calculations about the canal were flawed, that the canal would endanger water resources, and, importantly, that it would destroy thousands of acres of riverine forests, damage wildlife, and demolish the river's aesthetic beauty. The environment, FDE argued, needed to be included in calculations of federal construction projects. The activists won when President Richard M. Nixon, in the wake of their federal lawsuit, halted the canal in 1971. "A national treasure is involved in the case of the Barge Canal—the Ocklawaha River—a uniquely beautiful, semitropical stream, one of a very few of its kind in the United States, which would be destroyed by construction of the canal," Nixon declared. It was the first major grassroots environmental victory in Florida, and it set a national precedent.[28]

The project was dead, ensured later by a 1986 congressional deauthorization, but remnants of the project, already under construction, remain, including the Kirkpatrick Dam that blocks part of the Ocklawaha, creating a bleak, little-used Rodman Reservoir and impeding river navigation by boaters and by endangered fish and manatees. Efforts to remove the dam and restore the river continue today, led by FDE.

On a bright, cloudless winter day I joined Karen Chadwick, an FDE board member and certified boat captain, for a trip down the undisturbed part of the Ocklawaha. We launched from the dam and headed away from the concrete structure and noisy spillway into a peaceful winding path lined with dense vegetation and beauty. Chadwick, sporting a baseball cap, sunglasses, and a blue "Free the Ocklawaha" sweatshirt depicting an old steamboat, heads out on the river regularly, sometimes for fun but often to educate a curious public about the river and the barge canal project. A bald eagle circled overhead, and a noisy kingfisher flitted along our path as

Karen Chadwick regularly travels the waters of her beloved Ocklawaha River, advocating for its restoration. Courtesy of Bruce Hunt.

we motored along, admiring the brilliant green spiderwort and the maple trees, sporting red leaves while the other deciduous trees stood bare.

Chadwick had much on her mind. Recently the carcass of a young manatee was found—perhaps it was separated from its mother and succumbed to cold stress during a recent wintery snap. Manatees used to travel along the river, often heading into Silver Spring, where water temperatures stay a constant 72 degrees, far warmer than the 62 degrees recently registered in the Ocklawaha. The dam now prevents those travels; the only way to reach the spring requires negotiating locks that can be impediments to the mammals. Chadwick also was getting ready for an upcoming rally celebrating the anniversary of Nixon's edict; a group of kayakers were planning to gather at the dam with signs calling for its removal.

Peering into the sapphire sky, she smiled. "It's my church. Every time you go out it's different."[29]

Her keen eyes picked out a subtle rise on the river's shore: Davenport Landing, once the last stop before eastbound steamboats reached the St. Johns River. Here boats dropped off food and picked up wood to fire the engines for the return trip to Palatka. Anchoring on a rock, we hiked up a steep path, once traversed by wagons, and reached a series of kiosks recounting the human history of the area that began an estimated 12,000 years ago with Native people who disappeared long before the steamboat era. The Fillyaw family once had a homestead here where generations lived in the sandy scrublands, managing to survive on the land and river. We pushed through saw palmettos, heavy underbrush, and vines to find the grave of Thomas C. Fillyaw, a Confederate corporal who served with the Georgia Infantry. A rectangular granite marker offered his name and information (May 1830–Dec. 8, 1893), and the site was surrounded by a metal guardrail erected eighty years later. Fillyaw was the landing master during the steamboat heyday; now his gravesite is a destination for knowledgeable boaters and for intrepid hikers who come through the Ocala National Forest.

Perhaps Stowe stopped here on her journey, although the landmarks she knew have faded with time. Her family's last winter at the beloved Mandarin home was 1883–84. Calvin's health was "in too precarious a state to permit him to undertake the long journey from Hartford," wrote their son Charles. "By this time one of Mrs. Stowe's fondest hopes had been realized; and, largely through her efforts, Mandarin had been provided with a pretty little Episcopal church, to which was attached a comfortable rectory, and over which was installed a regular clergyman."[30]

Upon Calvin's death in 1886, Stowe asked the Episcopal Church of Our Savior to place a window facing the river in the sanctuary in his honor. However, the congregation was unable to raise the funds, owing to citrus freezes that caused "a reversal of Mandarin's fortunes." Stowe died in Connecticut in 1896, and the window project went unrealized until 1916, after a church committee secured funding and hired famed New York stained-glass artist Louis Comfort Tiffany to create it. The design: a view of the river as it might have appeared from Stowe's porch with an oak tree draped in moss. Lines from a Stowe poem were inscribed on it:

In that hour, fairer than daylight dawning,
Remains the glorious thought, I am with Thee.[31]

Tourists from around the world used to visit the church to see the window—they admired Stowe and Tiffany. Hurricane Dora in 1964 damaged the church, which was rebuilt as a replica of the original. The stained-glass window is gone—a large hickory tree fell during the storm and destroyed it. Still, Stowe's memory looms large at the site overlooking the St. Johns River.

"We take a lot of pride in that she was a founder because of her role in the abolition of slavery," said Rev. Joe Gibbes, the church rector. He pointed to a large live oak on the property that likely witnessed her presence. On Easter in recent years a local Black church participated in a service beneath its massive branches. "When that choir starts singing . . . I think of her."[32]

Farther down the road are more sites associated with Stowe. The Mandarin School building was burned and rebuilt and continued to offer classes until 1929. Stowe "was not always loved by everyone in Mandarin," noted church member Anne Morrow. "She was a Yankee." Today the building is home to the Mandarin Community Club, a nonprofit dedicated to beautifying and preserving the area.[33]

The Stowe house has been replaced by two enormous modern mansions. But pieces of it remain at the nearby Mandarin Museum & Historical Society. A painting by Stowe of magnolia blooms on silk as a gift to a neighbor was displayed, along with a chair and a decorative column once on her home's exterior. When the Stowes left, they declared anything left behind available to anyone who wanted it, local lore has it. "So, people took things," some of which are on display, said museum board member Sandy Arpen. A few Black families took gingerbread adornment from the house's exterior and used it over their doorways in her honor.[34]

Stowe's time in Florida seems a bit dreamlike in the early twenty-first century. Steamboats no longer ply the rivers—by the 1920s the business was dead, supplanted by railroad lines and the rise of automobile tourism. But her legacy lives on as her books remain in print and historians explore her influence on American history. Her original intention of rehabilitating Frederick dimmed quickly, and he disappeared in San Francisco in 1871. Of greater success were Stowe's community efforts in Mandarin through the school and church.

More than a century later, however, one can still find evidence beyond her writings of her love for Florida. The Hartford home where Stowe spent her final years before dying at age eighty-five is now the Harriet Beecher Stowe Center; it holds her papers and offers house tours for the curious. There, visitors can find reminders of Stowe's time in Mandarin: a photograph and a portrait of the airy riverfront house, a canvas with cheerful yellow jessamine and Spanish moss, and a panel of an orange tree branch adorned with bright fruit and white blossoms—the latter three painted by Stowe, perhaps on her wide veranda enjoying a sweetly scented breeze. In the bedroom hangs her small watercolor of a wildly mystical scene of palm trees, palmettos, and live oaks overhanging a watery swamp. It is a landscape akin to the "fairy-land" she found on the Ocklawaha River that many nights may have enfolded her with warm memories of her Florida paradise.

To share some of Harriet Beecher Stowe's experiences, visit these three sites in Mandarin, plus the Harriet Beecher Stowe Center in Hartford, Connecticut. To get to the Kirkpatrick/Rodman Dam and access to the Ocklawaha River, see the directions below.

Mandarin Museum and Schoolhouse

11964 Mandarin Road
Jacksonville, Florida 32223
(904) 268-0784
mandarinmuseum.net/visit/mandarin-museum

The Mandarin Museum contains exhibits that illustrate the history of the community of Mandarin, from its earliest Timucuan settlements to the current day. One section is devoted to Harriet Beecher Stowe and her husband, Calvin, and features displayed pieces from the Stowe's Mandarin home.
The St. Joseph's Mission Schoolhouse for African-American Children, a one-room schoolhouse built in 1898, originally stood adjacent to St. Joseph's Church about 3 miles east and was relocated to the Mandarin Museum property in 2015.
Hours: Saturdays: 9:00 a.m.–4:00 p.m.
Admission is free.

Episcopal Church of Our Saviour

12236 Mandarin Road
Jacksonville, Florida 32223
(904) 268-9457
oursaviourjax.org

Harriet Beecher Stowe and her husband, Calvin Stowe, had been conducting Bible studies in Mandarin since 1868, when in 1880 an Episcopal missionary, Reverend Charles Sturgess, was assigned to begin holding regular services there. Two years later the congregation constructed a church building on the St. Johns River waterfront, and the first regular services began in 1883. The Stowes were instrumental supporters of the church. Sadly, both the church building and a stained-glass window dedicated to Calvin were damaged beyond repair during Hurricane Dora in 1964. The new church, rebuilt on the existing site, is larger and pays architectural homage to the original. Although the Tiffany window was not replaced, other stained-glass windows along with much of the original interior furnishings that survived Hurricane Dora have been reused in the new church.

Mandarin Community Club

12447 Mandarin Road
Jacksonville, Florida 32223
(904) 268-1622
mandarincommunityclub.org
mandarinartfestival.org

The Mandarin Community Club occupies the building that once housed the Mandarin School founded by Harriet Beecher Stowe in 1872. The structure served as a school until 1929 and has been home to the Mandarin Community Club since 1936.

The Mandarin Community Club has held the Mandarin Art Festival on their grounds on Easter weekend every year since 1968, and this is a great time to visit the location. They also host the Third Thursday Lecture Series presented by the Mandarin Museum & Historical Society.

Harriet Beecher Stowe Center

77 Forest Street
Hartford, Connecticut 06105
(860) 522-9258
harrietbeecherstowecenter.org

The Harriet Beecher Stowe Center occupies two adjacent houses in the historic Harford neighborhood of Nook Farm (where Mark Twain was also a resident): an ornate Queen Anne Victorian architecture mansion, the Franklin Chamberlin House, now known as the Katharine Seymour Day (grandniece of Harriet Beecher Stowe) House; and a smaller Victorian Gothic cottage next to it that was the home of Calvin and Harriet Beecher Stowe and their family from 1873 to 1896 (other than winters, which they spent in Mandarin). The Center maintains the most comprehensive collection of her correspondences, manuscripts, and sketch books, as well as some of her original paintings and first-edition books. Special access to some of the collection is available by advance appointment. They also conduct daily guided tours of the home, which was renovated in 2017, and discuss Harriet Beecher Stowe's life and her influence on American society.

Hours: Open Wednesday through Saturday 9:30–5:00 and Sunday noon to 5:00, January through March except Easter, Thanksgiving, Christmas Eve, and Christmas Day.

Admission: $16 for adults; $14 for seniors; $12 for active military; $10 for children; under 5 free.

Ocklawaha River

Directions: From Palatka head south on Florida SR 19 approximately 10 miles; cross the bridge at the Cross Florida Barge Canal; and then turn right onto Rodman Dam Road and go 3 miles to the end.

At the Kirkpatrick/Rodman Dam and at the Rodman Recreation Area, there are two separate (boat and kayak/canoe) launch ramps that access the Ocklawaha River.

7

Middle/West Florida Travelers

Hopes in the Panhandle, 1765–1891

Wilderness. That was the best way to describe much of North Florida in the eighteenth and nineteenth centuries. Although there were bustling ports in St. Augustine on the Atlantic Ocean and Pensacola on the Gulf of Mexico, most of the land between the two was uncharted territory with vast tracts of pine forests, blackwater rivers, and swamplands inhabited by Native people.

The accounts of White travelers who journeyed through this area during this era offer glimpses into its history and natural resources and recount vastly different reactions—some glowing, others critical. But each wayfarer recognized his or her entrance into a landscape that few European wanderers and colonists had encountered.

Their explorations also reflected Florida's role as a pawn in the colonial ambitions and holdings of European nations, which greatly shaped its character, causing governmental instability as well as a rich blending of ethnic groups unlike many other areas of North America. From Spanish to British to Spanish to American hands, with an unsuccessful French claim as well, colonial control of the peninsula reflected the winds of wars waged largely on other turfs.

With the Treaty of Paris in 1763 ending the Seven Years' War (often called the French and Indian War), Spain ceded its long-held Florida holdings to Great Britain, receiving Cuba in return. The British divided their new holding into East Florida and West Florida (the latter of which stretched to the Mississippi River), becoming the fourteenth and fifteenth colonies—a little-heralded fact since these colonies remained on the loyalist side during the American Revolution. It was an advantageous possession for the British, who also held Canada; the new United States was sandwiched between the two.[1]

Most Spaniards fled the two new Floridas, which were meager possessions at best. A 1763 census listed St. Augustine, the capital of East Florida, with 3,046 people. It was a settlement of perhaps three hundred houses and featured a large masonry coquina fort guarding the harbor. Pensacola, the capital of West Florida, was even smaller, with a population of fewer than 800 people, comprising Native people, colonists, and prisoners. It had a wooden fort, but there was little agriculture or development—trade and government fueled its economy.

The British encouraged new settlers by offering free lands, a lure that brought celebrated American frontiersman Daniel Boone and some male relatives to the colony in 1765. They took a long, circular route from North Carolina to St. Augustine to Pensacola before returning north, a distance of more than 750 miles. Boone was looking at land prospects while hunting his way through the Southeast.[2]

The trip was a bust, with Boone's recollection making it "sound something like an extended bachelor party, featuring a good deal of flirting and cavorting with pretty serving girls and Seminole Indian maidens," notes historian John Mack Faragher. Hunting was miserable thanks to swamps, high water, and bugs. At one point Boone's brother-in-law was separated for several days "and almost starved before being found." The party was rescued by Seminoles who took them to their camp "and succored them with venison and honey."[3]

In Pensacola, the men sold animal skins, and Boone took a surprising step, buying a city lot. His son Nathan later reported that his father was willing to move to Florida, but Daniel's wife, Rebecca, refused, "unwilling to go so far from her connections and friends." Boone later gained fame in his explorations of the Appalachians, particularly Kentucky.[4]

A decade later, William Bartram, the intrepid Quaker botanist from Philadelphia, made a quick foray into the area on a whim. Bartram had been roaming the southeastern British colonial holdings since his 1774 East Florida sojourn, ending up in Mobile a year later waiting for a trip up the Mississippi River. To fill his time, Bartram hitched a ride with a crew sailing to Pensacola in search of a shipwreck and its potentially valuable goods. But they were too late—the wreck was stripped when they reached it—so they continued on to Pensacola. Bartram wrote in his *Travels* that along the way they camped on a beach, setting a driftwood fire to "keep up a light, and smoke away the musquitoes," awaking to a cool September morning.[5]

Bartram was a bit of a celebrity upon his arrival. Governor Peter Chester offered to cover Bartram's housing and expenses if he would stay and explore the colony's natural treasures. But Bartram declined, since accomplishing such work would "require the revolution of the seasons to discover and view vegetable nature in all her various perfections." Still recovering from a fever, Bartram had other plans and left with the ship's captain to catch passage into Mississippi.[6]

He did offer observations of Pensacola and its environs:

> This city commands some natural advantages, superior to any other port in this province, in point of naval commerce, and such as human art and strength can never supply. It is delightfully situated upon gentle rising ascents environing a spacious harbour, safe and capacious enough to shelter all the navies of Europe, and excellent ground for anchorage; the West end of St. Rose island stretches across the great bay St. Maria Galves, and its South-West projecting point forms the harbour of Pensacola, which, with the road or entrance, is defended by a block-house built on the extremity of that point, which at the same time serves the purpose of a fortress and look-out tower.[7]

Bartram described several rivers running into the bay but judged none to be navigable, noting some "spots of good high land, and rich swamps" that had "given rise to some plantations" growing rice, indigo, corn, sweet potatoes, and other products. There were several hundred homes, including the Spanish-built governor's palace, in Pensacola, which was defended by a tetragon-shaped fort housing officers, soldiers, and artillery. And, of course, he had a look at the native plants, noting "several curious non-described plants" growing on the nearby sand hills.[8] "Next morning early we arose from our hard sandy sea-beaten couch, being disturbed the whole night by the troublesome musquitoes; set sail, and before night returned safe to the city of Mobile."[9]

Today the naturalist's brief visit is commemorated with a small, shady waterfront space in the city's downtown historic district: William Bartram Memorial Park. Across from where he once camped is a small marina; on the other side, a busy road. Several Bartram markers have been placed in the Pensacola area, denoting his significance to history and to avid fans who follow his path (like me). However, this is the only marked site that he actually visited. Walking through adjacent Seville Square on a quiet, rainy afternoon, one can only imagine the hustle and bustle that Bartram encountered during his sojourn.

By 1784, Spain once again controlled Florida, the result of the Treaty of Paris, which ended the American Revolution. Most British citizens in the two Floridas fled the area. But the Spanish ownership was short-lived. As historian Charlton W. Tebeau wrote, "Quite early in the second occupation it became clear that Spain could not people, develop, and govern Florida effectively. It was equally obvious that it would fall to the United States unless some great power, possibly England, should intervene to prevent it. The struggle to control the destiny of Florida was far more than a local affair."[10]

European conflicts, including the War of 1812 between Britain and the United States and other colonies fighting for independence from Spain, "absorbed that country's energies and left little resources with which to protect Florida." As Spain ebbed in power, the United States' stature arose, forcing Spain to give up its control of the westernmost part of West Florida, which now extended only to the Perdido River near Pensacola. And the Americans had more plans to acquire the remaining land. Hostilities with the new United States were growing, fueled in part by freedom-seeking slaves taking refuge in Spanish Florida and concerns that British agents were arming Native people to fight American troops.[11]

During the War of 1812, Pensacola was seized by British troops, who used it to "stir up trouble with Creek Indians." Major General Andrew Jackson, who later would be elected the US president, attacked Pensacola, forcing out the British, and then headed to New Orleans, where Jackson sealed his fame by beating the British. Jackson came back to Florida in 1818, taking a Spanish fort at St. Marks to the east of Pensacola and opposing Seminole tribes during what became known as the First Seminole War (1816–19).[12]

These were audacious acts—Jackson and his armed troops invaded the lands of another sovereign state, and the US government "clearly approved" of his conduct. US Secretary of State John Quincy Adams argued that "Spain must either demonstrate power to govern and police the unruly population or turn the Floridas over to the United States."[13]

Among Jackson's militia was Davy Crockett, later known on TV as the "King of the Wild Frontier" for his exploits. Crockett was on furlough from fighting with Indigenous tribes but "wanted a small taste of British fighting," according to his autobiography. He joined a group that trailed Jackson's army by horse and by foot, arriving too late for the Pensacola battle. "That evening we went down into the town, and could see the British fleet lying in sight of the place," he wrote. "We got some liquor, and took a 'horn' or so, and went back to the camp." The next morning Jackson set out for New Orleans. Crockett's enlistment ended in 1815, and a decade later he was elected to the US House of Representatives from Tennessee, where he opposed Jackson's 1830 Indian Removal Act that forced Native people from southern US lands into areas west of the Mississippi River. Crockett's popularity soared in the 1950s, when an American television show depicted him as a fierce woodman who wore a coonskin cap; Boone also became a television icon in the 1960s.[14]

Tensions between Spain and the United States ultimately led to the 1819 Adams-Onis Treaty in which Florida became part of the United States. In 1821, shortly after the treaty was approved by the US government, Jackson was commissioned as Florida's military governor to "receive, possess, and occupy the ceded lands; to govern the Floridas; and to establish territorial government." President James Monroe wrote to Jackson that he had "full confidence" in Jackson's leadership. "Smugglers and slave traders will hide their heads; pirates will disappear, and Seminoles cease to give trouble."[15]

Jackson and his family, including his wife, Rachel, and their nephew and adopted son, arrived in Pensacola in June, but it was not what he expected:

Jackson was never happy at Pensacola. He disliked dealing with the Spaniards, who had six months to wind up their affairs. He had discovered that President Monroe had appointed the most important officials for the Territory without consulting him. It was summer and the weather was at times uncomfortably hot and humid. His personal quarters, a large two story house, very comfortably furnished, led Mrs. Jackson to pronounce Pensacola the most healthful place she had ever seen. The new governor, on the other hand, found some of the public buildings unusable.[16]

Actually, the pious Rachel Jackson's initial opinion of the city was dim. She made that clear in letters to her friend Eliza Kingsley back home in Nashville: "Oh, how shall I make you sensible of what a heathen land I am in? Never but once have a heard a Gospel sermon, nor the song of Zion sounded in my ear. . . . Oh, I feel as if I was in a vast howling wilderness, far from my friends in the Lord, my home and country. The Sabbath entirely neglected and profaned."[17]

Unlike Bartram, she found no beauty in the surrounding landscape, even complaining about the smell of magnolia tree blossoms:

Every step I have traveled on land is a bed of white sand; no other timber than longleaf pine on the rivers, the live-oak and magnolia. The most odoriferous flower grows on them I ever saw. Believe me, this country has been greatly overrated. The land produces nothing but sweet potatoes and yams. One acre of our fine Tennessee land is worth a thousand.

The General, I believe, wants to get home again as much as I do.[18]

A few weeks later she wrote to Kingsley after watching the official ceremonies ceding Florida from Spain with a dramatic change of national flags. Those who remained behind mourned when the Spanish leaders sailed away, she recounted. Then she returned to grousing that stores were open on Sundays and that she heard "swearing in the streets." She sent an army major to enforce a strict sabbath and was relieved when, the next week, "Great order was observed; the doors kept shut; the gambling houses demolished; fiddling and dancing not heard any more on the Lord's day; cursing not to be heard."[19]

Rachel's attitude about the landscape had softened as well:

Pensacola is a perfect plain; the land nearly as white as flour, yet, productive of fine peach trees, oranges in abundance, grapes, figs, pomegranates, etc., etc. Fine flowers growing spontaneously, for they have neglected the gardens, expecting a change of government. The town is immediately on the bay. The most beautiful water prospect I ever saw; and from ten o'clock in the morning until ten at night we have the finest sea breeze. There is something in it so exhilarating, so pure, so wholesome, it enlivens the whole system. All the houses look in ruins, old as time. Many squares of the town appear grown over with the thickest shrubs, weeping willows, and the Pride of China; all look neglected. The inhabitants all speak Spanish and French. Some speak four or five languages. Such a mixed multitude, you, nor any of us, ever had an idea of. There are fewer white people far than any other, mixed with all nations under the canopy of heaven, almost in nature's darkness.[20]

She did add that the town seemed to be "pure and wholesome" and that the "weather is oppressively warm to me, and raining every day. Sometimes the streets are two feet deep in water."[21]

Andrew Jackson wrote to a friend that he was hoping to leave Pensacola by October, noting that Rachel's health "is not good, and I am determined to travel here as early as my business and her health will permit, even if I should be compelled to come back to settle my business and turn over the government to my successor. I am determined to resign my office the moment Congress meets."[22]

Jackson did just that, giving up the governorship and returning to Tennessee, where he already might have envisioned a campaign for the presidency. Historian Herbert M. Domherty Jr. wrote that Jackson learned that Pennsylvania politicians wanted him to run for the office. Florida was "a long way from the main national political scene," perhaps making "presidential politics . . . another underlying factor in his decision to leave." He did depart with the recommendation that East and West Florida be unified and admitted "to the union as one state as speedily as possible."[23]

Jackson would become the seventh president of the United States, serving from 1829 to 1837 after a term as a US senator from Tennessee. He had helped shaped the territorial government of Florida and established county courts. It was time to realize his bigger ambitions.

Today, the pious Rachel Jackson might be horrified at how Pensacola has changed. The house where she lived at the southeast corner of Palafox and Intermedia became a World of Beer bar, and the downtown is home to many restaurants and night spots. Two entrepreneurs have even used her descriptive words to name their downtown venture: Perfect Plain Brewing Co. The brewery's website pays homage to Rachel's words, using them on its website. "Located in the heart of Downtown Pensacola, our mission is to create incredible experiences that make our beer, our brewery, and our hometown, Pensacola, unforgettable." The company's brewhouse offerings and a busy outdoor taco food truck at a recent lunch hour attested to local delight in the business, but it's doubtful that Rachel would have partaken.[24]

Florida officially became a US territory in 1822, and that July its Legislative Council convened for the first time in Pensacola; the next year the meeting was in St. Augustine. From the outset it was clear that this alternating of locations wouldn't work: the St. Augustine delegation took fifty-nine days to reach Pensacola by water, and, the following year, the Pensacola group was shipwrecked and "barely escaped death," noted historian Michael Gannon. "Not surprisingly, the principal decision made at the second session was to select a halfway location for a capital that would shorten the sea voyage and the twenty-eight-day overland crossing from St. Augustine to Pensacola."[25]

A committee decided that a representative of each of the Floridas would meet at St. Marks, located south of today's Tallahassee, on October 1, 1823, and then "proceed carefully to explore and examine" nearby areas to find

"the most eligible and convenient situation" for a capital between the Suwannee and Ochlockonee Rivers. The two designated scouts, Dr. William
Hayne Simmons of St. Augustine and John Lee Williams of Pensacola, were
required to keep notes about soils, streams, and the "local situation" of the
country.[26]

Simmons left St. Augustine on horseback on September 26, immediately
enduring rainy days and sickness. By October 1, he was no farther west
than the Alachua Savannah that Bartram had visited almost fifty years earlier. Simmons found it "a beautiful expanse of fresh and living verdure." He
had two guides, two pack horses, and ten days' worth of provisions as he
continued westward, crossing rivers and streams and describing a rolling
landscape and thick vegetation. They met Natives along the way—Simmons
gave two dollars to one to help secure a canoe crossing of the broad Suwannee River; the five horses had to be swum across one at a time. On October
10, Simmons reached St. Marks, but Williams was nowhere to be found.
The physician noted that the nearby pine land was high and dry and "would
form an eligible situation for a town."[27]

After a week of waiting, the restless Simmons rode west with the commander of the fort, Captain McClintock, in the hope of encountering Williams along the way. They camped, crossed rivers, and were entertained by
the owner of a plantation where there were crops of rice, sugarcane, and
cotton. On October 24, "hearing nothing of Mr. Williams," Simmons headed back, declaring that he had business in St. Augustine that needed his
attention.[28]

The next day, Williams arrived at St. Marks; the trip from Pensacola had
taken twenty-four miserable, frustrating days. He and the small boat's crew
encountered bad weather, unfavorable winds, and contrary tides; they also
took wrong turns into bays. But he'd also experienced the Gulf's bounty. At
Apalachicola Bay, Williams noted "armies of porpoises" and plentiful fish
and shellfish.[29]

Before us opened a fine, extensive sheet of water; on the left grass
meadows extended to the north and west, as far as the eye can reach.
The shores are sprinkled with beautiful keys or islets of cabbage or
cedar, whose intense verdure affords a comfortable relief from the
dazzling white sandy shores which we had passed. We found that this
flattering prospect, however, like many others in this uncertain world,
was calculated for show more than use. As darkness approached, our
brilliant landscape vanished, and a succession of oyster bars succeed-

ed in encircling us on every side, among which we were obliged to anchor, but we took vengeance on the oysters by roasting and eating great numbers of them.[30]

Williams, anxious to meet up with Simmons, on October 19 loaded up "as many articles as I could conveniently carry" and headed out to hike along the coast. After camping on the beach, he turned inland, and after toiling "among ponds, swamps and marshes, I grew faint from want of provisions, and had to shape my course eastward in order to reach the shore," where he ate a crab and oysters and "slept soundly till next morning." Williams fashioned a raft from driftwood and paddled across a bay, meeting up with his previous boat (now repaired) on the far shore. The crew shared their raccoon dinner with him. On October 24 he reached St. Marks but had to rest the next day, as they were "so exhausted by fatigue and hunger that we were unable to walk without great difficulty."[31]

Finally united, the official search for the new capital commenced, albeit three weeks late. Simmons and Williams scoured the local area, finding traces of an old Spanish highway and camping along the way. When they reached Tallahassee, they met Seminole chief Neomathla. When Williams showed Neomathla paperwork affirming his commission and expressed his desire to find a new site for territorial government, the "fine, stout Indian" became friendly, offering cigars and roasted nuts as well as lodging in a council house. In his records, Williams described watching young Seminole men and women playing a ball game—the women won—and a late evening of dancing and singing.[32]

During the next few days Simmons, Williams, and crew roamed the area, tracing streams south of the Georgia border, following Native trails, and noting the landscape. An "Indian hunter" at the price of a "quarter of a dollar" took them to the site of an old Spanish fort that Williams reported was "situated on a commanding eminence at the north point of a high narrow neck of highlands nearly surrounded by a deep ravine and swamp. The moat, parapet and bastians [sic] are strongly marked." Later in the day, they learned that the area once held many Spanish settlements. The searchers also sailed along the coast, looking for rivers and assessing navigation.[33]

After careful consideration, it was clear that Tallahassee was the best site. The men headed home; this time Williams's seaward journey to Pensacola took only three days. On March 4, 1824, Florida governor William Duval declared Tallahassee, the former Apalachee settlement where de Soto once wintered, to be the new state capital. The legislative session met there that year in a log building "where Indians leaned through the windows to hear the strange goings-on," Gannon wrote. Although now populated by Creek tribes, the location made for easier travel for Florida's Legislative Council, which created new laws to establish river ferries, "incorporate churches and towns," and construct roads and canals.[34]

A brick building was completed in 1845—just in time for statehood—and it remains the core of a larger building that served the state until 1978, when a twenty-two-story high-rise and accompanying complex were erected behind it. Some leaders, including the governor, wanted to demolish the old building, but it was saved and restored, thanks to historic preservation activists. Today the Historic Capitol's white facade, red-and-white awnings, and dome welcome visitors driving up Apalachee Parkway into the city. It houses a museum with two floors of exhibits about the state's political history that offer an opportunity to consider its colorful, and often difficult, past.

Tallahassee was depicted by poet and writer Sidney Lanier in his 1875 travelogue *Florida: Its Scenery, Climate, and History*. The guidebook, which described many parts of the state, was commissioned by the Atlantic Coastline Railway to lure tourists to the state, emphasizing its natural beauty and mild climate. The project was "reluctantly undertaken" by Lanier, who needed the income, but its lyrical tone and observations included "a wealth of factual information accurately presented by a perceptive observer and careful writer."[35]

In a chapter entitled "The Tallahassee Country or Piedmont Florida," Lanier noted that "no one with an eye either for agricultural advantages or for the spiritual beauties of hill-curves and tree-arabesques can do other than praise the happiness of their choice." As the train neared Tallahassee and the area that came to be known as Middle Florida, he found "long fences, generous breadths of chocolate-colored fields, spreading oaks, curving hills" and "ample prospects."[36]

Arriving in Tallahassee, Lanier rode a carriage to a "genuine old-fashioned tavern," where he took a room up a long flight of stairs. Lanier was mesmerized by a wide view of the rolling countryside with crops (he mentioned tobacco, cotton, corn, sugarcane, wheat, melons, and vegetables), homesteads, and farm buildings. It was a scene, he said, of "bounteous richness almost too large for their content."[37]

> And this indeed has always been the tone of things—not only of the hills, but of the social life—in Tallahassee. The repute of these people for hospitality was [a] matter of national renown before the war be-

tween the States: and even the dreadful reverses of that cataclysm appear to have been their force in vain against this feature of Tallahassee manners; for much testimony since the war—to which this writer cheerfully adds his own—goes to show that it exists unimpaired.[38]

Perhaps Lanier's hype of southern hospitality was meant to soothe the worries of potential travelers from the North concerned about the social atmosphere a decade after the end of the Civil War. He noted that the "people are poor and the dwellings need paint and ready money is slow of circulation, yet it must be confessed that the bountiful tables looked like anything but famine, that signs of energy cropped out here and there in many places, and that the whole situation was but a reasonable one for a people who ten years ago had to begin life anew." His southern sympathies—Lanier served in the Confederate Army—remained clear.[39]

Lanier continued his travelogue by describing various buildings and businesses in Tallahassee, including the Capitol Building; he noted that the city, with a population of 2,500 to 3,000, had a post office, a telegraph office, two newspapers, and churches "of all the main denominations." Lanier stayed at the City Hotel, newly refurbished and opposite the Capitol Building on the west side of Adams Street; the hotel burned a decade later.[40]

Outside the city, Lanier visited several lakes and exulted about Wakulla Spring, located 15 miles south, which he said was "one of the most wonderful springs in the world." He traveled there by train and then carriage, finding it enchanting. The spring was "thrillingly transparent" with a "mosaic of many-shaded green hues."[41]

It is one hundred and six feet deep; and as one slowly floats face downward, one perceives, at first dimly, then more clearly, a great ledge of white rock which juts up to within perhaps fifty feet of the surface, from beneath which the fish come swimming as if out of the gaping mouth of a great cave. Looking down past the upper part of this ledge, down, down through the miraculous lymph, which impresses you at once as an abstraction and as a concrete substance, to the white concave bottom where you can plainly see a sort of "trouble in the ground" as the water bursts up from its mysterious channel, one feels more than ever that sensation of depth itself wrought into a substantial embodiment.[42]

This site is now preserved as Edward Ball Wakulla Springs State Park, named for a financier who once used the property as a retreat. Ball built the then-luxurious Wakulla Springs Lodge in 1937 to take advantage of the idyllic location and proximity to the freshwater spring, touted as the largest and deepest in the world. The site has been popular ever since, drawing many Hollywood filmmakers—think Tarzan and *Creature from the Black Lagoon*—and travelers who, like Lanier, have exulted at its enchanting waters. When Ball died in 1981, the property went to a trust that sold it to the state in 1986.

During a visit there, a friend joined me for a hike into the 6,000 acres of surrounding riverine forest that offer peace and views of the spring and the river into which it empties, headed south to join the St. Marks River. We were attending a history conference at the lodge, which offers a restaurant, soda shop, and swimming areas for day visitors. A late afternoon river cruise provided a chance to peer into the spring and watch alligators and a myriad of wading birds on the river's banks, all activities Lanier would have enjoyed.

Near the end of his Tallahassee chapter, Lanier made a pitch for settlement, stating that the area's agricultural land is rich and affordable and that the local climate "has been found exceedingly beneficial to consumption"— a claim of healthfulness that propelled much of the state's early tourism. Lanier also briefly described West Florida, noting that it was "sparsely inhabited" and lesser traveled because of its inaccessibility by rail. At Apalachicola he observed a town of 400 to 500 residents, "now little more than the shell of a once prosperous city," its shipping of cotton being supplanted by railroad lines. "Its fish, and particularly its oysters, are celebrated for their excellent flavor," he wrote.[43]

Two important American artists also visited the Pensacola area—one of them finding great beauty, the other disappointment.

George Catlin, a painter who focused much of his work on portraits and scenes of Native people on the vanishing frontier, came to the area in the winter of 1834–35, having recovered from a dangerous fever. Four years earlier, Catlin started traveling west to visit different tribes, many of them in the Great Plains, hoping to paint them on canvas before they were removed due to encroaching settlement. He sketched or painted some five hundred works from his journeys, exhibiting them in the United States and Europe, and published a number of books recounting his adventures.

In the second volume of his *Letters and Notes on the Manners, Customs, and Condition of the North American Indians,* Catlin wrote about his Florida visit, extolling its natural beauty: "The sudden transition from the ice-bound regions of the North to this mild climate, in the midst of winter, is

Noted artist George Catlin, visiting the Pensacola area in the winter of 1834–1835, painted this scene of a Seminole family encamped near the enormous sand dunes of Santa Rosa Island. Courtesy of the Smithsonian American Art Museum.

one of peculiar pleasure. At a half-way of the distance, one's cloak is thrown aside; and arrived on the ever-verdant borders of Florida, the bosom is opened and bared to the soft breeze from the ocean's wave, and the congenial warmth of a summer's sun."[44]

Catlin noted that "Florida" meant a "country of flowers" and that "Perdido," the name of the river on its western boundary, meant "River of Perdition." He described looking into its "black water" into what seemed to be dangerous and gloomy depths. On shore was loveliness:

Florida is, in a great degree, a dark and sterile wilderness, yet with spots of beauty and of loveliness, with charms that cannot be forgotten. Her swamps and everglades, the dens of alligators, and lurking places of the desperate savage, gloom the thoughts of the wary traveller, whose mind is cheered and lit to admiration, when in the solitary pine woods, where he hears nought but the echoing notes of the *sand-hill cranes*, or the howling wolf, he suddenly breaks out into the open savannahs, teeming with their myriads of wild flowers, and palmettos; or where the winding path through which he is wending his lonely way, suddenly brings him out upon the beach, where the rolling sea has thrown up her thousands of hills and mounds of sand as white as the drifted snow, over which her green waves are lashing, and sliding back again to her deep green and agitated bosom.[45]

Catlin painted a scene set among the dunes on Santa Rosa Island, a barrier island south of Pensacola, that were 50 or 60 feet high. It depicted a Seminole family "encamped, catching and drying red fish, their chief article of food." The canvas, dominated by enormous white mounds of sand with the family in the foreground, now is owned by the Smithsonian American Art Museum.[46]

Today Santa Rosa Island's massive dunes mostly have been replaced with hotels and high-rise condominiums that appeal to tourists along a 26-mile area dubbed the "Redneck Riviera." But interspersed in the development are sections of Gulf Islands National Seashore that provide public beach access and a glimpse into Catlin's inspiration. At the farthest westerly section of the island, a two-lane road stretches between white sand so fine it feels like one is walking in flour. At the tip are the remnants of Fort Pickens, part of a series of fortifications built near Pensacola to regulate and protect its shipping port and navies dating from the Spanish colonial period.

The seashore is full of history that includes fort ruins and interpretative signage. It includes the Naval Live Oaks Area, created in 1828, now the oldest US federal tree reserve (its live oaks were prized for wooden shipbuilding before the Civil War) and 15 miles of the Florida National Scenic Trail. Deep in the Naval Live Oaks Area lies a 2.4-mile white sand path known as the Andrew Jackson Trail—the last remnant of the road that once connected Pensacola to St. Augustine. In 1824, shortly after Florida joined the United States, a two-year construction project began on the almost 400-mile road, a venture that opened the interior of Florida to the White homesteaders who would soon flock to the state, increasing tensions with tribes that already called it theirs. The tree-shaded path now provides a visual memory of this era, despite the sound of pines and lapping waves to the north and distant automobile traffic to the south. Catlin would be astounded.

Of the nearby city of Pensacola, Catlin repeated claims that it was a place of "good health" and recommended it for winter and summer visitation:

> The town of Pensacola is beautifully situated on the shore of the bay, and contains at present about fifteen hundred inhabitants, most of them Spanish Creoles. They live an easy and idle life, without any energy further than for the mere means of living. The bay abounds in the greatest variety of fish, which are easily taken, and the finest quality of oysters are found in profusion, even alongside of the wharves.

Government having fixed upon this harbor as the great naval de-pot for all the Southern coast, the consequence will be, that a vast sum of public money will always be put into circulation in this place; and the officers of the navy, together with the officers of the army, stationed in the three forts built and now building at this place, will constitute the most polished and desirable society in our country.[47]

Recognizing that another war in Florida was impending—the Second Seminole War broke out in 1835—Catlin decided to head up the Arkansas River to travel into the Rocky Mountains "under the protection of the United States dragoons." In closing, he wrote that he would "hail the day with pleasure, when I can again reach the free land of the lawless savage; for far more agreeable to my ear is the Indian yell and war-whoop, than the civilized groans and murmurs about *'pressure,' 'deposits,' 'banks,' 'boundary questions'* &c; and I vanish from the country with the sincere hope that these tedious words may become obsolete before I return. Adieu." Catlin later painted a regal portrait of one of the great warriors of the Second Seminole War, Osceola, during the chief's prison stay in South Carolina shortly before his 1838 death.[48]

Heralded avian artist John James Audubon briefly visited Pensacola in 1837 while hoping to embark on a lengthy trip down the Gulf coast of Florida. Five years earlier he had been elated with the wealth of bird life in southern Florida, but this time his plans fizzled: he only got as far as one day in Pensacola.

Hopping a ride on a steamer from Mobile, Audubon arrived in Pensacola to a "most rascally house called 'Collin's Hotel.' May your star never shoot you there!" he wrote on March 3, 1897, to Rev. John Bachman, a Charleston, South Carolina, naturalist and friend. Using some letters of introduction, Audubon and a companion were welcomed onto the frigate USS *Constellation,* where the commodore gave them a tour, poured some "first rate" wine, and shared a "bottle of Copenhagen *Snuff* that would make your nostrils expand with pleasure, and draw tears from your eyes—the stuff is so potent." They returned to the hotel, where they contemplated the rainy weather. Audubon's observations and words:

> Pensacola is a small place at present; principally inhabited by Creole Spaniards of the lowest Class, and some few aimiable [*sic*] & talented famillies [*sic*] of Scotch, and Americans.—The place is said to be *perfectly healthy.* The country is deeply sandy, and mothering but pine Barrens exist for about 80 miles back.—The Bay is grand and of good

depth—The Bar at the entrance about 22 feet admits of Vessels of great Burthen—this is guarded by two powerful fortifications.—The Naval Depot or Navy Yard is 9 miles before the Village, we had not time to visit it.—Fish is abundant, and there I saw I think the finest oysters ever observed by me in any portion of the southern country.—Deer, Wild Turkeys and smaller Game is said to be very plentiful.[49]

Audubon wrote that a new town is "laid out for sale and an *Immense* Hotel is now being erected there" but reported that "the back country is so poor, and the want of some navigable stream so great in my opinion, that I have great doubts" about boasts about its future development. He walked around the area but found no new birds and returned to Mobile the next day. Of the glowing accounts of the healthfulness of the region, Audubon, who had endured bugs and swamps on earlier treks into Florida, was skeptical, declaring that he would never "seek refuge (much less health) in either the lower parts of Alabama or any *Southern States.*"[50]

The lure of healing, however, wooed many northerners to Florida—among them Laura Ingalls Wilder, who later became a celebrated author for the *Little House on the Prairie* book series. But in 1891, all Wilder and her family wanted was to improve the recovery of her husband, Almanzo, who had lingering health issues and paralysis from a stroke following a bout of diphtheria three years earlier. The family hoped the warm Florida climate would be better than what they had endured in South Dakota and Minnesota.[51]

As did many others of the era, the Wilders believed the prevailing myths, perpetrated by tourist and railroad interests (Lanier among them), that Florida was a land of sunshine, health, and productive soil. In a shameless tract, W. D. Chipley, founder of the Pensacola & Atlantic Railroad line that transported the Wilders to Florida, claimed that in "Florida may be found locations suited to tastes and desires of every would-be resident, and every production the agriculturalists may desire to grow." His 1880s publication *Facts about Florida* claimed that there was nothing to cause malaria or yellow fever and that "the whole region is equally secure from death-dealing diphtheria and typhoids"—an assertion that certainly would have caught the Wilders' interest. That this was patently false didn't matter, and settlers who endured malaria and yellow fever outbreaks certainly would have taken issue with that boast.[52]

Nevertheless, the Wilders headed to Florida with their four-year-old daughter, Rose, in October 1891. They joined Laura Wilder's cousin Peter Ingalls, who had a new wife and a homestead near Westville, Florida, close to the Alabama border. Wilder briefly mentioned the Florida jaunt in positive terms, but Rose, in an award-winning short story written three decades later, depicted a fairly miserable experience.[53]

Although Rose Wilder Lane's 1922 short story "Innocence" is fiction, the descriptions and parallels to the Wilders' experiences are notable. In the story, a family of three travels by rail to Florida to live near "Uncle Charley," who, they discovered, was newly married to a mysterious local woman. The young narrator, Mary Alice, describes the landscape as "piney woods" where the white sandy road curved around "straight, tall gray trees that had no branches." It was the land of towering longleaf pine that attracted many settlers to the area for the lumber business. The child goes to sleep every night listening to the aeolian song of the pines, which "had no leaves, only long things like red and brown darning needles. She must not go far from the house—there were snakes in the piney woods." While her father worked to dig a well and plant crops, Mary Alice was left to play in the mud and watch lizards and ants in the yard.[54]

Mary Alice and her mother find the land dark and foreboding and the local female population unfamiliar, even dangerous. When Charley's new wife offers the child a treat, her mother feeds it to a chicken that dies. Combined with the mutilation of their cow and other factors, the family packs up and leaves; Charley refuses to join them despite their pleas.[55]

As Wilder biographer Caroline Fraser notes, the story is a "plaintive glimpse of Rose's relationship to her parents, particularly her mother, whose deep unhappiness makes her sharp and punitive, eroding the rapport mother and daughter originally share." Fraser notes that the Wilders never filed for a homestead, heading to De Smet, South Dakota, in August 1892, unable to tolerate Florida's humidity.[56]

In the 1930s and 1940s, Wilder began to pen books about her prairie childhood, garnering good reviews and attention; Rose edited them, and the books inspired a popular television series that aired from 1974 to 1982. Wilder attracted a huge fan base, including Alene Warnock, who traveled to Westville with her husband to fill in gaps about the author's life there. Warnock, who died in 2011, dug up courthouse records and interviewed descendants of Peter Ingalls. She visited a local church and looked at grave sites, gathering stories along the way. But she never found the exact site of

Seeking a more healthful home for her ailing husband, author Laura Ingalls Wilder briefly moved to Westville, Florida, in 1891—a site now commemorated by a historical marker. Courtesy of Bruce Hunt.

the Wilder family home. "It is quite evident from what we learned that the climate did not bring about the improvement in health which the Wilders sought," she wrote. After moving back north, their "health did improve, Laura living to be 90 years of age, Almanzo 92."[57]

In 2005, an Ingalls Wilder historian and researcher, John Bass, of Shreveport, Louisiana, along with the Holmes County Historical Society, erected a historical marker on the roadside near the Ingalls' homesite to tell the family's story. Bass researched the information for the marker, raised money, and then financed most of it as a "labor of love." It inspired an annual "Picnic in the Piney Woods" gathering of Ingalls descendants and Wilder fans.[58]

Bass organized the Ingalls-Wilder-Lane Historic Alliance in 1995 with a goal of setting up markers at each of the family's prairie homesites, an outgrowth of his childhood affection for Ingalls's writings. "Reading the books and then watching the show . . . I wanted to know what happened next and what's there now," Bass said. "I wanted to see where they lived." A fount of knowledge and enthusiasm about the family, Bass has become friends with many of Peter Ingalls's heirs.[59]

On a foggy February day, with the help of Google navigation and Bass's directions, I found the marker, a large metallic sign adorned with gold writing documenting the Wilders' time in the area. At the top is a black-and-white photo of Laura and Almanzo with narrative of their lives on both sides. I bypassed "No Trespassing" signs to get close to the monument, now in a quiet wooded lot with a few picnic tables nearby. They may have been here a short time, but the beloved family is not forgotten.

The Wilders, like many other travelers in the Florida Panhandle region, had come in the hope of fulfilling their dreams but did not expect what they experienced—some good, some bad. Two centuries later, Florida can still be that way.

Sites visited by or related to explorers of Middle and West Florida, mentioned in this chapter:

William Bartram Memorial Park
211 Bayfront Parkway
Pensacola, Florida 32502
cityofpensacola.com/Facilities/Facility/Details/Bartram-Park-17

Scenic walkways wind through 2.5-acre Bartram Park, and the William Bartram Trail passes through here as well. It is situated on an inlet off Pensacola Bay, a short walk to Pensacola's downtown district.

Perfect Plain Brewing Company
50 East Garden Street
Pensacola, Florida 32502
(850) 471-8998
perfectplain.com

Florida Historic Capitol Museum
400 South Monroe Street
Tallahassee, Florida 32399
(850) 487-1902
flhistoriccapitol.gov

Hours: Monday through Friday: 9:00 a.m.–4:30 p.m.; Saturdays: 10:00 a.m.–4:30 p.m.; Sundays and holidays: Noon to 4:30 p.m. (closed Thanksgiving Day and Christmas).
Admission is free; however, donations for educational programs are appreciated.

Wakulla Springs State Park
Wakulla Springs Lodge
550 Wakulla Park Drive
Wakulla Springs, Florida 32327
(850) 421-2000
(855) 632-4559 reservations
thelodgeatwakullasprings.com

Fort Pickens Area and Naval Live Oaks Area at Gulf Islands National Seashore on Santa Rosa Island.
(850) 934-2600
nps.gov/guis/index.htm

Fort Pickens directions: Take exit 12 from I-10 to I-110 South; take exit 1B to Gregory Street East; merge onto 30 East Chase Street; turn left onto Bayfront Parkway/US 98 East; merge onto SR 399 to beaches, cross toll bridge ($1.00); turn right onto Fort Pickens Road.

Naval Live Oaks directions: Take exit 12 from I-10 to I-110 South; take exit 1B to Gregory Street East; merge onto 30 East Chase Street; turn left onto Bayfront Parkway/US 98 East. Stay on US 98 for 4.1 miles. National Seashore Headquarters is located on the right.

Laura Ingalls Wilder Memorial
Holmes County Road 163
Holmes County, Florida

The Laura Ingalls Wilder historical marker is located on the west side of Holmes CR 163, 2.6 miles south of the Alabama–Florida state line; or 1 mile north of Florida SR 2.

8

Ingraham Everglades Expedition

The Myth and Allure of "Conquering" the Everglades, 1892

In the nineteenth century, Florida's natural beauty drew many writers and tourists seeking a vast subtropical region unlike any other in the United States. The state was a magnet for adventure, a place where explorers, often wealthy White men from northern states, could encounter some of the last remaining wilderness in the country: the vast, watery Everglades. That Native people had lived in and adjacent to the area for centuries didn't dampen enthusiasm for these arrogant expeditioners, although embracing Native knowledge certainly would have been useful.

Stretching from the peninsula's center to its southern tip and covering almost 11,000 square miles, the Everglades were an expanse of shallow, slow-moving freshwater characterized in large part by the presence of sawgrass, an aptly named razor-edged plant that grew in vast expanses. While much of the young country's wilderness had been explored and mapped—in 1893 historian Frederick Jackson Turner declared the US frontier closed—the Florida wetlands remained mysterious to the greater world. They weren't unknown to the Native people who hunted and fished in the watery refuge. But to the thinking of most Americans, the Everglades were wastelands with no useful purpose.

In 1892, one notable expedition assembled, determined to master the Everglades and, its members hoped, to find a route by which rail lines could cross them. At the same time, the trip might provide a stronger picture of how the wetlands could be drained and turned into an agricultural Eden to grow tropical fruit, sisal hemp, sugarcane, tobacco, and rice.

The Ingraham Everglades expedition—also known as the Everglade Exploring Expedition—was led by John E. Ingraham, forty-one, president of the South Florida Railroad Co., and financed by hotelier and railroad magnate Henry B. Plant. The goal: surveying a path between Fort Myers on the

John E. Ingraham led an ill-equipped expedition into the interior of the Everglades in 1892, hoping to complete a survey for a future rail line from Fort Myers to Miami. Photograph from the James Edmundson Ingraham Papers, P. K. Yonge Library of Florida History, Special and Area Studies Collections, George A. Smathers Libraries, University of Florida.

Gulf coast southeasterly to Miami on the Atlantic Ocean. Plant had connected Tampa with Jacksonville through his rail line; now he plotted the possibility of taking rails across the southern end of the state.

It was a daunting task. They were to "cross and survey the Glades as no white expedition had done since the Indian wars," wrote Miami author Marjory Stoneman Douglas in *The Everglades: River of Grass*. And, as she noted, the three Seminole Wars waged in Florida during the early half of the nineteenth century left behind many cautionary tales of hardship and woe.[1]

In his account of field life from 1836 to 1838 during the Second Seminole War, US Army surgeon Jacob Rhett Motte wrote of "marching over the burning sands; wading in morasses and swamps waist deep, exposed to noxious vapours, and subject to the whims of drenching rains or the scorching sun of an almost torrid climate"—an "arduous service" that sent many men "home with ruined constitutions" should they survive disease or "an Indian bullet." Low on drinking water, Motte and company traversed across pine barrens where coral-rock soil cut through boots and lacerated soldiers' feet "as if we were walking over a surface from which protruded a thick crop of sharply pointed knives."[2]

This place was inhospitable to humans, Motte thought, except for the Seminoles. Hundreds of Seminoles had fled into the Everglades to resist a forced migration to Indian Territory west of the Mississippi River, today's Oklahoma. They adapted to the landscape, living on tree islands while farming, hunting, and fishing. It became a home where they navigated the wetlands on dugout canoes and established trading networks with amenable White settlers.

In his memoir, Buffalo Tiger, the first chairman of the Miccosukee Tribe (the tribe split from the Seminole Tribe in 1962 and gained separate federal recognition), related how his people found beauty and sustenance in the Everglades—a far cry from observations by White explorers and soldiers:

> We know plants and trees, both north and south. We know the animals and birds. We know which fish live in freshwater and which live in saltwater. We had no boundaries on this land, no fences. We were always free. All wildlife and human life could freely wander. Since Breathmaker put this land for us to live on and care for, money cannot buy land. We are not supposed to buy or sell even a cup of muck. Many of our people have fought and died for us to keep our land.
>
> When we came down here, they found there were a lot of things people could eat. There were five different types of *yokche,* or freshwater turtles. They found things that come out of the ground that we could eat, too, like a kind of potato and coontie. There were plenty of cabbage palms. We could find seven different types of wild fruits that we could eat that grew either in the sand or out in the Glades at different times of the year.[3]

This knowledge gave Native people a great advantage over newcomers. During the wars, as army troops advanced, the Seminoles evaded them by disappearing into hiding places in a "country rendered almost impenetrable by the wide spread morasses and everglades, the dense hammocks and fastnesses that cover its surface, in which no troops in the world could operate, but which afforded a safe shelter to the Indians," Motte recalled.[4]

Capt. John T. Sprague wrote of an 1842 scouting group of marines in the Everglades that had to return for lack of water. "The fatigue and privation undergone by this detachment was so great, that private Kingsbury fell in his trail, and died from sheer exhaustion," he wrote. It was grueling work that resulted in few victories.[5]

Once Seminole conflicts and the Civil War subsided, the Everglades lured White explorers as well as land speculators gambling on the state's desire and ability to drain the wetlands. "For its part, Florida was beginning to generate excitement as the region's land of enchantment," writes historian Jack E. Davis, noting that at least nine Everglades expeditions were

launched in the late nineteenth and early twentieth centuries. It was attrac-
tive to those who wanted to prove their prowess: "Florida therefore stood as
a remnant of a powerful American experience. If the Everglades happened
to be good for nothing else, they offered a last opportunity for men with
a wistful hunger to be explorers without the burden of traveling abroad."[6]

Two greatly publicized Everglades treks were sponsored by the *Times-
Democrat,* a New Orleans newspaper. The first, in 1882, explored the upper
reaches of the system from the Kissimmee River to Lake Okeechobee and
from there westward down the Caloosahatchee River to the Gulf of Mexico.
The articles chronicling the expedition were well-received and reprinted
in many northern newspapers. A year later the newspaper sent a dozen
men, including a writer and artist, into the northern Everglades to continue
south. They followed a river that flowed out of Lake Okeechobee through a
pond apple forest and, ultimately, into thick sawgrass, learning the hard way
that there were no easily navigable waterways in the wetlands.

"It was discovered that in this country, in a State which can boast of being the first colonized of any portion of the Union, there existed a region, of
which less was actually known than of the interior of Africa," the newspaper
declared. The purpose of the trip was

> not one merely of adventure; it was designed for useful and prac-
> tical purposes. It was desired to find the character of the immense
> region of Southern Florida, known as the Everglades, covering mil-
> lions of acres, to discover the quality of its soil, and to what crops
> and purposes it was best suited. To test the possibility of draining
> this immense region, and thus giving millions of acres to cultivation.
> To discover the condition and manner life of the Indians who have
> sought refuge there. And finally, at the request of the Western Union
> Company, to test the practicability of constructing a telegraph line
> down the peninsula.[7]

Early on, the crew discovered an unwelcoming landscape:

> They had imagined that this saw-grass region was only ten miles
> wide, and that in a week, or at least ten days, they would be in deeper
> water. But at the end of ten days the character of the country was
> completely unchanged. It was the same desolate saw-grass desert.
> They found the country utterly devoid of game of any kind. A death-
> like oppressive stillness prevailed everywhere. There were no fish in

the water, no birds in the air; even the air itself seemed to be without life or motion.

The situation of the men grew worse day by day. They had to toil onward, waist deep, in the mud and water; with leeches clinging to their legs until the water around them was dyed a deep red; with thousands of bugs pestering and bothering them; with prickly plants to bruise and poison them, and with the water alive with moccasins. Rest at night, cuddled up in the canoes, was scarcely pleasant, for the moccasins had a way of crawling into the boats to get warm and comfortable. It was thought for a big day's journey to travel a mile and a half in twenty-four hours.[8]

Eventually the team found deeper water and moved south down the Shark River into White Water Bay and into the Gulf of Mexico. The newspaper reported that the journey was "much harder than was imagined" and had shown that the sawgrass extended 100 miles south of Lake Okeechobee. Laying the telegraph line was deemed "impossible." As for drainage, the newspaper declared that many islands might be cultivated but the rest of the Everglades "are of no value agriculturally. We regret to learn this, but it is better that it should have been brought out now, instead of the world being encouraged into the mistaken belief that the Everglades could be redeemed."[9]

It was sage advice, but the Ingraham Everglades expedition was unworried, perhaps blinded by its members' dreams of glory—an echo of the De Soto expedition. They were undaunted and unprepared.

Alonzo Church, twenty-one, the expedition's compassman and one of three men to write narratives (Ingraham and trip secretary Wallace R. Moses also kept accounts), romantically anticipated a land of Seminoles and abundant wild game. The Everglades, Church wrote, held "that glamour that unexplored regions shroud themselves in and which to an ardent fancy have all the attractions that the imagination can bring forth. The opportunity of joining an expedition for exploring this region was therefore eagerly embraced despite the advice of friends who had been upon the border of this country, and the wishes of relatives that I should not run the risks of such an undertaking."[10]

Twenty-two men set out with two flat wooden skiffs, two canvas canoes, provisions for twelve days, guns, tents, axes, cooking equipment, and a set of rules: no liquor, no "obscene jests," and no excessive profane language.

Covering almost 11,000 square miles, the Everglades once stretched across the southern part of the peninsula, providing a sheet flow of freshwater that fed the unique environment. Courtesy of Bruce Hunt.

The men were expected to maintain "uniform mildness of demeanor and cheerfulness of manner." These orders, among others, were read to the group in its first camp in Fort Myers on March 14. The next day the men set out, marching across mostly prairie, but before the week's end they encountered a heavy storm, hours of wading, and temperatures that dropped as low as 38 degrees. They were cold and wet and had only just begun, leaving one to wonder how long those rules about language and comportment were enforced.[11]

Survey teams, carrying chains and equipment to plot the route—intended to be a nearly straight line—left daily after breakfast. The rest of the crew followed, mostly pulling the boats while trudging along with packs on their backs. Measurements were kept of temperature, water depth, and soil, which consisted, for the most part, of thick submerged muck atop hard rock. When the sawgrass became thick, some members set it on fire to ease the boats' passage.

By the second week, the men were slogging sometimes armpit-deep through water, muck, and sawgrass—likened to "a vast expanse of wheat field near harvest time"—often having to abandon boats temporarily along with extra clothing, tools, and cooking utensils to push forward. When possible, they camped on small, dry islands that sometimes bore evidence of Seminoles. This was not an empty wilderness but peopled lands. "Mosquitos and red bugs b-a-d," Ingraham wrote. Three days later, he noted: "Saw grass impossible to get boats through without too heavy work, or by abandoning boats. Packing supplies on men's backs found impracticable on account of bogging."[12]

Moses, forty-five, wrote in the official expedition journal that the men walked beside the wooden boats so they could pull themselves out of muck when necessary. One day, he reported, "the bog is fearful and it sometimes seems as though it would be easier to stay in it than to go on. Both legs up to the waist frequently become imbedded in the same hole in the mud, and to extricate ones-self with from 30 to 50 lbs. of weight on the back requires strength and time."[13]

Church was so exhausted one day that he sat in the mud for two hours before he could muster enough strength to continue toward an island camp. Church slowly "bogged" along, "my feet working like suction pumps in the mud, stopping now and then to blow and to wonder where the strength for the next step was coming from. . . . Just as the sun set, I saw a little smoke curl up from the island and I knew that our Captain had reached it and was doing his best to cheer us on. About dark I reached the goal for which I had been making and was happy to stretch myself on the ground once more. Weariness is no name for the suffering I underwent and comfort no expression for my sensations of pleasure when I threw myself down on the ground by the fire." Church later mused that the best treatment for a discontented, bored man is "to take a trip through the Everglades—if it doesn't kill it will certainly cure him." He added:

> A day's journey in slimy, decaying vegetable matter which coats and permeates everything it touches, and no water with which to wash it off, will be good for him, but his chief medicine will be his morning toilet. He must rise with the sun when the grass and leaves are wet with dew and put on his shrinking body his clothes heavy and wet with slime and scrape out of each shoe a cup full of black and odorous mud—it is enough to make a man swear to be contented ever afterwards with a board for a bed and a clean shirt once a week.[14]

Under such conditions, the expedition often didn't accomplish its daily goal of 5 miles—one day only moving 1,100 feet. By March 28 its members were out of flour and meal, having "only grits and beans left, but all men seem to do well," Ingraham wrote, noting that they were out of wood "so cooking next to impossible." The group changed directions several times to accommodate the landscape but continued to use survey gear to try to map the path. But the route wasn't as straight as anticipated, and by the end of two weeks food was becoming scarce. The expedition was in real trouble. On April 1, Ingraham wrote:

> Having been longer crossing the saw grasses than we anticipated, we are now reduced in food very considerably, and but for young cranes, young water turkey and cooters, we would have suffered seriously for food. We have had nothing but grits and rice for 8 days, no bread. No one can leave the line to hunt for fear of bogging and being lost. Have seen many Indian signs, but no Indians. . . . At this camp survey had to be temporarily suspended by reason of the broken down condition of the men, who are unable to work in the saw grass, and to the lack of food, making it necessary to proceed to Miami as speedily as possible to procure new supplies so that the survey can be resumed.[15]

Moses kept accounts of food, noting that the group supplemented supplies by shooting birds, catching fish that jumped in the boats, and eating turtles—many of them found when men stepped on them. Still, he wrote, hominy and game only met about "one half the amount craved." That could sustain life but was not "muscle producing sufficient to meet the excessive labor required in this expedition." Moses was startled one day while writing notes when "an inquisitive moccasin," estimated to be 5 feet long, attempted to crawl up his left shoulder. Moses rolled away quickly, and the snake took cover in a rubber plant's roots.[16]

On April 2, the men found deeper water flowing to the southeast and hoped it meant they were headed toward the Miami River and their destination. Their sign: a floating piece of a flour sack.

The men were heartened two days later when they spotted a Seminole tribesman and immediately "stood on their boats, waved their hats, cheered, and shouted 'come on, old man, come on' in the most frantic manner," wrote Church. The man, named Billy Harney, said the group was 25 miles northwest of Miami and offered an escort there—a trip that would take one or two days by water. With such news, Church said, "our faces fell several feet because at the rate we had been going it would take us five days to get there and we had only enough rations, at half allowance, for two days more." Ingraham went with Harney to his camp, hoping to get provisions, and returned with the decision that a few members, including expedition

A Seminole man, perhaps in a dugout like this tribe member, helped the Ingraham party find their way out of the Everglades after many perils and problems. Courtesy of State Archives of Florida.

leader Capt. John Newman and Ingraham, would go ahead and the rest would follow. They had been rescued by a knowledgeable Seminole.[17]

The advance group headed to Miami and were welcomed April 5 at the riverside home of Julia Tuttle, often referred to today as the "Mother of Miami." Tuttle, a widow from Cleveland, Ohio, purchased the 640-acre site of Fort Dallas, built during the Seminole Wars on the north side of the river, and made it her home in 1891. She became a huge advocate for the area, trying repeatedly to entice Henry Flagler to extend his Florida East Coast Railway line to the area—something he did in 1896. Legend has it that she sent him orange blossoms by mail after the devastating freeze of February 1895 that killed citrus crops in North Florida; the blossoms were proof that Miami was a subtropical wonder free of cold temperatures. Whatever the truth, Flagler visited the area, was charmed, and opened his posh Royal Palm Hotel there in 1897.

The day Ingraham reached Miami, the rest of the crew began following his path. While dragging a wooden boat through the sawgrass, Church recalled, the men saw an island and then a joyful sign: a pair of pants hanging from a tree. They were on the right track. To their great cheer, the next morning Newman returned with food with which they made a feast of bacon, beans, rice, tomatoes, and coffee "to which we did ample justice." The group pushed on and the next night enjoyed another big meal, which did not go down well, according to Church: "our hearty meals, after such long abstinence, made nearly every one sick and none of us were able to sleep."[18]

The next morning the remainder of the crew traveled down the Miami River, carrying boats around its rocky rapids, and arrived at Fort Dallas, where an American flag flew. Church recalled: "For the first time in my life I felt that the stars and stripes really represented something to me; I felt that I had been in a foreign country and had come back to the comforts and blessings of home. Those of our party who had preceded me looked fresh as roses; and soon, with the help of soap, water and clean clothes, I made myself appear half-civilized."[19]

They had made it. Ingraham and a few others stayed a few days in the area, sightseeing with Tuttle, while other team members headed home. Ingraham soon went to work for Flagler, helping with the expansion of the East Coast Railway and Flagler's hotel business.

Five years later, wealthy gentleman-adventurer Hugh Willoughby, forty, made another Everglades crossing, this time starting farther south in the Ten Thousand Islands on the west coast of Florida and crossing east to Miami. Willoughby, an ex-lieutenant with the Rhode Island Naval Reserve and avid yachtsman, prepared meticulously, consulting accounts of previous expeditions (including Ingraham's notes), studying Seminole methods of cooking and travel, and taking along an experienced Everglades hunter-guide, Ed Brewer.[20]

Brewer, Douglas noted, "was glad to be guiding for Mr. Willoughby at the moment, because he had heard that Captain Dick Carney, the sheriff, was as usual looking for him with a warrant for selling liquor to the Indians." Although he was "warned by some of my friends that he was a dangerous character, I preferred to rely upon my own judgment of human nature than on unproved stories about him," Willoughby wrote.[21]

It was a good decision.

Willoughby, aided by Brewer's expansive knowledge, traversed the Everglades during fifteen days in early January 1897. They paddled and poled their canoes, zigzagging when necessary to head east. Willoughby charted scientific and mapping observations while collecting data and specimens of flora and fauna for the University of Pennsylvania. He observed that the Everglades were composed of slow-moving water. In his 1898 narrative of the trip, Willoughby described the ecosystem, showing an enlightened view:

The popular impression has always been that the Everglades is a huge swamp, full of malaria and disease germs. There was certainly nothing in our surroundings that would remind one of a swamp. Around the shores of the little islands the mud may be a trifle soft, but pure water is running over it, and no stagnant pools can be found. In the daytime the cool breeze has an undisturbed sweep, and the water is protected from overheating by the shade the grass affords. Water-plants of various kinds and several varieties of fish and reptiles keep the balance of life, as in a self-sustaining aquarium. As will be seen by the analysis, this water is quite wholesome to drink. . . . I had no hesitation in drinking it whenever the canoe stopped, taking two or three glasses at a time, when thirsty from the exertion of poling.[22]

The men had plenty of adventures, encountering snakes, bugs, sawgrass, and birds. Willoughby complained about nighttime noises, particularly that of bellowing frogs and screeching limpkins, that shattered his rest. "When do these birds sleep? or do they ever sleep?" he lamented. At one island deep in the wetlands the men found an old, abandoned Seminole camp. "I felt for once in my life that I had reached ground never before touched by a white man and in my enthusiasm took my little New York Yacht Club flag from my pocket and Brewer christened the island Willoughby Key." Seagrape Hammock in the Shark Valley area of Everglades National Park may be that island.[23]

Willoughby's resulting book was well-regarded and was reprinted several times, no doubt because it appealed to the Romantic mythology of a wild, unconquered Everglades. "It may seem strange, in our days of Arctic and African exploration, for the general public to learn that in our very midst, as it were, in one of our Atlantic coast States, we have a tract of land one hundred and thirty miles long and seventy miles wide that is as much unknown to the white man as the heart of Africa," he wrote.[24]

The ensuing decades heralded a collective determination to drain the Everglades, using newly developed technology to make dreams of agricultural expansion a reality. "The drainage of the Everglades would be a Great Thing. Americans did Great Things. Therefore Americans would drain the Everglades," Douglas recounted, noting that no ecological studies of the system would come until the mid-twentieth century. "They saw the Everglades no longer as a vast expanse of saw grass and water, but as a dream, a mirage of riches that many men would follow to their ruin."[25]

The first big bust occurred in the 1880s, when the State of Florida sold Philadelphia businessman Hamilton Disston 4 million Everglades acres in return for $1 million—an amount that would settle state debts. In return, Disston promised to drain and "improve" the seeming wastelands and profit from selling reclaimed lands. At the same time, Flagler and Plant were plotting their railroads, buoyed by drainage plans and hoping to profit from resulting tourism and commerce. By 1887, however, state officials realized that Disston's grand promise would never become a reality. Disston dug more than 80 miles of canals, including one that connected the Caloosahatchee River to Lake Okeechobee, but the hope that he could drain all the Everglades died. Disston returned north, dying of a probable heart attack in 1896.

As the twentieth century dawned, Floridians clamored continually for the Everglades to be drained. Napoleon Bonaparte Broward declared, during his successful 1904 campaign for governor, "It would indeed be a sad commentary on the intelligence and energy of the people of Florida to confess that so simple an engineering feat as the drainage of a body 21 feet above the level of the sea was beyond their power." Water will run downhill, he told audiences—surely that would be the solution.[26]

Drainage and development schemes took their toll on the Seminole and Miccosukee Tribes. New settlers competed for animal hides, once an important tribal product, and overhunting diminished these resources. Tribal members were forced to take "what jobs could be found in the new economy, often working as farmhands or laborers." Canoe routes were lost to land drainage, and developers swooped in to buy lands that the tribes used. Tribal leaders, working with the Friends of the Seminole, an advocacy group, sought land and by 1938 had three reservations of more than 80,000 acres.[27]

The history of efforts to drain the Everglades and the toll on Seminole and Miccosukee people is long and complicated, deserving of more attention than this chapter can offer. But central to these early attempts was the lack of technology and funding to revamp the wetlands—a problem resolved with future feats of engineering. Decades later, irreversible environmental destruction made it clear that these were far-reaching accomplishments of tragic proportions.

The first grand step in reconfiguring the system was the immense $20 million Herbert Hoover Dike, built to contain the waters of Lake Okeechobee, which once flowed in high water from the southern part of the lake into the Everglades. Unfortunately, as hurricanes in 1926 and 1928 proved, high water levels from the lake could be unleashed with deadly force, killing thousands—mostly poor farmworkers who lived in the area. To prevent this from recurring, the US Army Corps of Engineers (hereafter referred to as the Corps) from 1932 to 1938 built a 143-mile earthen levee around the lake that reached almost four stories in height. Water from the lake was diverted in other directions, exposing mucklands where expanses of vegetables and sugarcane could be grown. It was the hoped-for agricultural Eden. It was also a turning point: as Michael Grunwald notes, the dike signaled that the primary objective in the Everglades "would no longer be drainage, but flood control."[28]

At the same time, there were efforts to save some parts of the lush flora and fauna found in the Everglades. Botanists had long extolled the diversity of trees, plants, and orchids in the wetlands and, foreseeing coming development, worried about the future. John Kunkel Small warned in the 1920s that human progress could be destructive. Nature's changes are "slow, and, as a rule, orderly, and results are usually finished—constructive—and satisfactory, while man's methods are crude and rapid, and result in great disorder," he wrote. "This is indicative of Florida's tomorrow. Yesterday, a botanical paradise! Tomorrow, the desert!"[29]

Small's worries and those of other naturalists inspired the Florida Federation of Women's Clubs (FFWC) to save a lush hammock island in the lower Everglades. By getting private land donated and tirelessly lobbying state legislators to add acreage to the project, the women (even before they could vote) in 1916 created Royal Palm State Park, the first state park in Florida and the first in the nation created by women's clubbers. In 1947 the FFWC donated it to be part of Everglades National Park (ENP), the first national park created for biodiversity, not scenery. Ernest Coe, a landscape architect, campaigned tirelessly for years to achieve the national park, assisted by many others, including Douglas.

Douglas, originally from Boston, arrived in Miami in 1915, fleeing a bad marriage. She learned to love the Everglades, recalling flocks of birds reaching "30,000 to 40,000 in one swoop." But she was realistic about the inhospitable swarms of bugs, noting that "knowing the Everglades does not necessarily mean spending long periods of time walking around out there. Unlike other wilderness areas, where the naturalist is a hiker, a camper, and explorer, the naturalist in the Everglades must usually appreciate it from a distance." When approached by a publisher to write a book about the Miami River, Douglas persuaded him that the bigger story was the Everglades. She coined the phrase "river of grass" to explain the sheet flow that cascades southerly down the state and got a book deal. Her very readable book, published a month before the national park was dedicated, became a bestseller and remains in print today.[30]

With the creation of the national park, many believed that the most important part of the Everglades was saved; the rest could be developed for tropical agriculture. What they didn't anticipate was that the park, located on the southernmost tip of the state and the Everglades system, needed water from the north that had been diverted by the Hoover Dike and would be interrupted even more by an imminent plumbing project of enormous proportions.

Initially Douglas and most Florida leaders were enthused about a massive Corps project in 1948 called the Central and Southern Florida (C&SF) project, which promised to create 2,000 miles of levees and canals from the Kissimmee River in the north all the way to the national park. The project was "designed to control just about every drop of rain that landed on the region, in order to end the cycle of not-enough-water and too-much-water that had destabilized the frontier and stifled its growth," writes Grunwald. "This was truly Flood Control and Other Purposes—not only saving lives and property, but reclaiming land, storing water, and promoting economic growth. The C&SF project would subdue the Kissimmee valley into a cattle empire, the upper Glades into an agricultural empire, and center Glades into giant reservoirs, and the eastern Glades into famers and suburbs that would offer the postwar version of the American Dream."[31]

By 1971 the Corps and C&SF project achieved that mission, reducing the Everglades system by half, but the environmental consequences were obvious and devastating. The once-serpentine Kissimmee River had been channelized into the lifeless Canal C-38. Water flow was diverted from the system, and the national park was threatened by poor water quality and quantity. Pollution from agriculture, especially sugarcane, and urban areas damaged the natural systems as well. The wading bird population that awed early visitors dropped by 90 percent, and many of the system's most charismatic animals, including crocodiles, manatees, and the Florida panther, were placed on endangered species lists because of their low numbers. Invasive plant and animal species, including stands of Brazilian pepper plants and Australian pines that grow in dense monocultures, dramatically altered habitats.

Native culture and water transportation in the Everglades system was irreparably changed. Seminole Tribe member Pete Tiger in 1956 observed: "In the old times we could paddle our canoes for many days and hunt the deer and the alligator. Now the white man has drained the Glades with his canals to make fields for his tomatoes and sugarcane. Our canoes cannot run on the sand and it is forbidden to cross the white man's fences. And the deer and the alligator each day go farther away."[32]

Douglas was outraged at the condition of her beloved Everglades. Since penning her book about it, she had led a lively writing life that produced poetry, short stories, and novels. Challenged in 1969 by local activists to get involved in protection battles, Douglas, seventy-nine, founded the Friends of the Everglades (FOE), a grassroots advocacy group that has been involved in a myriad of issues ever since. It was also the beginning of Douglas's rise to become an activist icon of the environmental movement—a role she filled until her death at age 108.

Seeing the damage caused by the C&SF, Douglas changed her mind about the project and Everglades drainage and began to work tirelessly to save what remained of the system. "Douglas wanted those who controlled policy and whose actions disrupted a healthy environment to do the same. She carried this message as she oversaw to a significant degree the emergence of a united and unprecedented effort to try to save and even repair not just a part—a lake, hammock, marsh, or park—but an entire ecosystem," writes Davis.[33]

The Miccosukees also stepped up to protect their lands polluted by agricultural pumping. Starting in the 1990s, they filed lawsuits against the state and the federal government to force improvements in water quality. "The vigilance of the Miccosukees has been responsible for some of this success; the Everglades saved their ancestors, and they have helped to return the favor," Grunwald notes, adding that "the tribe has replaced the U.S. government as the defender of Everglades water quality, litigating to force Florida to live up to its obligations."[34]

Everglades crises in the late twentieth century, boosted by a growing public consciousness about the environment, gave rise to a new approach: *restoration*. That generated another program and acronym: CERP—the Comprehensive Everglades Restoration Plan—that came with a pledge of $7.8 billion in state and federal funding.

CERP was devised and adopted in 2000 in a rare bipartisan congressional act that demonstrated an evolved understanding and appreciation for the Everglades. The clamor to drain the wetland system was long gone, replaced by scientific appreciation for its ecological value and worldwide affection. The national park is a World Heritage Site and an International Biosphere Reserve, having become "the ecological equivalent of motherhood and apple pie."[35]

The CERP plan—ironically led by the Corps—is designed to undo as much of the C&SF project and other development damage as possible, with recognition that there will never be a return of the pristine Everglades. It includes a thirty-six-year program, with more than sixty flexible engineering parts that will improve hydrology in the system. Unfortunately, the constituencies relying on Everglades water include agriculture (prominently sugarcane), the national park, Seminoles and Miccosukees, nearby nature preserves, and booming urban areas where some 8 million people turn on their taps daily and expect an unlimited flow. And there is no end in sight to growth: in 2020, the population of Miami-Dade was 2.7 million, a dramatic increase from 4,094 in 1900. There are many moving parts and different groups assessing, advising, and implementing CERP, but some promising results have been realized.

The three-phase reconstruction of Tamiami Trail is a prime example. The road, constructed to link Tampa and Miami in the 1920s, acted as a levee, cutting off sheet water movement in much of the southern peninsula, leading to fires, drying, and an upset of the ecosystem in Florida Bay. The Tamiami Trail plan includes new bridges to elevate the waterway, allowing billions of gallons to move more naturally. However, the water flow will still be heavily regulated by dikes and massive water structures, keeping humans in charge.

And big problems remain: Biscayne National Park to the east as well as Everglades National Park and Florida Bay at the southern tip of the peninsula lack enough freshwater to keep their estuaries robust; water quality and quantity in natural areas affect wildlife, especially wading and nesting birds; and polluted discharges from Lake Okeechobee have repeatedly caused problematic algal blooms that kill biota and upset residents and tourism businesses.

"The Everglades National Park is at the bottom of the pipe—the last priority for water. That's why the park is so dry and where there has been such a dramatic drop in the keystone species like birds and alligators," said Tom Van Lent, an Everglades scientist and advocate. "We estimate that the park gets about half of the water it used to on average. It's more or less in a state of perpetual drought."[36]

The main goal of restoration is to "take what we have left in Everglades National Park and the part near the Big Cypress and see if we can make it look like what Willoughby saw," said Van Lent, who has studied the explorer's path. "And what that's going to take is a lot more water. That's the goal of Everglades restoration—to put more water in the Everglades system. . . . To fix it—and we can fix it—we need more water. We need a river of water."[37]

Willoughby's route, easily determined by his careful observations and maps, today traverses mostly the national park. Van Lent, who created a Google map using the explorer's data, notes that a boat passage on the same route would be impossible—much of the wetlands are gone. "The Everglades is so much drier except in a very wet season. That's the sad fact—you can't boat it and must take a car," he said. Still, there are ENP sites that look very much like the photos Willoughby took such as watery sawgrass scenes, including Seagrape Hammock (Willoughby Island), visible from a viewing tower in the park's Shark Valley area. But a few miles farther east the urban chaos of Miami would be unrecognizable to Willoughby and members of the Ingraham expedition, who could never have imagined what the Everglades would become.[38]

Today the system is fully managed by humans for urban areas and agriculture more than for wildlife. When I take students on Everglades field trips, they are amazed by all the towering machinery, dikes, and structures that manipulate the water flow. Ironically, the system's northernmost headwaters are in the Disney World property—perhaps the state's best example of managed, unnatural nature in the state with its human-made lakes and plastic topiaries.

As we walk along the massive Hoover Dike, now touted as a biking and hiking path, students gaze into the horizon, absorbing the vastness of Lake Okeechobee. Driving through miles and miles of sugarcane from an industry known as Big Sugar because of its prominent political influence makes clear the enormity of the agricultural empire that has replaced much of the Everglades. The soil did prove rich, as Ingraham and others hoped, but only temporarily; once it was drained and exposed to the air, it oxidized and literally began to disappear. Today the once-rich soil must be enriched by fertilizers and pesticides to increase crop yields. And, despite artificial marshes created in the late twentieth century to absorb and clean excessive fertilizers, chemicals continue to dirty water in some parts of the system, including Lake Okeechobee, Everglades National Park, and Florida Bay, where regular algal blooms occur and seagrass beds are imperiled.

The CERP project includes plans for improving the Kissimmee River system and creating more water storage areas north of Lake Okeechobee, said Paul Gray, science coordinator for Audubon Florida's Everglades Restoration Program. When there are high water levels today from as far north as the Orlando area, water flows quickly through the Kissimmee into the lake. If lake levels get too high, threatening the dike's structural integrity, the Corps flushes the excess into the St. Lucie and Caloosahatchee canals for offshore dispersal. That dumps valuable freshwater that might be needed in later droughts—something more storage could prevent. "They [Corps] don't have time to be environmentalists; they lower the lake when the water levels get too high." Despite all the costs, delays, and need for federal-state financing and cooperation, Gray is "very optimistic" about CERP. "Everybody wants to fix this."[39]

He notes that the Kissimmee River restoration has taken forty years, with most of its initial advocates now dead. But Gray, who lives near the river, is the beneficiary of their work. "I realize that I'm not going to get these projects done in my lifetime or my career, but if I can get them started, that will be worthwhile."[40]

Tracing the Ingraham Everglades expedition in today's world is a challenge. Fort Myers and its surrounding area are now more concrete than prairie and sawgrass. The Caloosahatchee River, which once had 10-foot-high rapids, has lost its wild serpentine upper self and now is little more than a straight ditch for Lake Okeechobee releases. Traversing to Miami now is best accomplished by automobile, not canoe.

My "best guess" route started in downtown Fort Myers at the wharf site where Ingraham and company likely unloaded their boats from Tampa and readied near an abandoned military fort around which the city was growing. Those structures are long gone, and the riverfront has been filled in with soil and multistory buildings so that the original site on the southern edge of the waterway is almost two blocks from the water. Rae Ann Wessel, a local limnologist, naturalist, and historian, joined me to talk about how the river changed on a muggy summer morning.

"The river was the highway," she said, looking across a broad expanse now crossed by I-75. Once, there was no bridge and the best passage was upriver by ferry. Disston's work, which included blasting the rapids and falls, and subsequent dredging and flood control changed the river's very nature.[41]

"The Caloosahatchee was a beautiful river and a rich estuary that we have diked and channeled and polluted" in the modern era, Wessel said. "I find beauty in it, but it's a heavy sadness knowing what we've lost." Flood control, which destroyed the rapids and resulted in three locks and dams on the river, was a "no brainer" at the time, since government associated it with protecting the public health, safety, and welfare. But if she could travel in time, the ancient river would be one of her stops. "I'm so sad that I can't—except through books and histories—see the Caloosahatchee as it was."[42]

From downtown Fort Myers, the Ingraham group would have followed rutted, sandy cattle trails into the interior, a trip that was "very, very rough."[43]

To head in that direction, I traveled southeasterly on SR 82, once a cattle trail but now a mishmash of traffic lights and subdivisions metastasizing into former prairies. At the farming city of Immokalee, the route turns south along SR 29. Starting high and dry, the two-lane road cuts a rural path, eventually moving into ancient wetlands that abut the 26,000-acre Florida Panther National Wildlife Refuge, a federally managed area purchased in 1989 to protect the rare feline.

Flashing lights on signs remind drivers that this is a panther-crossing area—an important warning since car collisions annually are the primary cause of panther deaths. It is a grim fact among a bit of good news in Florida: panthers, reduced in number in the 1970s to between 20 and 30, have rebounded to an estimated 120 to 230 adults. Still, 27 were killed on roads in 2022, which would account for up to 10 percent of their population—bad news for a critically endangered species. To that end, many roads in South Florida are being reconfigured to include wildlife underpasses so that panthers and other animals can travel safely. The grassy underpasses are visible from SR 29, and I offer a prayer that the panthers will use them in their treks to find food and love.

South of the panther refuge is the adjoining Fakahatchee Strand Preserve State Park, a place of true magic proclaimed to be "the Amazon of North America." The "strand" is actually a 20-mile-long linear swamp forest in the western Everglades where dark freshwater trickles south, eventually reaching the estuaries of the Ten Thousand Islands. It is no way pristine—loggers built raised beds through the area for railway trams to remove lumber in the 1940s through the 1960s—but the water here still moves in a natural way, and the tropical plant life, which includes seventy-three species of endangered, threatened, or commercially exploited species, is stunning.

A tour through Fakahatchee with biologist Mike Owen is the experience of a lifetime. Owen arrived here in 1993 and has been taking people on swamp walks ever since, estimating that some six thousand have slogged with him in thigh-deep water, using a stick or pole to help their passage. The walks rarely go farther than a mile. But once you step into the cool liquid, gaze into the thick overstory of trees, and, with Owen's astute guidance, begin to spot the rare orchids, you have entered another world, a tropical dimension of Florida.[44]

"There are lots of superlatives in Fakahatchee," says Owen, whose sheer enthusiasm for the lush plant life radiates into his visitors, who join in his survey of species. Solo hikers easily can get lost if they wade into the waters, he notes, recalling the case of a Miami secretary who spent two nights mucking about before her rescue; she later joined him on several walks. "The thing that we learn above all else is patience. . . . [Y]ou really can't do anything fast out there. And humility—the place is big and wild and potentially dangerous. Patience and humility are two things you need in wild areas."[45]

One of the wilder remnants of the Everglades system is the Big Cypress National Preserve. The federal preserve covers 1,139 square miles, roughly the size of Rhode Island. It is a freshwater swamp ecosystem that extends southward to Tamiami Trail. It was created in 1974, when environmentalists challenged a project to build a jetport there—the very crisis that led to Douglas's activism. One runway was built, but the rest of the jetport project was scrapped when political winds changed, leading to creation of the preserve, which, incidentally, Coe always believed should have been included in Everglades National Park.

An airboat ride through the Big Cypress, north of ENP, is the easiest way to observe what the Ingraham expedition encountered. The large, shallow-draft boats, popular among tourists, are propelled by airplane-sized engines that roar through the sawgrass and water, making smooth, seemingly easy trips. Ingraham and company could have made the desired straight line with these boats in far less time. Although I abhor the noise, airboats are the best means to explore this backcountry and see wildlife seemingly numb to the racket; human passengers wear noise-reducing headsets. Massive alligators, wading birds, and (to my delight) endangered Everglades snail kites barely take notice of the boat as it zips by, offering a view of sawgrass interspersed with cypress stands that stretched to the horizon. I shuddered to think how the expedition slogged through such a landscape.

My travels continued eastward along I-75, known in these parts as Alligator Alley. Cars whiz by, their drivers barely noticing the low, golden sawgrass landscape—the true realization of Ingraham's mission to find a transportation route across the Everglades. Signs announce that the road passes by the Big Cypress as well as Miccosukee and Seminole reservations. A few rest areas offer some views of nature—one even has an elevated viewing station—and, happily, there are many wading birds to be seen. Still, most of the road is a long path of asphalt edged by wide ditches and interspersed occasionally by wildlife underpasses for the panthers I never see. A brief jog onto the Palmetto Expressway and then onto US 27 and the path heads southeast into the concrete confusion of Miami.

A few more turns and the Miami River loomed, barely more than a concrete-lined canal that heads through downtown Miami into glittering Biscayne Bay. Several circuitous trips over Miami River bridges, one steep parking garage, and a short walk later, I reached the site of Fort Dallas and Tuttle's home that so elated Ingraham and Church. No flag or food—just a fenced lot, with decaying wooden buildings and a sign that declares this to be Fort Dallas Park.

The river is no longer the clear, 4-mile tropical waterway that the expedition paddled. The rapids were dynamited to improve river navigation, and subsequent dredging and pollution fouled it forever. It is now part of the Great Wall of Miami—high-rises that soar from sea level, connected on the ground by a paved river walk that offers lunchtime respite for overly air-conditioned office workers. Large pleasure yachts slowly motored by as I peered into the dark water and saw floating debris and trash.

Looking up, I glimpsed Tuttle's likeness reproduced in bas relief on the nearby Brickell Avenue bridge. Her left hand holds a sun hat, and her right rests on a basket of citrus offered up by a man; two others work in a background grove. Behind her image loomed a towering buidling, an indication, perhaps of Miami's future. Looking down, I spotted a strange sight—a massive gray manatee has swum up to stick its head into a drainage culvert to munch on algae. A passerby said manatees are here in the river frequently, sometimes in groups, and they are visible from her condominium tower.

It seemed to be the last vestige of wildness, a faint reminder of what the Everglades once were.

To approximate the Ingraham expedition's route across the Everglades, travel southeast from Fort Myers on SR 82 down to SR 29, then south through Immokalee. From here, there are no roads that continue along their original diagonal route. Instead, continue south to I-75/Alligator Alley, then east into Miami.

Visit these places along the way for a better appreciation of the Ingraham expedition's and other Everglades explorers' experiences:

Centennial Park
2000 West 1st Street
Fort Myers, Florida 33901
(239) 321-7045
cityftmyers.com/facilities/facility/details/centennialpark-9

Although none of the three chroniclers—John Ingraham, Alonzo Church, and Wallace Moses—recorded the precise spot from which their Everglades expedition began, it was likely on the south shore of the Caloosahatchee River, at the wharf in downtown Fort Myers where the two US 41 bridges cross the river today. To visit the start, the waterfront Centennial Park is a good place to begin. A scenic walkway runs along the river, and the park contains some modern art sculpture and statues, including a fountain with

statues of Thomas Edison, Harvey Firestone, and Henry Ford; and a statue commemorating African American soldiers who served in the Second Regiment Infantry of the Union Army during the Civil War.
Hours: Open 7 days a week.

Fakahatchee Strand Preserve State Park

137 Coastline Drive
Copeland, Florida 34137
(239) 695-4593
floridastateparks.org/parks-and-trails/fakahatchee-strand-preserve
-state-park

Fakahatchee Strand Preserve State Park is a wonderland often called Florida's Amazon that offers many opportunities for visitors, including biking, birding, and guided tours and swamp walks. Endangered Florida panthers have been spotted on its trails, stalking deer that populate the park. Contact the park for information about tours.
Hours: Open seven days a week.
Admission: $3 per vehicle.

Big Cypress National Preserve

33100 Tamiami Trail East
Ochopee, Florida 34141
(239) 695-2000
nps.gov/bicy/learn/the-first-national-preserve.htm

Created in 1974 to save it from a proposed commercial jetport, the Big Cypress National Preserve is a 729,000-acre freshwater swamp ecosystem that is part of the larger Everglades. The Seminole and Miccosukee Tribes call the preserve home and use the area as their ancestors did, including erecting chickee shelters on tree islands. Hiking, fishing, camping, canoeing, and hunting as well as forestry and gas and oil extraction are allowed. There are a large variety of ranger-led programs, and several commercially permitted groups lead water and ground tours of the preserve. See the preserve's web page for a list of approved tour companies.
There are several good overlook points along the I-75/Alligator Alley stretch, some with elevated observation towers:
Mile Marker 70: Trail Head, Big Cypress National Preserve
Mile Marker 63: Florida Trail Crossing, Collier County Service Plaza
Mile Marker 35: Broward County Rest Area

Everglades National Park
nps.gov/ever/planyourvisit/placestogo.htm

There are four official entry ways into Everglades National Park:

1. Everglades City, south on SR 29. This is also the official gateway to the Ten Thousand Islands.
2. Shark Valley, about halfway across Tamiami Trail (US 41). You can bicycle or ride a tram south to the observation tower.
3. Royal Palm Park, west of Homestead on SR 9336, the park's main road. Turn left at signs for the Anhinga Trail, a great short hike with exceptional opportunities for wildlife viewing.
4. Flamingo is at the southern end of the park. Enter on SR 9336 and follow the main park road to its end. There is a marina and put-in for kayaks and canoes as well as a nearby waterfront and campground.

Fort Dallas Park/Julia Tuttle Homesite
84 South West 3rd Street
Miami, Florida 33131

Fort Dallas Park, on the banks of the Miami River in downtown Miami, was originally a plantation that was commissioned as a military post in 1836. In 1891 Julia Tuttle purchased the property and made it her family's home. John Ingraham, a friend of Tuttle's, concluded his Everglades expedition here. Today the property is fenced off and not accessible. There is a historical marker along the riverfront walkway located next to the property and, on a nearby bridge, a likeness of Tuttle.

9

Stephen Crane

A Journalist's Adventure, 1897

Stephen Crane arrived in the bustling city of Jacksonville, Florida, in 1896 with much to prove. Although he had been greatly lauded for his Civil War–era novel *The Red Badge of Courage,* Crane's ego was bruised by criticism that he had never been in conflict and had not personally experienced the danger and consequences of war. Determined to overcome that knock on his reputation, the twenty-five-year-old traveled south in hopes of finding adventure as a journalist observing the fighting in Cuba between colonial forces and those seeking independence from Spain.

What he experienced, however, exceeded his expectations—a harrowing shipwreck off the Florida coast, a thirty-hour paddle in a wooden dinghy overloaded with four people, and fodder for a short story that would be praised by noted writers Ernest Hemingway, Joseph Conrad, and H. G. Wells.

The tale of Crane's Florida shipwreck is little-remembered, other than in some school classrooms, but it offers a glimpse into the perilous shipping passages near the peninsula's Atlantic coast and the importance of lighthouses and houses of refuge—rescue stations—along what was once a mostly deserted landscape. It also involves the raucous world of illegal gunrunning, a brothel madam who captured a writer's heart, and the story of a young man trying to maximize the few years he had on this earth.

When Crane arrived in Florida in the late nineteenth century, the state was largely wilderness. The 1890 census tallied its population at 391,422. By contrast, New York had more than 6 million residents; even neighboring Georgia had 1.8 million. That same year, Duval County, the home of Jacksonville, counted 26,800 people—the most of any state county; what would become Miami-Dade County had 861. With Florida's inland a mix of wetlands, scrub, and pine forests, interior travel—indeed, almost all transportation—was best accomplished by boat along rivers or saltwater passages. Jacksonville's location at the meeting of the northbound St. Johns River and the Atlantic Ocean made it an important, bustling port.

Crane, on assignment for the Bacheller-Johnson news syndicate, arrived in the city on November 28, 1896, joining up with an assortment of eager journalists hoping to secure passage and report about the Cuban conflict. Almost two years earlier Crane had traveled to Mexico and the American West for the syndicate, which paid Crane ninety dollars for a serialized, shortened version of *The Red Badge of Courage,* leading to the book's national publication. He had talked to farmers suffering from drought, celebrated Mardi Gras in New Orleans, visited hot springs in Arkansas, observed life in Mexico, and written about cowboys and saloon fights.

While in Nebraska, Crane, twenty-four, visited the office of the *Nebraska State Journal,* where he met a college junior named Willa Cather who would go on to great literary acclaim. She later remembered him as a "slender, narrow-chested fellow" who said he was heading to Mexico to report for the syndicate "and get rid of his cough." Cather watched Crane with interest, noting that he was the "first man of letters I had ever met in the flesh." She was greatly disappointed in his shabby appearance, recalling that Crane "was thin to emaciation, his face was gaunt and shaven, a thin, dark moustache straggled on his upper lip, his black hair grew low on his forehead and was shaggy and unkempt." Crane hung around town and the newspaper office, seemingly morose and discouraged, before leaving. "Now that he is dead it occurs to me that all his life was a preparation for sudden departure," she wrote in 1900. "I remember once when he was writing a letter he stopped and asked me about the spelling of a word, saying carelessly, 'I haven't the time to learn to spell.'"[1]

In fact, Crane was suffering from tuberculosis, a scourge that for centuries had been considered a hereditary disease and had taken the lives of many famous artists. Several members of Crane's family had it, but the journalist also might have contracted it while investigating conditions of tenements in New York City, where the disease was rampant. Knowing he likely would die young created "his almost obsessive need to take risks and test his limits."[2]

When he arrived in Jacksonville, Crane checked into the St. James Hotel as "Samuel Carleton" to hide his identity, which by then had international proportions as his novel went from serialization into several reprintings to meet readers' demands. *The Red Badge of Courage,* highly praised in the United States and Europe, "redefined American war fiction," becoming the

Cora and Stephen Crane met in Jacksonville, Florida, shortly after he arrived in the hope of advancing his writing career through adventure experiences. Courtesy State Archives of Florida.

"touchstone against which other war novels are judged," writes historian Paul Sorrentino, adding that Crane's attempt at anonymity failed. "Within days of arriving in Jacksonville, Samuel Carleton was rumored to be a syndicate journalist headed for Cuba or an army veteran planning military tactics." Crane spent much of his time carousing in local bars, gambling, and mixing with locals while planning his voyage.[3]

Soon after his arrival, Crane's fate took an important turn when he met Cora Ethel Eaton Howorth, thirty-one, known as Cora Taylor, who was running a business known as Hotel de Dreme. It got its name from the former owner, Ethel Dreme, and Taylor, described as a "small, plump blonde," ran it as a high-end brothel/nightclub/gambling house located in downtown Jacksonville in an area known for such franchises. Also referred to as Hotel de Dream, Taylor's business was reputed to be the city's finest; it was located on Ashley Street and served a wide clientele, including news reporters. It wasn't the only such establishment Crane visited, but it became central to his life as his relationship with Taylor deepened.[4]

Jacksonville in 1896 was a raucous city of contrasts. Founded in 1821, it had survived Seminole Indian War battles (some city trees were still scarred by bullet holes from the skirmishes), four occupations by Union forces during the Civil War, fires that periodically hit the city, and yellow fever epidemics that devastated the population. After Reconstruction, the city was remodeling itself as a destination for rich northern tourists escaping dismal winters. The New York Giants would arrive for spring training in

March; a year later the city got its first "sky-scraper" at six stories tall. Residents engaged with visitors by holding fairs and expositions and bringing their goods to town for sale. But there was a dark side as well: "when virtue clashed openly with vice, when local political elections were at once the best entertainment and the most serious business in town." Liquor flowed freely, as did cattle and pigs, which roamed the streets rooting through garbage. Holidays brought out gun-toting men on horseback who unloaded celebratory pistols.[5]

Like the rest of Florida, Jacksonville had big ambitions but, in reality, was a frontier town of legal and illegal activities, offering excitement for a man like Crane who fevered for it.

When Crane was introduced to Taylor by a journalist friend, she happened to be reading his recently published novel, *The Little Regiment*. Later, he gave her his novel *George's Mother* and signed it "To an unnamed sweetheart," setting in motion a love affair that would end only with his death in 1900. Taylor in many ways was the ultimate survivor for a woman of her era, her talents and dreams circumscribed by patriarchal society and hemmed in by strict moral codes. When she met Crane, she had been divorced twice and was separated from her third husband, Capt. Donald William Steward, an English aristocrat who refused her request to divorce. She had, however, remained independent, taking up the surname Taylor, perhaps for business purposes in Jacksonville.[6]

Crane, who had endured an earlier scandal in which it was revealed publicly that he had lived with a woman in a New York City brothel, may have viewed Taylor with a sympathetic eye and appreciated her ability to overcome obstacles. His first book, *Maggie: A Girl of the Streets,* published in 1893, featured a young woman and her travails in poverty, which included being forced into prostitution and, ultimately, committing suicide. The book was gritty, brutal, and tragic; Taylor, however, had used her business acumen to avoid an ending such as Maggie's. The book was criticized for being crude, but it was Crane's big step into realistic writing, resulting from research conducted on urban streets.[7]

Crane hustled his way through Jacksonville, landing a space among the crew of twenty-eight men on the SS *Commodore,* a fishing steamer known for its speed. That the boat, owned by wealthy Cuban expatriates, would be carrying weapons to aid insurrectionists in the Cuban conflict—something banned by the US government—did not deter Crane or the ship, which had been impounded twice before for illegal activities. This would be the ship's fifth attempt to reach Cuba.

Filibustering—the illegal smuggling of arms—was an American tradition in the nineteenth century, as the United States attempted to gain power by helping to overthrow colonial powers, especially Spain, in different rebelling countries in the Caribbean, Central America, and South America, writes historian Kimberly Lane Eslinger: "American opportunists used expeditions to unstable countries for personal gain, but undermined American foreign relations at the same time." The United States repeatedly tried to outlaw the practice without much success.[8]

In June 1895, the United States had taken an official position of neutrality in the ongoing battles between Spain and Cuba. However, many Americans supported Cuba's move to independence and helped by smuggling weaponry to the rebels, led by José Martí. Their actions led to their vessels being called "filibusters," notes Sorrentino, and Jacksonville was a prime place for organizing such ventures: "Operating out of a cigar store, Cuban nationalists planned filibustering expeditions and supplied misinformation about the boats in order to deceive the US government, Spanish authorities, and Pinkerton spies hired by the Spanish" to investigate suspected filibusterers.[9]

It also created great opportunities for journalists seeking to enhance their reputations.

"At the time of the Cuban Revolution, American newspapers were warring for readership," writes Eslinger. "More sensational headlines splashed across the papers each day, as reporters sought bigger and more exciting stories. The Cuban Revolution and the illegal filibustering expeditions offered an opportunity that few reporters or papers could resist. Many up-and-coming correspondents of the day traveled to Jacksonville, Florida, where they could secretly sign onto a filibustering crew and then send their stories home."[10]

In a post-shipwreck article, Crane wrote that Jacksonville was the center of filibustering operations and was very "pro-Cuban in the most headlong fashion." Enthusiasm about such ventures made it easy to find crews for smuggling boats. "The romance of it catches the heart of the lad," he wrote. "The same lad who longs to fight Indians and to be a pirate on his own account longs to embark secretly at midnight on one of these dangerous trips to the Cuban coast."[11]

Despite efforts by federal authorities, gunrunning was profitable in Florida, a state that deserved its reputation as a frontier where lawlessness could match any tale of the American West. One of the peninsula's most colorful politicians, Napoleon Bonaparte Broward, boasted about using his steamer, *Three Friends*, to support Cuban revolutionaries. In his bid to become governor, an office he held from 1905 to 1909, Broward's election materials stated that he had captained the boat on several 1896 trips, "conveying war materials to the Cubans." Broward, a former Duval County sheriff, was a proud lawbreaker and later would become Florida's governor.[12]

By the time Crane arrived in Florida, Cuba was the "storm center of the Western Hemisphere," with some twenty-seven expeditions reaching the island despite US patrols off the Florida coast to enforce neutrality. Besides the possibility of being intercepted, the filibusters also had to contend with Florida weather; one boat had gone down in January 1896 in a storm and rough seas, losing more than half its crew.[13]

Florida's long Atlantic coastline was known for its menacing reefs and treacherous storms. The lucky survivors of shipwrecks who made it to shore—as Jonathan Dickinson in 1696 came to learn—found sparsely pop- ulated stretches of sand and little food, water, or shelter but a plethora of flesh-biting bugs. To aid stranded sailors, the federal government erected ten shelters, known as houses of refuge, in 1875–86 that extended south from St. Augustine. The houses of refuge were staffed by low-paid keep- ers whose job it was to keep an eye out after storms for shipwrecks (years could pass between incidents), render any needed aid, and help victims to safety. The keepers and their families lived mostly quiet lives in spartan conditions (it could be a 24-mile trip to get supplies) with just one boat pro- vided by the government. Some keepers or their family members worked with the US Postal Service, establishing offices at the houses of refuge and transporting mail up and down the coast. With the dawn of the twenti- eth century, railroads began replacing ship transportation along the coast, making the houses of refuge unneeded. By 1915, two of them were closed; the eight remaining facilities were incorporated into the newly created US Coast Guard. Today, Gilbert's Bar House of Refuge, located on Hutchinson Island, is the sole remainder of this era and is a popular museum.[14]

Four lighthouses along the east coast also gave warning to navigators. Central to the Crane tale, one lighthouse was located at Mosquito Inlet, since renamed Ponce Inlet. It was completed in 1835 but never lit because of a lack of oil; hurricanes that year eroded sand at its base, Indian warriors burned it, and it collapsed a year later. But the light was crucial for travelers trying to negotiate the inlet's tricky channel and bar. The US government bought land for a new lighthouse and hired engineers, who completed it in 1887. The 175-foot-tall lighthouse, painted a distinctive brick red so it could be recognized at night, offered mariners guidance between Daytona Beach and New Smyrna Beach; during Prohibition in the 1920s it was also a navigation asset to rumrunners. Today the Ponce de Leon Inlet Lighthouse, which includes a museum, with its bright coloring and height—it is the tallest lighthouse in Florida—serves as a landmark to passersby and is listed with the National Register of Historic Places.[15]

A trip along this hazardous coast to arm an uprising was just the type of real-life drama that Crane hoped would pay off with colorful firsthand stories of smuggling and war. Stretching into his youth, Crane had encountered several life-threatening situations and managed to defy them. In 1895 he had written a poem for his collection *The Black Riders* that expressed his need to take everything from life:

There was a man who lived a life of fire.
Even upon the fabric of time,
Where purple becomes orange
And orange purple,
This life glowed,
A dire red stain, indelible;
Yet when he was dead,
He saw that he had not lived.[16]

On New Year's Eve, Crane boarded the *Commodore,* registering himself as a seaman at a monthly salary of twenty dollars. The boat, at 123 feet in length and weighing 178 tons, was loaded with illegal cargo. Eslinger notes that estimates of the value of the ship's cargo varied between $3,000 and $10,000. "Allegedly, *Commodore* had fifteen tons of arms, dynamite, and war matériel aboard when she sank" with additional Mauser, Winchester, and Remington rifles. Crane joined the crew of more than two dozen, which included Cubans.[17]

In a newspaper article in the *New York Press* a week later Crane described the loading: "The Commodore lay at her dock in Jacksonville and negro stevedores processioned steadily toward her with box after box of ammunition and bundle after bundle of rifles. Her hatch, like the mouth of a monster, engulfed them. It might have been the feeding time of some legendary creature of the sea. It was in broad daylight and the crowd of gleeful Cubans on the pier did not forbear to sing the strange patriotic ballads of their island."[18]

It did not take long for the boat to encounter trouble. Less than 2 miles from port on the St. Johns River, an "atrocious fog caused the pilot to ram the bow of the Commodore hard upon the mud and in this ignominious position we were compelled to stay until daybreak," Crane wrote. Ironically, the US revenue cutter *Boutwell,* charged with stopping filibusters, came to the rescue, towing the *Commodore* off the sandbar and toward the Atlantic Ocean. After the *Commodore* took on an open sea pilot at Mayport, the boat once again beached. "The Boutwell was fussing around us in her venerable way, and, upon seeing our predicament, she came again to assist us, but this time, with engines reversed, the Commodore dragged herself away from the grip of the sand and again headed for the open sea," Crane wrote. And then the *Boutwell*'s captain wished the crew a "pleasant cruise."[19]

That was not to be.

No one checked whether the two groundings had caused any injury to the boat, but as the evening progressed in open water it became clear that the hull was damaged, leading the boat to take on water. Crane, recalling that he was too excited to sleep, witnessed the chaos that ensued: "I sat down in the corner of the pilot house and almost went to sleep. In the meantime, the captain came on duty and he was standing near me when the chief engineer rushed up the stairs and cried hurriedly to the captain that there was something wrong in the engine room. He and the captain departed swiftly."[20]

Water was flooding the engine room. Crane was sent down with buckets to help bail, but the work was futile, and soon the ship's whistle was blowing. Lifeboats were lowered to transport the crew away. Crane refused to get on the three lifeboats and stayed until the very end. "Valiantly, Crane helped to calm the crew and kept watch on the bridge with binoculars, searching the horizon for land," Sorrentino recounts. "When he began slipping on the uneven deck, he removed his new shoes, threw them overboard, and said 'Well, Captain, I guess I won't need them if we have to swim.'"[21]

At last, he climbed into a 10-foot dinghy along with Captain Edward Murphy, oiler William "Billie" Higgins, and cook/steward Charles Montgomery, who couldn't swim. It was a very risky situation—the seas were rough, threatening to capsize the dinghy, and the captain had a broken arm. Nearby, a few crew members still on the *Commodore* tried to fashion makeshift rafts, while others stoically remained on board. The dinghy tried to tow the rafts, but when it became clear that they would capsize the dinghy, the cook released the towline, the raft occupants lost to the sea. Crane watched the *Commodore* sink in what he reported was "silence, silence and silence."[22]

Crane's short story "The Open Boat" begins at this moment, omitting details of the wreck to focus instead on the ordeal of the four men fighting to survive in the dinghy. The opening lines are ominous:

> None of them knew the color of the sky. Their eyes glanced level, and remained upon the waves that swept toward them. These waves were gray, except for the tops, which were white, and all the men knew the colors of the sea. The line between sky and water narrowed and widened, and fell and rose.
>
> A man likes to take a bath in a bigger area than this boat could provide. These waves were frightfully rapid and tall; and each boiling, white top was a problem in the small boat.
>
> The cook sat in the bottom, and looked with both eyes at the six inches of boat which separated him from the ocean. He had bared his fat arms as he worked to empty the water from the boat. Often he said, "God! That was a bad one." As he remarked it, he always looked toward the east over the rough sea.[23]

Crane and Higgins took turns at the oars, carefully exchanging seats as needed and trying to aim the boat toward the beacon at the distant Mosquito Inlet Lighthouse. Waves lurched the boat up and down and flooded it, often washing over the men. Crane wrote that initially the lighthouse could only be seen at the top of a swell and "was exactly like the point of a pin." After hours of rowing and creating a sail from a coat held between the two oars, the men finally could see the coast—first as a black line but then as distinguishable sand and trees. Finally, the lighthouse loomed large along with a house on the shore and they began to anticipate someone coming to their aid in a larger rescue boat.[24]

> Slowly and beautifully the land came out of the sea. The wind came again. Finally a new sound struck the ears of the men in the boat. It was the low thunder of waves beating the shore. "We'll never be able to reach the lighthouse now," said the captain. "Swing her a little more north, Billie."[25]

The oiler did as instructed, and the men's hopes rose as "the nearness of success shone in their eyes." But the ordeal was far from over. No one arrived on the shore to help—the nearest life-saving house was 20 miles away, unbeknownst to them. The previous two lifeboats, filled with Cuban crew, had made it to shore and been helped by the lighthouse's keeper. Many believed Crane had drowned; instead, the four men in the dinghy kept paddling, now heading north of the inlet toward Daytona Beach.[26]

The lighthouse at Ponce Inlet, now a museum, served as a beacon for Crane and other survivors after the *Commodore* sank in 1897 off the Atlantic coast. Courtesy of Bruce Hunt.

They kept rowing north, trying to determine the best way to approach the shore without capsizing. When they finally decided to head for shore, the men paused to assess the danger.

There was a sudden tightening of muscles. There was some thinking.

"If we don't all get to shore," said the captain, "—if we don't all get to shore, I suppose you fellows know where to send news of my finish?"

Then they briefly exchanged some addresses and instructions. As for the thoughts of the men, there was a great deal of anger in them. They might be summed up this way: "If I am going to lose my life to the sea—if I am going to lose my life to the sea—why was I allowed to come this far to see sand and trees?"[27]

But the waves were too rough, and they headed seaward to calmer waters. Still no one came out to the beach to help. Higgins and Crane kept pulling the oars, an exhausting proposition after so many hours. When people did arrive on the beach, the men couldn't distinguish what or if they were being sent signals. Then daylight dimmed, and they faced another night at sea. As Crane wrote, "A night on the sea in an open boat is a long night."[28]

As January 3, 1897, dawned, they spotted several dark houses on the shore but no people. With their weakened state and after almost thirty hours at sea, the men decided they had to save themselves by rowing toward shore and taking their chances with the surf. They expected the boat to swamp or capsize at some point when they would have to jump away from it and swim for shore. And that's exactly how it happened, Crane remembering the water as "icy." The story's descriptions of the final minutes in the water are dramatic and tragic. A man on the shore ran out to help save the cook and dragged Crane to shore at the captain's command. The oiler, Higgins, didn't make it, his body left lifeless in the waves; likely he hit his head on the boat or an oar before drowning. A large group of people came out to rescue the men, carrying blankets, clothes, and coffee. Crane concludes: "When night came, the white waves rolled back and forth in the moonlight, and the wind brought the sound of the great sea's voice to the men on the shore. And they felt that they could then understand."[29]

Crane had escaped a watery death, landing on shore in Daytona Beach near where the Main Street Pier stands today. However, the rest of the world presumed he was dead, and his fame put this predicted tragedy into headlines. Early newspaper reports proclaimed that he had gone down with the ship. *COMMODORE SINKS AT SEA* screamed one headline for an article that reported that twenty members of the crew had made it safely to shore while the fates of the rest were unknown but bleak. Cora Taylor received a note that an empty boat had been found but with no Crane. She frantically checked with friends at the port and local newspaper, finally hearing from Crane by telegram that he was alive. She wired back: "Thank God your [*sic*] safe have been almost crazy." Crane stayed in Daytona Beach to see Higgins buried, and Taylor caught the first train out of Jacksonville, joining him there the morning of January 4; the couple returned to the city via train that day.[30]

Two days later Crane sent his news service an account of the filibustering trip, but it didn't include the drama of the days at sea. He saved that for his short story, written at various Jacksonville venues and published in 1898. It was dedicated to Higgins, Murphy, and Montgomery.

For decades after the event, questions lingered about the cause of the *Commodore*'s sinking. Newspapers speculated about "possible sabotage, suggesting the someone opposed to the Cuban insurrection had tampered with the pumps," writes Sorrentino. Others focused on "mechanical failure and human error" to avoid any thought of "dissension within the Cuban community in Jacksonville." The chief engineer was accused of being drunk; certainly, the repeated groundings before the boat reached the ocean likely were responsible.[31]

Crane apparently didn't waste time worrying about it. After recuperating at the St. James Hotel in Jacksonville and writing his initial news account, Crane's thoughts returned to his desire to be a war correspondent. His targeted venue: Greece, where an impending war with Turkey promised the journalistic action he sought. But this time Crane wasn't going alone—Taylor was joining him to pursue her desire to become a writer. After being feted by the London literati (Taylor stayed discreetly in the city), the couple headed to Paris, eventually arriving in Greece on April 8. The expected war broke out nine days later, but it lasted only a month, and Crane never witnessed the hoped-for grand campaign, although he did report about some battles. The war was a "series of retreats and rearguard or defense actions," but ultimately Crane witnessed what he wanted—warfare "as he had imagined it," writes historian R. W. Stallman. Taylor, however, claimed to be the first female war correspondent to go to a front, using the byline "Imogene Carter" to pen articles for the *New York Journal* such as "War Seen through a Woman's Eyes." In 1899 Crane published a novel, *Active Service,* set in the

Greco-Turkish War with a reporter as one of its chief characters, clearly based on his experiences in this short undertaking.[32]

After the war, the couple, calling themselves Mr. and Mrs. Crane (theirs was a common-law relationship since she was not divorced), lived in England, where he was celebrated for his literary accomplishments. To deal with rising debts, Crane wrote a series of stories and then headed off to report for the *New York World* on the Spanish-American War in Cuba in 1898, caused by official US intervention in the Cuban independence war and the sinking of the USS *Maine* in Havana harbor. The brief war lasted from April to October, but it gave Crane the opportunity to witness the United States militarily opposing a European power. But by the end of the conflict Crane had contracted yellow fever or malaria—or both. He ultimately returned to England, where his health worsened from tuberculosis and fever. A trip to a German Black Forest spa for treatment did no good, and, while there, Crane often sank into visions in which he once again was aboard the rocking open boat, paddling for his life. Taylor wrote to a friend, "It is too awful to hear him try to change places in the 'Open Boat.'"[33]

On June 5, 1900, Stephen Crane died at age twenty-eight, a passing that was widely lamented. The *London Spectator* proclaimed that Crane "was a writer of singular force and originality, whose studies in the psychology of peril had the quality of clairvoyance nothing short of magical." William L. Alden wrote in the *New York Times* that Crane's death "is a serious loss. In his way he was unique. Whether he had done his best work in 'The Red Badge of Courage,' or whether he would in time have surpassed even that brilliant book we shall never know." Crane's body was returned to England, and then Taylor sailed with the casket to New York for the funeral. He was laid to rest in the Evergreen Cemetery in Hillside, New Jersey.[34]

Taylor lived another decade, her life taking tumultuous turns befitting a novel. Since there was no legal marriage, she was unsuccessful in gaining royalties for Crane's work and could not sell her own writing. Facing mounting bills in England, she avoided creditors by returning to the United States. She reportedly had a breakdown in 1901 and then traveled around the South, eventually returning to Jacksonville, which had recently endured a devasting fire. In 1902 she built a high-end brothel known as "The Court," returning to the business she operated before meeting Crane. She once again was known as Cora Taylor or "Miss Cora."

Three years later (and three months before the death of her estranged husband) she remarried—Hammond McNeil was twenty-five and she was forty—and the marriage quickly fell apart because of her husband's jealousy and violent temper. Two years into the marriage, McNeil shot a man he believed to be her paramour and was charged with murder but acquitted by a jury on the plea of self-defense. Taylor hurried to England to avoid testifying against her husband; he later sued for divorce, claiming that she had beaten him on several occasions. She suffered a stroke in 1910 and died a few months later, collapsing after helping push a car that was stuck in the sand. She is buried in Jacksonville with a marker inscribed: Cora E. Crane 1868–1910.[35]

In a sense it was Taylor who helped solve the puzzle seventy-five years later about exactly where the *Commodore* went down.

In 1985, Elizabeth Friedmann, then an adjunct English professor at Jacksonville University, was researching Taylor's colorful life for a book and had used "The Open Boat" in her classes. Her curiosity and sense of adventure led Friedmann, a scuba diver and magazine writer, to wonder where the shipwreck might be. She contacted Don Serbousek, a Volusia County diver and explorer, to muse about searching for it. As it turned out, Serbousek had been diving around a wreck identified by fishing charts as a Spanish-American War–era ship for the previous two decades. He had collected a few artifacts such as glass and parts of a pipe, many of them encrusted with marine life, but the wreck's location in 70 feet of murky water some 12 miles off the coast of Ponce Inlet made it difficult to explore. Friedmann's research turned up a list of materials that were on the *Commodore;* using that, they set out to see if the wreckage was the famed boat.[36]

"He said that he knew where it might be—he had dived around artificial reefs in the area and had seen a site," Friedmann recalls. When they found it, "All you saw were pieces of things," she said. "There are online videos of it. You don't see a ship—you see pieces of things." While diving there for the first time, Friedmann looked back to shore and saw the lighthouse—the same guidepost Crane used. It gave her confidence they were in the right place.[37]

At the announcement of the ship's possible discovery, doubters began to weigh in, demanding absolute proof that it was the *Commodore.*

After dozens of trips, divers found rifles, bullets, a brass pulley, and a 170-pound pump. What they didn't find was a money belt with seven hundred dollars in Spanish gold purported to have been ditched by Crane before he left the boat. "It was fun. Just the fact of finding the shipwreck was cool," Friedmann said during a trip to the Ponce de Leon Inlet Lighthouse. A museum at its base tells the story of the *Commodore,* of filibustering, and

Elizabeth Friedmann, a sports diver and English professor, first saw the *Commodore*'s wreckage in 1986 and worked for years to help verify its authenticity. She is writing a book about Cora Crane. Courtesy of Bruce Hunt.

of houses of refuge. And it displays many artifacts now attributed to the *Commodore* wreck.[38]

The wreck's discovery was of special interest to academics. "I was invited to a Crane conference at Virginia Tech, and I knew there would be several Crane scholars there whose works had been critical to my research," Friedmann said. To express her gratitude, she took some bullets from the wreck and gave them to these professors as souvenirs. "You would have thought I had given them gold doubloons," she said, adding that some framed the bullets to display in their offices.[39]

Final verification of the shipwreck's identity came in 2005 with publication of historian Kimberly Lane Eslinger's master's thesis at East Carolina University. Eslinger, a professional underwater archaeologist, carefully compared information about the ship's history with the wreck site and 180 artifacts found at the site.

Today there are few local reminders of Crane's harrowing experience. The unmistakable lighthouse still stands, attracting paying visitors who climb 203 steps to its top for a 360-degree view. Friedmann joined me there one day to talk about Crane and explore the museum and its displays about Crane with information she helped pen. The museum also offers information about the houses of refuge along the state's shores, and, of course, there is a gift shop. Boaters and beachgoers are used to the towering landmark, but few would suspect its role in Crane's near-death drama.

The coast where Crane swam to safety is more than 11 miles north of the lighthouse and now a public beach, swarming with sunseekers and cars that roll down its wide, sandy path. Bright umbrellas, lifeguard stations, and numerous people bouncing in the waves next to the looming Main Street Pier, built in 1925, make it hard to imagine a time in which it was a desolate stretch of sand and dunes. Cresting whitecaps in the green-hued waves along with signs warning of rip currents, however, are a reminder of how rough the water easily can become, especially for four men in a wooden boat.

More than a century ago, an exhausted, aching Crane, wearing a soaked seaman's shirt and dungarees, fell onto that sand, feeling as if he had "dropped from a roof." He had escaped death, giving him the opportunity to write one of literature's greatest short stories. But too soon Crane's life would be over, marking the end of an extraordinary existence and literary career.[40]

Visiting Stephen Crane locations:

Ponce de Leon Inlet Lighthouse & Museum
    4931 South Peninsula Drive
    Ponce Inlet, Florida 32127
    (386) 761-1821
    ponceinlet.org

    Directions: The Ponce de Leon Inlet Lighthouse & Museum is 12 miles south of Daytona Beach. Follow Atlantic Avenue/A1A until just before the end of Atlantic Avenue, and then follow the signs west for several blocks.

At 175 feet, Ponce de Leon Inlet Lighthouse is the tallest lighthouse in Florida, and the third-tallest in the United States, behind Cape Hatteras Light, North Carolina (207 feet) and Cape Charles Light, Cape Charles, Virginia (191 feet). It became operational in 1887, took three years to construct, and cost the lives of four construction workers. The Ponce de Leon Inlet Lighthouse Preservation Association formed in 1972 and began operating the site as a museum (while simultaneously it was, and still is, a functioning lighthouse). That same year the lighthouse and its ancillary structures were listed on the National Register of Historic Places. Visitors who climb the 203 steps to the top of the tower are rewarded with a stunning view, not just of the lighthouse grounds but also of the Halifax River, the Atlantic Ocean, and the beach. The lighthouse keeper's home houses the main museum, where visitors can learn about both the original construction and the restoration of the lighthouse tower. In addition, they have on display an extensive collection of artifacts brought up from the sunken SS *Commodore.* Stephen Crane credits the Mosquito Inlet Lighthouse (the name was changed to Ponce de Leon Inlet Lighthouse in 1926) in his short story "The Open Boat" for guiding him and three crew members toward shore following the harrowing sinking of the *Commodore* in 1897.

Hours: Open daily 10:00 a.m.–6:00 p.m. (closed Christmas Day and Thanksgiving Day); 10:00 a.m.–9:00 p.m. in the summer months.

Admission: $6.95 for adults; $1.95 for children under 11.

Daytona Beach Pier

1200 Main Street
Daytona Beach, Florida 32118
codb.us/index.aspx?nid=529

Parking at:
Breaker's Oceanfront Park
13 South Atlantic Avenue
Daytona Beach, Florida 32118

Directions: From Daytona take International Speedway Boulevard across the bridge onto Daytona Beach; turn left (north) on South Atlantic Avenue/A1A; go 0.5 miles to Main Street.

The precise location where Stephen Crane and two of his fellow crew members crawled onto the beach in 1897 is unknown (a third crew member drowned when their dinghy capsized before making it to shore); however, the best guess seems to be somewhere close to where the Daytona Beach Pier is today. The original 600-foot Daytona Beach/Keating Pier would be constructed two years later by Thomas Keating and would burn down in 1920. The 1,000-foot pier that is there today was its replacement, built in 1925 on the same site, and featured a two-story casino. The City of Daytona purchased the pier in 2004 and began refurbishing it in 2009. It reopened in 2012 with a Joe's Crab Shack Restaurant as the pier's main anchor business.

Hours: The pier opens at 7:00 a.m.; Joe's Crab Shack opens at 11:00 a.m. and closes at midnight.

Parking fee at Breaker's Oceanfront Park is $1.25 per hour.

Gilbert's Bar House of Refuge

301 Southeast MacArthur Boulevard
Hutchinson Island, Stuart, Florida 34996
(772) 225-1875
houseofrefugefl.org

Directions: From Stuart, cross over onto Hutchinson Island via Southeast
Ocean Boulevard/A1A (north); then turn right (south) onto Southeast
MacArthur Boulevard for 1.5 miles.

In the late 1800s, much of Florida's Atlantic coastline, particularly the southern half, was very sparsely populated. Shipwrecks and other sea vessel ca-
lamities were commonplace, so between 1876 and 1885 a US government
federal agency called the United States Life-Saving Service constructed ten
house of refuge stations along Florida's beaches. Nine were on the Atlantic
coast; the farthest north was just south of St. Augustine, and farthest south
was near Miami. One other house of refuge was constructed on Santa Rosa
Island, on the Gulf of Mexico near Pensacola. The closest house of refuge to
where Stephen Crane swam ashore would have been one just built the previous year, 50 miles south, near what is now Canaveral National Seashore.
Only one house of refuge remains today: the Gilbert's Bar House of Refuge,
at the south end of Hutchinson Island. It was commissioned in 1875, with
construction completed in 1876, on one of Florida's rare shoreline rocky
(compacted shell) bluffs (hence the "Bar"). It was operated by the US Coast
Guard through World War II and in 1955 was acquired by the Martin County
Historical Society to be turned into a maritime museum. The Historical
Society petitioned to have the location added to the US National Register
of Historic Places in 1974, and it underwent an extensive renovation the
following year. The museum offers both guided and self-guided tours, and
features exhibits of lifesaving equipment, along with displays that tell the
history of local shipwreck rescues.
Hours: Monday through Saturday: 10:00 a.m.–4:00 p.m.; Sunday: 1:00
p.m.–4:00 p.m. (closed New Year's Day, Easter, Fourth of July, Thanksgiving,
and Christmas Day).
Admission: $8 for adults; $7 for seniors; $6 for children; under 6 free.

10

Zora Neale Hurston

Collecting and Celebrating Florida Stories, 1927–1939

Zora Neale Hurston was aglow with good fortune. Cruising down the highway, she steered deep into her beloved Florida, tasked with a mission dear to her heart: collecting the lore and music of African American workers. It was something she loved to do, and now it would help earn a college degree and, eventually, a steady income.

"I was glad when somebody told me, 'You may go and collect Negro folklore,'" she wrote in *Mules and Men,* her 1935 compilation of tales. When asked where she wanted to work, her answer was immediate: Florida. It was a place "that draws people—white people from all over the world, and Negroes from every Southern state surely and some from the North and West.' So I knew that it was possible for me to get a cross section of the Negro South in the one state. And then I realized that I was new myself, so it looked sensible for me to choose familiar ground."[1]

Hurston packed up her camera and notepad and headed to Eatonville, Florida, the all-Black city north of Orlando where she grew up. No one would care that she was getting a degree at fancy Barnard College in New York City or that she rubbed elbows with Harlem's artistic crowd; in Eatonville she would be "just Zora." Better than that, the city was familiar and safe and held great treasures for someone interested in writing and anthropology. And Hurston's background gave her special access to the community.

> I hurried back to Eatonville because I knew that the town was full of material and that I could get it without hurt, harm or danger. As early as I could remember it was the habit of the men folks particularly to gather on the store porch of evenings and swap stories. Even the women folks would stop and break a breath with them at times. As a child when I was sent down to Joe Clarke's store, I'd drag out my leaving as long as possible in order to hear more.[2]

Noted author and anthropologist Zora Neale Hurston took many trips around the state to collect the lore and music of its African Americans—something she was uniquely qualified to accomplish. Courtesy of State Archives of Florida.

Hurston claimed Eatonville as her hometown—and spiritually it truly was—but she actually was born on January 7, 1891, in rural Notasulga, Alabama. The next year her parents, Lucy and John, left their lives as sharecroppers and started a new future in the town, which was incorporated in 1887 and lays claim as one of the oldest all-Black cities in the United States. Although it was located in a state that was a hotbed of Jim Crow restrictions and dangers (Florida had the highest per capita lynching rate in the nation in 1882–1930) and many of its residents worked as laborers or domestics for White bosses, the city offered its residents breathing space and a level of independence from the threatening outside world. It was a place where "racism was no excuse for failure," writes Hurston biographer Valerie Boyd. "Here, individuals could sink or swim on their own merits."[3]

The family prospered, growing to eight children, and soon was able to use John Hurston's earnings from carpentry work to buy 5 acres, where he built a two-story, eight-room home in the small city where church, school, and stores were an easy walk. John became a respected member of the community, serving as pastor of churches in nearby Sanford and then Eatonville's Macedonia Baptist Church. He was the city's mayor from 1912 to 1916.

"We lived on a big piece of ground with two big chinaberry trees shading the front gate and Cape jasmine bushes with hundreds of blooms on either side of the walks," Hurston recalled in her autobiography *Dust Tracks on a Road.* "There were plenty of orange, grapefruit, tangerine, guavas and other fruits in our yard. We had a five-acre garden with things to eat growing in it, and so we were never hungry."[4]

The real "heart and spring" of Eatonville was across the street at Joe Clarke's store, where men "sat around on boxes and benches and passed this world and the next one through their mouths. The right and the wrong, the who, when and why was passed on, and nobody doubted the conclusions," Hurston wrote. "For me, the store porch was the most interesting place that I could think of. I was not allowed to sit around there, naturally. But, I could and did drag my feet going in and out, whenever I was sent there for something, to allow whatever was being said to hang in my ear." The men's "lying" sessions, when they strained "against each other in telling folks tales," were a favorite event. These memories served her well in later years.[5]

Tragedy struck when Lucy died in 1904. It was a crushing blow to thirteen-year-old Hurston to lose the woman who had nourished her creativity, exhorting her children "at every opportunity to 'jump at de sun.' We might not land on the sun, but at least we would get off the ground. Papa did not feel so hopeful."[6]

It was the beginning of what Hurston would call "my wanderings," which took her to school in Jacksonville, where she cleaned to help pay the bills, and back to Eatonville, where she clashed with her father's new wife (at age twenty Zora beat her stepmother soundly before leaving town) and lived in the homes of different relatives and friends. She tried school a few times, worked as a maid for a traveling theater company, waitressed, and, in 1917, lied that her age was sixteen instead of the actual twenty-six (lying about her age was a practice throughout her colorful life, which included three marriages and divorces) in order to attend college preparatory classes in Baltimore. She moved to Washington, DC, to attend Howard University, an all-Black school, in 1919. There she honed her writing skills, which served her well when she left the university without a degree and earned money writing for Black magazines, working her way to New York City and into the community of African American artists during the 1920s, an era since dubbed the Harlem Renaissance.[7]

In 1926, after meeting the founder of the all-female Barnard College, Hurston won a scholarship there and hoped to finish a degree. It changed the course of her life.[8]

At the suggestion of a college adviser, Hurston took some anthropology classes, which led her to work with Franz Boas (Hurston referred to him as Papa Franz), a Columbia University professor and national leader in the field. She was inspired by a desire to study the lore and music of Black people of her youth and others in the South. Boas, aware that Hurston was about to finish her degree, helped her get a 1927 fellowship to collect African American folklore for six months. She headed to Florida, stopping first in Jacksonville, where she bought a used car that she nicknamed "Sassy Susie." Then it was off to Eatonville, a "city of five lakes, three croquet courts, three hundred brown skins, three hundred good swimmers, plenty guavas, two schools, and no jail-house."[9]

She was delighted the minute she drove into town—there on the store porch were six men playing a game and telling stories. When Mayor Hiram Lester hollered his greetings and asked if she was home to stay, Hurston replied:

> "Nope, Ah come to collect some old stories and tales and Ah know y'all know a plenty of 'em and that's why Ah headed straight for home."
>
> "What you mean, Zora, them big old lies we tell when we're jus' sitting around here on the store porch doin' nothin'?" asked B. Moseley.
>
> "Yeah, those same ones about Ole Massa, and colored folks in heaven, and—oh, y'all know the kind I mean."[10]

She explained to the skeptical group that the stories "are a lot more valuable than you might think. We want to set them down before it's too late" and they are forgotten.[11]

Just as she'd expected, Hurston found plenty of people happy to share tales—some almost competing for her attention. They took her to a "toe-party," which involved women standing unseen behind a curtain and sticking out their toes. Then men paid a dime for the toes they liked, obligated to treat the lady to anything she wished for the duration. Partners could split up, leading to other toe bids. "Well, my toe went on the line with the rest and it was sold five times during the party," she recounted in the clever anecdote. Dancing and feasting on chicken, rabbit, peanuts, and chitterlings ensued, as did drinking of "coon dick," described as "raw likker" by Hurston, who wrote that as "it touched my lips, the top of my head flew off." Later, she drove a car loaded with sleepy people back to Eatonville.[12]

The next day, "the gregarious part of the town's population" once again gathered on the store porch and "told stories enough for a volume itself,"

During a 1935 research trip, Hurston and Rochelle French listened to Gabriel Brown play his guitar in Eatonville, Florida. Courtesy of State Archives of Florida.

she wrote. "Some of the stories were the familiar drummer-type about two Irishmen, Pat and Mike, or two Jews as the case might be. Some were the European folk-tales undiluted, like Jack and the Beanstalk. Others had slight local variations, but Negro imagination is so facile that there was little need for outside help."[13]

She went to the nearby St. Lawrence African Methodist Episcopal (AME) Church to "hear the testimony and the songs" as well as tales about churches and preachers, including one tale by Ellis Jones:

"Ah knowed a man dat was called by a mule."

"A mule, Ellis? All dem b'lieve dat, stand on they head," said Little Ida.

"Yeah, a mule did call a man to preach. Ah'll show you how it was done, if you'll stand a straightenin."

"Now, Ellis, don't mislay de truth. Sense us into dis mule-callin' business."[14]

With that, Ellis launched into a tale of a man who mistook a mule's instruction as God encouraging him to become a preacher and a second tale about a preacher so frustrated with the lack of response from the congregation that he threatened them with a gun to get them to bow. Others, while laughing, chided him for fabricating the story.

"Naw, dat ain't no lie!" Ellis contended, still laughing himself.
"Aw, yes it 'tis," Gold said. "Dat's all you men is good for—settin' 'round and lyin'. Some of you done quit lyin' and gone to flyin'."

Hurston, writing to express the dialects and inflections of the vernacular, recorded many conversations and stories—even a prayer she heard lifting from the church. She recounted tales like "why women always take advantage of men" and songs, including that of John Henry, "the king of railroad track-laying songs." The latter would serve Hurston well in her next venue. Here's the first stanza of nine that she recorded about the popular African American folk hero known for his superhuman ability to hammer into rock:[15]

John Henry driving on the right hand side,
Steam drill driving on the left,
Says, 'fore I'll let your steam drill beat me down
I'll hammer my fool self to death,
Hammer my fool self to death.[16]

The trip to Eatonville was fruitful for Hurston, who admitted that her job was not easy, but her race gave her insight and access that Whites could not acquire:

Folklore is not as easy to collect as it sounds. The best source is where there are the least outside influences and these people, being usually under-privileged, are the shyest. They are most reluctant at times to reveal that which the soul lives by. And the Negro, in spite of his open-faced laughter, his seeming acquiescence, is particularly evasive. You see we are a polite people and we do not say to our questioner, "Get out of here!" We smile and tell him or her something that satisfies the white person because, knowing so little about us, he doesn't know what he is missing. . . .

The theory behind our tactics: "The white man is always trying to know into somebody else's business. All right, I'll set something outside the door of my mind for him to play with and handle. He can read my writing but he sho' can't read my mind. I'll put this play toy in his hand, and he will seize it and go away. Then I'll say my say and sing my song."[17]

After more than a week of hearing tales in Eatonville of "saw-mill and turpentine bosses and prison camp 'cap'ns' set to music" Hurston decided that she "had to visit Polk County right now" and readied to leave. "A hasty good-bye to Eatonville's oaks and oleanders and the wheels of the Chevvie split Orlando wide open—headed south-west for corn (likker) and song," she wrote.[18]

In reality, Hurston's life took a detour, first taking her back to New York. Boas was disappointed in her collections, and Hurston felt she was being rushed in her work. By the end of 1927, however, she had a new sponsor: Charlotte Mason, a wealthy New Yorker, who offered to pay Hurston to continue collecting southern folklore through 1928, with a possibility of it extending into the next year. Mason, known as "Godmother" to those she supported, was interested in anthropology but too sickly to conduct it herself. "An able-bodied Zora Hurston, then, was hired to do the research for her," Boyd writes, adding that her contract required Hurston to collect "'music, poetry, folk-lore, literature, hoodoo, conjure, manifestations of art and kindred subjects' among Negroes in the South." Hurston acknowledged Mason's backing, calling her the "world's most gallant woman." Hurston also had received her bachelor's degree from Barnard.[19]

Her new trip started in Mobile, Alabama, where she interviewed a former slave, eighty-six-year-old Cudjo Lewis, for an article; her manuscript was posthumously published in 2018 as *Barracoon: The Story of the Last "Black Cargo."* Then she hit the road for her next Florida folktale adventure, making a quick stop in Eatonville.

Traveling to new places suited Hurston. As a child she had climbed a chinaberry tree and scanned her world: "It grew upon me that I ought to walk out to the horizon and see what the end of the world was like." She spent the rest of her life searching for knowledge that, she admitted, "took me into many strange places and adventures. My life was in danger several times." The research trip to Polk County was a case in point.[20]

Although "the little Chevrolet was all against it," in February 1928 Hurston, thirty-seven, drove to Loughman, home of the Everglades Cypress Lumber Company. Ignoring signs that it was private property, Hurston, who carried a pistol for protection (this was the Jim Crow South) found lodging at a company-owned boardinghouse run by a Mrs. Allen. The sawmill folk were cordial but initially wary of Hurston, hindering her folklore collections. Then she discovered why: her shiny car made locals suspect that she was a detective or revenue agent—a real concern since some of the workers were dodging the law. In response, Hurston created her own lie: she was a bootlegger on the run. "So I was hiding out. That sounded reasonable. Bootleggers always have cars. I was taken in," she recalled. She lessened concerns about her fashionable dress by explaining, in lingo far from her Barnard world, that her "man brough me dis dress de las' time he went to Jacksonville."[21]

Eatonville was a piece of personal heaven; this new setting was anything but.

"The sawmill and turpentine camps managed by the Everglades Cypress Company were much like the camps that flourished in north and central Florida after the Civil War," writes historian Tiffany Ruby Patterson, adding:

> Here migrants from all over the South and immigrants from Europe worked for a wage in a restricted, almost prison-like environment. Straw bosses and overseers kept a watchful eye on workers even during their leisure hours, controlled accounts at the company store (ensuring the perpetual debt of workers), and herded workers into the woods at daybreak. Yet Hurston found that the camps nevertheless were home to a diverse community of honest workers, family men, fugitive murderers, knife-wielding good-time girls, Christian mothers (also sometimes wielding knives), hard-living gamblers, jackleg preachers, and hoodoo charlatans. Together they created a rick folk tradition of stories, songs, folktales, and jokes.[22]

Loughman was a company town, and the sawmill was king. Originally known as Lake Locke, it was founded in 1883, when railroad lines arrived, creating access to the area's rich forests and swamps that held virgin pine and cypress. The longleaf pine, which once stretched for more than 60 million acres across the southeastern United States (today only 2 percent still exists), was a prime source of lumber. The trees, which could rise 50 to 110 feet and live as long as five hundred years, were cut and hauled to sawmills to provide construction materials for a growing state. Virgin cypress was even more impressive. Thriving in standing water, the trees could be 25 feet in circumference and up to 150 feet tall, and some were more than six hundred years old. Felling cypress, because of their location, was difficult work, wrought with additional concerns about wetland denizens such as poisonous moccasin snakes and alligators.

The Everglades Cypress Company's predecessor (Everglade Cypress Lumber Company) was established in 1905 and a year later was employing about 300 men and producing 200,000 feet of lumber daily. Labor included cutting and hauling trees and also operating the sawmill that processed the wood for shipment out by rail. By 1910 the company employed 721 people and boasted two years later that it had the largest payroll in the state. When Hurston visited, the mill and lumber operation was on its last legs; it closed in 1928. Its workers were more than 90 percent Black.[23]

After gaining the confidence of the community, Hurston got to work. At a big dance and bonfire the next Saturday night (a payday), Hurston joined in the festivities, which featured plenty of food, guitar playing, liquor, and square dancing. Outside the building she discovered a group "standing around and woofing and occasionally telling stories." Standing on a table, she sang the popular tune "John Henry" along with the others, gaining entry into the "inner circle. I had to convince the 'job' that I was not an enemy in the person of the law; and, second, I had to prove that I was their kind. 'John Henry' got me over my second hurdle," she wrote. Soon she was sharing her car with others and traveling the county.[24]

> After that I got confidential and told them all what I wanted. At first they couldn't conceive of anybody wanting to put down "lies." But when I got the idea over we held a lying contest and posted the notices at the Post Office and the commissary. I gave four prizes and some tall lying was done. The men and women enjoyed themselves and the contest broke up in a square dance with Joe Willard calling figures.
>
> The contest was a huge success in every way. I not only collected a great deal of material but it started individuals coming to me privately to tell me stories they had no chance to tell during the contest.[25]

It also gained Hurston the chance to watch the lumber laborers and collect their stories.

> Cliffert Ulmer told me that I'd get a great deal more by going out with the swamp-gang. He said they lied a plenty while they worked. I spoke to the quarters boss and the swamp boss and both agreed that it was all right, so I strowed [sic] it all over the quarters that I was going out to the swamp with the boys next day. My own particular crowd, Cliffert, James, Joe Willard, Jim Allen and Eugene Oliver were to look out for me and see to it that I didn't get snake-bit nor

'gator-swallowed. The watchman, who sleeps out in the swamps and gets up steam in the skitter every morning before the men get to the cypress swamp, had been killed by a panther two weeks before, but they assured me that nothing like that could happen to me; not with the help I had.

Having watched some members of that swamp crew handle axes, I didn't doubt for a moment that they could do all that they said. Not only do they chop rhythmically, but they do a beautiful double twirl above their heads with the ascending axe before it begins that accurate and bird-like descent. They can hurl their axes great distances and behead moccasins or sink the blade into an alligator's skull. In fact, they seem to be able to do everything with their instrument that a blade can do. It is a magnificent sight to watch the marvelous co-ordination between the handsome black torsos and the twirling axes.[26]

Before dawn broke the next day, Hurston listened as the "shack-rouser" man, Dick Willie, sang to wake up the crew:

Wake up, bullies, and git on the rock. 'Tain't quite daylight but it's four o'clock.
Wake up, Jacob, day's a breakin'. Git yo' hoe-cake a bakin' and yo' shirt tail shakin'.[27]

Hurston also traveled to area phosphate mines to observe the laborers and hear their stories of working in pits that also yielded up bones of long-departed creatures along with the mineral valued for fertilizers. Hurston also collected children's tales and games and held another lying contest. The Polk County stories are rich, colorful tales, covering topics from how the porpoise got its crosswise tail to why there are so many mosquitoes and storms in Florida. They also highlight a number of strong personalities, perhaps none as vibrant as Big Sweet, a "large and portly" woman who joined Hurston in her local travels and ruled the camps. Hurston was warned that Big Sweet was a formidable foe who could "handle a knife with anybody." Big Sweet wasn't mean, a friend advised, she just "don't stand for no foolishness, dat's all," Hurston wrote. "Right away, I decided that Big Sweet was going to be my friend." Hurston offered her a ride in her car, and soon they were getting along. And friends of Big Sweet got her protection:[28] "We shook hands and I gave her one of my bracelets. After that everything went well for me. Big Sweet helped me to collect material in a big way. She had no idea what I wanted with it, but if I wanted it, she meant to see to it that I got it. She pointed out people who knew songs and stories."[29]

When Big Sweet invited Hurston to return to Loughman, Hurston agreed, hoping to attend some Saturday-night festivities. Big Sweet warned Hurston to avoid any confrontations, particularly with a jealous woman named Lucy who had it out for Hurston. Big Sweet warned that Lucy "mean tuh slip up on yuh sometime and hit yuh uh back hand lick wid her knife and turn her hand over right quick and hit yuh forward wid it and pull it down." Hurston went anyway and was enjoying hearing new songs, when Lucy, carrying a knife, came her way and a fight broke out—Big Sweet was there with her own knife to protect Hurston. "Run you chile! Run and ride! Dis is gointer be uh nasty ditch," one man warned.[30]

"Curses, oaths, cries and the whole place was in motion. Blood was on the floor," Hurston recounted. "I was in the car in a second and in high just too quick," she recalled. "Jim and Slim helped me throw my bags into the car and I saw the sun rising as I approached Crescent City." It had been a productive visit, but now Hurston was hours away, heading to a new adventure in New Orleans.[31]

Years later, Hurston penned a musical, *Polk County,* featuring Big Sweet along with sawmill experiences and the music of its workers. The play never made it to Broadway during her lifetime but was produced in 2002 in Washington as part of the modern revival of her work.[32]

By 1938 Hurston was back in Eatonville, renting a house where she could concentrate on writing a book based on her two years of travels and findings in Haiti and Jamaica. She was full of ideas, and the manuscript was finished by March, with publication scheduled for seven months later. In the meantime, she found steady work and reliable pay from a program set up through the federal government to help writers during the Great Depression.[33]

The Federal Writers' Project (FWP) was part of the Works Progress Administration (later renamed the Works Projects Administration), created as part of New Deal programming to get Americans back on their feet. The FWP, founded in 1935, aimed to publish guidebooks for every state, with special "Negro Units" set up in Florida, Louisiana, and Virginia. Hurston was hired to write for the Florida unit, based in Jacksonville, and was tasked with collecting stories about Black life. It was a mission, given her work at folklore collection, for which she was deeply qualified.[34]

As Boyd notes, despite Hurston's "impressive credentials, including two Guggenheim fellowships and three published books, Hurston was not officially given a slot on the editorial staff of the Florida Writers' Project and she was certainly not paid an editor's salary." In fact, she was hired at sixty-three dollars per month, less than her White male counterpart Stetson Kennedy, a twenty-year-old junior interviewer who assumed Hurston had the same pay.[35]

Kennedy recalled learning that Hurston would be joining the effort, announced to the staff by Carita Dogget Corse, the Florida FWP director. "Not only was Zora signing on, but she would soon be paying a state visit to the state office," Kennedy recalled. "Unaccustomed as we were to receiving blacks of any description, Corse cautioned us that Zora had been lionized by New York literary circles and was consequently given to 'putting on airs,' including the smoking of cigarettes in the presence of white folks, and we would therefore have to make allowances. And so Zora came, and Zora smoked, and we made allowances."[36]

Folklore, the "boiled-down juice of human living," still was a relatively unmined field, and Hurston recognized the riches the state held. "Folklore in Florida is still in the making. Folk tunes, tales, and characters are still emerging from the lush glades of primitive imagination before they can be finally drained by formal education and mechanical inventions," she wrote for the FWP. "In folklore, as in everything else that people create, the world is a great big old serving platter, and all the local places are like eating plates."[37]

Working from her home in Eatonville, Hurston collected her paycheck while collecting stories from different parts of Florida for FWP publications. She often disappeared for weeks, and her work was "sporadic," Kennedy recalled, but when prompted to produce work, she always came through. "In response to my letters, we would receive a thick packet of fabulous folksongs, tales, and legends, possibly representing gleanings from days long gone by. We did not care how, where, or when Zora had come by them—each and every one was priceless."[38]

Hurston took some time off in October 1938 to celebrate the publication of her new book, *Tell My Horse,* in New York City. Back in Florida in December, she resumed her FWP work with an added assignment: tape recording Black Floridians' reminiscences, stories, and songs. Hurston had made recordings in folklore collections years earlier and now used that experience. She wrote a report, "Proposed Recording Expedition into the Floridas," that "outlined recording possibilities" in four major areas of the state, Boyd writes, adding that Hurston got a raise to $79.50 per month with the new project.[39]

However, in 1939 Florida, sending out a biracial team to make recordings was impossible. "Those were the days when so innocent a gesture as a white man lighting a black woman's cigarette could get them both lynched," Kennedy wrote. "The solution, handed down to me from above, was to send Zora ahead as a sort of 'talent scout' to identify informants."[40]

In late spring, Hurston headed to Cross City, a small town along Florida's Big Bend coastline, to gather material from workers at the Aycock & Lindsey Company, touted in the late 1920s as the largest turpentine operation in the world, its main product used in a variety of items from paint to medicine. The company provided worker housing and food as well as rail lines to collect its product; in 1928 it was reported to employ 1,400 men and operate eleven turpentine stills.[41]

This was big business with tentacles that reached far beyond local economics.

"Timber and turpentine were the first major mechanized industries to take root in the Big Bend of Florida, and one could argue timber is still the dominant economic force in the area," according to historian Josh Goodman:

> Unlike agriculture (including cattle raising), which had dominated the local economy before 1900, turpentine and timber attracted outside capital to these places. To work trees for timber and naval stores you needed capital investments, infrastructure, etc., which could only come from outside money. The same people who started turpentine operations in counties like Dixie and Taylor also started banks, grocery stores, utility companies, and other businesses to serve the growing population of workers and their families. Railroads snaked into the area because there were logs and barrels of turpentine to ship; sometimes the railroads were actually owned by some of the same people as the timber and turpentine operations. This influx of capital and the businessmen who wielded it helped modernize the Big Bend region and shape its institutions.[42]

Aycock & Lindsey, "ruled by the comely, gun-toting 'Miss Catherine'—employed more than three hundred turpentine workers and held them and their families in virtual slavery," writes Boyd. Hurston "quickly won the trust of the laborers, who supplied her with ample amounts of song and lore, as well as an earful of horror stories: The white camp bosses regularly beat the workers, the turpentiners said, and they forced themselves on any woman they wanted. If the woman's husband dared protest, his surliness would earn him a beating—or even murder. Black bodies were often weighted down with cement, the laborers told Hurston, and dumped into the Gulf of Mexico."[43]

The industry was ebbing in the late 1930s but still employed thousands of people in remote areas, many without running water or education. These workers "left few written accounts of their lives," making their folklore "one of the few barometers of their attitudes and feelings about themselves," observes Pamela Bordelon.[44]

And Hurston, changing again into the guise of the community, was there to record it.

Turpentining was a harsh, exhausting year-round business that relied on intimidation and isolation as well as debt peonage to gain and control workers, amounting to economic slavery. Operating mostly in rural longleaf pine forests that once stretched across the southeastern United States, laborers made V-shaped cuts into the lower sections of trees, reaching the flow of resin. Weekly, workers revisited the trees and created new hacks to keep the flow moving, a process known as chipping. The resin was collected by men known as dippers, poured into barrels, and then processed into turpentine spirits and rosin, which were used in a variety of products, including paint and varnish.

Hurston described the process in "Turpentine Camp—Cross City," a brief FWP essay:

> Well, I put on my shoes and I started. Going up some roads and down some others to see what Negroes do for a living. Going down one road I smelt hot rosin and looked and saw a "gum patch." That's a turpentine still to the outsider, but gum [patch] to those who work them.
>
> It was not long before I was up [in] the foreman's face talking and asking to be talked-to. He was a sort of pencil-shaped brown-stained man in his forties and his name was John McFarlin. He got to telling and I got to listening until the first thing I knew I was spending the night at his house so I could "Ride the Wood" with him next morning and see for myself instead of asking him so many questions. So that left me free to ask about songs go [sic] the turpentine woods.
>
> "No, Ma'am. they don't make up many songs. The boys used to be pretty ad [sic] about making up songs but they don't do that now."

"If you don't make up songs while you are working, don't you all make some up round the jook?"

"[No ma'am], its like I told you. Taint like saw-mills and such like that. Turpentine woods is kind of lonesome."[45]

After McFarlin got his eighteen-man crew moving by 6:00 a.m. the next day, he got a horse for Hurston, and the two rode out to the woods to watch the turpentine work. Hurston wrote about the four different types of labor that went into the process: the chippers, pullers, dippers, and a woodchopper.[46]

The chipper is the man who makes those little slanting cuts on pine trees so that the gum exudes, and drains down into the box. He has a very sharp cutting tool that heavily weighted in the handle and cunningly balanced so that he chips at a stroke. The company pays a cent a tree. We stopped and watched Lester Keller chip because he is hard to beat anywhere in the world. He often chips 700 or more trees a week.[47]

Hurston described each step in the process but omitted the brutality she witnessed.

"Turpentine operations were located deep in the woods, which provided cover for manufacturers, who controlled and disciplined their workforce with methods similar to those of slavery," writes Patterson, adding that company-owned housing and commissaries kept workers "conveniently" in debt. In their research, "Hurston and Stetson Kennedy found some of the most wretched conditions."[48]

Accounts from a legal case involving a nearby turpentine operation, Blue Creek, run by the Wisconsin-based Putnam Lumber Company, also painted a devastating scene. Witnesses in the case against camp manager W. Alston Brown told federal investigators that Blue Creek "provided employees with shanties and a commissary that carried virtually everything deemed necessary for life in the camp, including furniture," writes historian Robert N. Lauriault. "Workers were required to make all their purchases from the commissary, and, indeed it would have been difficult for them to have done otherwise as they were almost without exception prohibited from ever leaving the camp on the basis of supposed debts owed to Brown. The camp was surrounded by barbed wire, and one or two guards patrolled the perimeter regularly." Brown controlled the workers and their families through threats and whippings.[49]

Another Putnam Lumber Company camp in the Dixie County community of Shamrock operated in the same brutal fashion, with the collusion of local officials. In 1924, Lewis Barker, an African American turpentine worker, was beaten and shot to death. Indicted for his murder: a deputy sheriff, a Putnam employee—described as a "prison guard"—who was awaiting retrial for the murder of a man in a different camp, and four others.[50]

Two years before Hurston's visit to the area, the Shamrock camp reportedly held several hundred workers "behind a fence complete with guarded gates," wrote historian Jerrell H. Shofner. "No one entered or left without approval of the guards. Nor were those who reported this condition moved by humanitarian impulses. Officials of Cross City complained that their merchant constituents were being deprived of a market because the Putnam Lumber Company would not let them in or the workers out. The merchants alleged that this was denying them a portion of the camp trade so that the company's store would benefit."[51]

When Kennedy and his recording team arrived in Cross City, he was surprised to see "Good scout Zora" still at the camp, perhaps disturbed by what she had learned. He wrote:

> It was unusual that she had not departed prior to our arrival, and unusual that she had turned in a page of cryptic handwritten notes such as "a hand tried to run away last week, and the sheriff had all the roads guarded" . . . "there is a grave not far from here of a hand they beat to death" . . . "a woman told me she cooks, cleans, washes and irons all for $2.25 per week."
>
> After recording some songs around an open campfire at night, I picked up on Zora's leads by putting on my cap as director of Social-Ethnic Studies and asking questions about such things as peonage and the commissary system. When I did, my informants promptly posted sentries.
>
> "Don'st you know that in this country nobody can make you work against your will?" I asked.
>
> "They do do it," came the laconic reply. "And if you tries to leave, they will kill you; and you will have to die, because they has folks to bury you out in them woods."
>
> After I had recorded a good deal of such as this, a sentry dashed into the firelight, whispering:
>
> "Here come The Man—sing somethin quick!"
>
> As we drove off through the gates of the Cross City camp and the

woodsrider bade us farewell, he asked, "Who was that colored gal who came in here ahead of y'sall? She was right smart for a colored girl.—Of course, I figured she was about three-fifths white."

The terrorism was real, not fancied, and a constant in the recording of the folk material in those days, at least in the South.[52]

Kennedy and others also heard about the abuses, but "they were folklorists, not government agents, so there was little they could do," Boyd writes. "When Hurston left Cross City, she reportedly wrote to Miss Catherine about the irregularities, but her disclosures could not have been news to the head of the company. In any case, nothing was ever done—and Hurston might have counted herself lucky to get out of town unharmed."[53]

In August Hurston left the FWP, joining the faculty of the North Carolina College for Negroes to help it develop a drama department. Hurston's work in staging productions of folk theater as well as her growing literary reputation—her new novel *Moses, Man of the Mountain* was published in November—provided new opportunities to broaden her already wide horizons. But her teaching experience ended a few months later, caused in part by her desire to collaborate on a play in New York and conflicts with the college president, who didn't adopt her curriculum suggestions. Her life and career took many twists in ensuing years, including publication of her autobiography, *Dust Tracks on a Road,* and a novel, *Seraph on the Suwanee*—both reflecting her fieldwork discoveries; a brief stint as a Hollywood studio writer; writing as a newspaper columnist and reporter; substitute teaching; and, when strapped for cash, working as a maid. She suffered in later years from hypertensive heart disease and in October 1959 suffered a stroke that left her in a St. Lucie County, Florida, nursing home. Three months later she died from another stroke, a sad ending for a dazzling, complicated woman who cleared her own path through life's brambles.

The author of seven books, dozens of stories, and the stager of plays and folklore events, Hurston had been "the dominant black woman writer in the United States" at one point in her life, notes historian Henry Louis Gates Jr. Then her career lapsed into "dark obscurity," ending with a "disastrous final decade."[54]

The world took little notice of her passing, but the Fort Pierce community showed its love for her. More than one hundred Black residents and a handful of Whites gathered for a service that celebrated her career as a writer and anthropologist. But once her body was interred in an unmarked grave in the segregated cemetery, Hurston and her work faded much like a sunset in her beloved Florida: a bright, brilliant flash ebbing into darkness. Her papers were burned by people cleaning out her home; a passing Black deputy saved many from the flames.

In 1973 celebrated author Alice Walker placed a formal marker on the once-forgotten grave, declaring Hurston "A Genius of the South"—an act that helped resurrect her literary reputation. Sixty years after her death, Hurston is treasured as an esteemed American author by modern writers, academics, and readers who delve into Hurston's works, discovering rich, descriptive tales of Black life in the American South and the Caribbean. They are the products of Hurston's extensive travels, particularly in Florida, where she gathered material for novels and collections of folktales that had been largely overlooked until she arrived on the scene with her camera, notepad, and recorder. And though she didn't keep a specific narrative journal of any one trip, her works illuminate three important areas of Florida: the unique African American community of Eatonville in Central Florida; the sawmill town of Loughman in Polk County; and the hardscrabble turpentine operations of Cross City in North Florida. Revisiting the areas using her descriptions provides a glimpse into a time and places now fading into history.

Today Loughman is little more than a crossroads of four-laned highways that funnel workers from their homes into Orlando's theme park and entertainment districts. Sitting near the border of Polk and Osceola Counties, there are only a few traces of the large, bustling complex that Hurston encountered. Trains still run on the tracks that once hauled milled wood, and bricks are poking through the asphalt of Old Dixie Highway (marked as Old Tampa Highway) that parallels it. The shady drive is quiet, and warning signs posted on the few homes along the way speak of a community unfriendly to strangers. One landmark, erected in 1930 after Hurston's visit, still attracts wayfaring travelers—a large stone column that (incorrectly) declares a welcome to Polk County (it's actually inside Osceola County). Another error: the word "CITRUS" is spelled "CITURS" on one side, providing amusement for many wayfarers. But the big mill operation, commissary, worker housing, and associated businesses are long gone, leaving behind new-growth pines and cypresses in the region's natural areas and a new Publix grocery store and shopping center on the main highway.

The brutal turpentine business that once bustled in Cross City also has vanished. One of the few reminders is a green metal roadside sign proclaiming "SHAMROCK" along US 19 near a drainage ditch and a fast-food restaurant at the north edge of the city. Across the busy four-lane highway are some chain retailers but no historical markers to recall the industry's past.

In her travels Hurston might have passed but not stopped at the thirty-six-room Putnam Lodge a few blocks north. The two-story wooden hotel, built in 1927–28, was part of the "company town" of Shamrock and "accommodated tourists, transients and company executives and clients," according to the hotel's website, which goes on to claim that "Shamrock provided its residents and employees with comfortable homes, a commissary, a store comparable to 'any city department store,' two schools, two hotels, the Shamrock Dairy Farm, and an ice plant producing 18 tons of ice daily. The lodge is representative of a time of local timber supremacy and economic prosperity." It is doubtful that any of the people Hurston interviewed stepped foot in the business.[55]

A good site to immerse in all things Hurston is Eatonville, now part of the ever-expanding Orlando metropolitan area. A two-lane road runs through the city of a little more than 2,000 residents, who proudly proclaim the community to be one of the nation's earliest self-governing African American cities. And in recent decades Hurston's growing fame has added to its charm.

N. Y. Nathiri learned about Hurston while growing up in Eatonville but didn't realize the writer was a "global icon" until the 1970s, when Hurston's literary talents were "rediscovered" and celebrated anew. Up to that point, Hurston was a local success story. Nathiri's grandmother, Addie Mae "MaMa" Gramling Johnson, was friends with Hurston and would talk about the writer to "let us know that because we came from a small town it didn't mean we couldn't achieve," said Nathiri. "She was a role model."[56]

To some Eatonville residents, Hurston "may have been a source of consternation," but in "our family she was celebrity," according to Nathiri, who never met the writer and didn't read a Hurston book until she was twenty-five years old. "She visited with my grandmother and took an interest in her children, teaching my Uncle Sam to play bridge and seeking a swimming scholarship for my Uncle Gus at Rollins College."[57]

It was MaMa who first introduced me to Zora Neale Hurston. Zora's stories were the same ones she would tell me at bedtime. I couldn't wait to be scared to death by Raw-Head-And-Bloody-Bones and The Boogey Man. Zora's sayings were an integral part of my grandmother's conversations. When I would ask too many "what if" questions, she'd reply, "If a bullfrog had wings, he wouldn't bump his head so hard." As I grew older, MaMa would explain how women had "the keys to the kitchen." She encouraged me to think for myself and take "no wooden nickels."[58]

Today Nathiri is executive director of the Association to Preserve the Eatonville Community, Inc. (PEC), a nonprofit that serves as the umbrella for a number of Eatonville causes, including the annual Zora!—the Zora Neale Hurston Festival of the Arts and Humanities—and the Zora Neale Hurston National Museum of Fine Arts. She was one of the founders of the Zora! Festival, which draws people from across the globe every January to celebrate the author in a monthlong series of events. The street-front museum, located close to where Hurston once lived (now a fenced-in lot devoid of her beloved trees and flowers) and to Joe Clarke's store (now a soul-food restaurant), also brings in Hurston fans who are visiting the area. The museum offers a brochure with a walking tour of Eatonville, noting many sites depicted in her books.

One of the sites is the St. Lawrence AME Church located on Kennedy Boulevard, the main east-west road through town, and a short distance from the Hurston homestead. Across the street is a dilapidated wooden building, the original 1881 AME church, where Hurston's father preached every other Sunday to a Baptist congregation that shared the building until it could afford its own site.

One sunny morning, Wanda Randolph, a missionary and member of St. Lawrence, worked with others to distribute food to community members hit hard by COVID-19 issues. "This is a blessing from God that we are able to help," she said.[59]

The church no longer owns the original building but takes pride in the modern facility, built in 1974, that houses a remarkable collection of original paintings by noted artist Andre Smith that depict Eatonville residents and relate to Psalm 23. Randolph said that visitors to the area increase in January during the Hurston festival and in February during Black History Month. Often tours of the church are offered during those months.[60]

Nathiri remembers getting ready to close the museum one day in the 1990s when a "middle-aged White man breezed in . . . and said 'I just had to stop.'" The man had read Hurston's masterpiece, *Their Eyes Were Watching God,* and realized while driving in inclement weather on nearby I-4 that he was near Eatonville. He stayed "maybe ten minutes, but he just had to stop," Nathiri said, because Hurston "had touched him in such a way." Visitors "want to connect with Zora Neale Hurston's hometown, with her Eaton-

Hurston's grave in Fort Pierce, Florida, is a pilgrimage site for visitors from across the globe who often leave food offerings and trinkets. Courtesy of Bruce Hunt.

ville. It's an emotional tie—it really speaks to the creative genius of that artist. It speaks to the power of artistry," she said. "Eatonville is Zora Neale Hurston's hometown, and she made it a literary destination."[61]

That acclaim includes a number of sites that memorialize the author's life, including the walking tour of Eatonville and a historical marker in her hometown of Notasulga, Alabama. Other signage in Sanford, Florida, as well as Baltimore, Maryland, and West Palm Beach, Florida, gives tribute to her talents and visits there. In 2016, the City of St. Augustine, one of the writer's regular haunts, renamed a downtown greenspace Zora Neale Hurston Memorial Park; a nearby home on King Street where she rented a room while finishing *Dust Tracks on a Road* is recognized as a National Historic Landmark with a large roadside marker.

Hurston "has deeply influenced at least two generations of writers and readers of all colors and cultures," writes Boyd, adding that her "success—in her lifetime and posthumously—legitimized the kind of intimate narratives that are now taken for granted in African-American literature." "But because of the way she *lived*, Zora Neale Hurston irrevocably changed the world. And now, at last, she is getting the acclaim she has long deserved."[62]

On a sun-drenched November afternoon, Hurston lies at rest in a quiet spot in Fort Pierce's Black community. A marble headstone declares her to be "A Genius of the South," and two pillars with bronze images of her declares the entrance into the Garden of Heavenly Rest Cemetery. A large information marker proclaims this as one of eight sites, along with three large kiosks, that compose the Zora Neale Hurston Dust Tracks Heritage Trail, a city project. Other spots include the newspaper office that published her articles and a Black school where she taught, signals of her rise in stature in recent decades. The community, which also holds an annual Hurston festival, plans to turn the nursing home where she spent her final days into a museum to celebrate her work and that of other members of the African American community.

She is not forgotten. On this day, the concrete cover over her grave serenely soaks up the sun's warmth as nearby wildflowers bloom. Surely, she is smiling.

To share some of Zora Neale Hurston's experiences, visit these locations:

Zora Neale Hurston National Museum of Fine Arts
344 East Kennedy Boulevard
Eatonville, Florida 32751
(407) 647-3307
hurstonmuseum.org

In addition to displays of artwork from African-descent artists, the Hurston Museum contains Eatonville historical and cultural exhibits. It opened in 1990.
Hours: Monday through Friday: 11:00 a.m.–2:00 p.m.
Admission is free.

St. Lawrence African American Episcopal Church
549 East Kennedy Boulevard
Eatonville, Florida 32751
(407) 644-1021

Across the street from the original 1881 building that housed the first St. Lawrence AME Church, this building is actually the church's third and was built in 1974. It contains eight paintings by resident artist Andre Smith that were donated in 1936 and originally displayed in the church's second building.

Loughman, Florida, Old Tampa Highway "Citurs" Center Monument (also known as Polk County Citrus Center Monument)

Directions: From I-4, take exit 58 (CR 532/Osceola Polk Line Road), and go east for about 4 miles. Turn south onto Old Tampa Highway. The monument is 0.6 mile on the right, at 6668 Old Tampa Highway.

Zora Neale Hurston Grave Site

Garden of Heavenly Rest Cemetery
Avenue S and North 17th Street
Fort Pierce, Florida 34950
cityoffortpierce.com/400/Trail-Marker-4

11

Marjorie Kinnan Rawlings

Harmony in Rural Florida, 1931

It began one spring night as two friends commiserated about life's unexpected turns, their musings lubricated by provisions from a local moonshiner. Despite her success at writing, Marjorie Kinnan Rawlings's personal life was a wreck. She had taken a huge risk, spending her inheritance to buy a ramshackle wooden house in rural Florida surrounded by 72 acres of orange groves. Her husband, Charles, was gung-ho for the 1928 move from cold Rochester, New York, hoping that sales of the golden fruit would provide income while the pair devoted time to their writing careers.

Now, five years later, he was unhappy with country life and feeling constrained in pursuing stories he favored about yachting, boating, and the sea. The stormy marriage was failing and her latest book was not coming together, Rawlings confessed to her drinking pal, Dessie Smith. Although Rawlings loved her life in the hamlet of Cross Creek, she had "lost touch with it" and found that "the difficulties were greater than the compensations," she later wrote in her autobiographical *Cross Creek*. "I talked morosely with my friend Dessie." What to do?[1]

Smith, a backwoods Cracker with superb hunting and fishing skills and a penchant for adventure, offered a solution—get away from it all with a long river trip, something she had yearned to do for years. "We'll take that eighteen-foot boat of yours with a couple of outboard motors and put in at the head of the St. John's River," Smith said. "We'll go down the river for several hundred miles."[2]

Rawlings agreed, "for the Creek was torture." Until the next morning, when, possibly suffering the aftereffects of drinking, she tried to back out. But Smith was having none of it—she could taste the long-dreamed-of trip and knew Rawlings "was a good cook and a fine companion, even on the hunting, so I kept her feet to the fire," she recalled. "And so, we went." Smith

Marjorie Kinnan Rawlings moved to rural Cross Creek, Florida, in 1928 to concentrate on her writing career, eventually winning the 1939 Pulitzer Prize and international readership. Her neighbors could hear her typing from her front porch desk. Courtesy State Archives of Florida.

steered the wooden boat, fished for dinner, and shot available protein; Rawlings was in charge of cooking and navigation; her equipment included a Dutch oven, charts, and a compass she later discovered wasn't working because the iron pot under her seat threw it off.[3]

For nine days the women traveled on the north-flowing river, and from it arose one of the great "buddy" stories of Florida literature. Rawlings first published it as a magazine article in 1933 and then incorporated it as the "Hyacinth Drift" chapter in *Cross Creek*, her 1942 compilation of essays about her life, neighbors, and adventures. Upon their return, Rawlings soon shed her husband and rediscovered her love of writing and of the North Florida landscape. Six years later she received lasting acclaim and the 1939 Pulitzer Prize for *The Yearling*, a best-selling tale of a young boy and his pet deer growing up in the area's hardscrabble scrub.

Rawlings and Smith met soon after the writer moved to Cross Creek. Neighbors, afraid that the couple might starve to death, especially after the bottom fell out of the orange market, sent Smith over to offer instructions on hunting and fishing; most locals supplemented their diets with local wildlife. The women felt an instant connection, and their friendship, despite some rocky moments, lasted a lifetime. Rawlings described her comrade:

> She is an astonishing young woman. She was born and raised in rural Florida and guns and campfires and fishing-rods and creeks are corpuscular in her blood. She lives a sophisticate's life among worldly people. At the slightest excuse she steps out of civilization, naked and relieved, as I should step out of a soiled chemise. She is ten years my junior, but she calls me, with much tenderness, pitying my incapabilities, "Young un."[4]

As the departure drew close in early March 1933, Rawlings wrote to her literary agent, Maxwell Perkins, about their adventure:

> I plan to take possibly a very foolish trip, beginning this coming Wednesday or Thursday. Another woman—an amazingly capable sportswoman—and I are going down the St. John's River by rowboat with outboard motor. . . . But as a Cracker friend says, "No fool, no fun." All this strenuous out-door stuff is new to me since coming to Florida. I've taken to it naturally, but my chief claim to capability in such matters lies only in being game for anything. So wish me luck.[5]

Perkins replied, "That trip down the river sounds mighty dangerous, but also fascinating."[6]

As they left the launch at SR 50 near Christmas, Florida, Smith, twenty-six, was thrilled.

"Young un," she called, "it's mighty fine to be travelling." The women believed they were at the headwaters of the St. Johns; in fact, the 310-mile river begins farther south in Indian River County. It is slow-moving with its tea-colored waters dropping only 27 feet on the way to Jacksonville and its outlet into the Atlantic Ocean. The transformation is remarkable—from a vast, barely navigable marsh to a clearly defined path among high, sandy banks to a wide, forested waterway to the center of the major city of Jacksonville. The river often expands and contracts, with portions of it widening into enormous lakes. Indeed, the Seminoles call it Welaka, meaning "river of lakes" or "big water." Before the advent of railways in the late 1800s, the river was the central corridor of transportation in Florida's interior. Rawlings and Smith knew its long history and had camped along its banks long before this trip. Now they hoped to see most of it in one long journey.[7]

Smith whistled as she cranked up the three-horsepower motor and drove into the grassy expanse of what is probably the state's best-named waterway: Puzzle Lake. "It was startling to discover that there was in sight literally nothing else," wrote Rawlings. "Far to the west, almost out of sight to the east, in a dark line like cloud banks was the distant swamp that edged this fluid prairie." There was no clear navigable path, and even standing up in the boat revealed "the rest of the universe. And the universe was yellow marsh, with the pitiless blue infinity over it, and we were lost at the bottom." Rawlings described it as a "spread of flat confusion" and a "labyrinth." After trying several routes, the women realized they had lost the channel. As evening approached, they made camp, using oars and Smith's rifle to prop up netting in a failed attempt to ward off swarms of bloodthirsty mosquitoes. "You can get more good out of a .22 rifle than any other kind of gun," Smith declared.[8]

After a restless night under the moon's glare, Rawlings awoke with new energy. "Marsh and water glittered iridescent in the sun. The tropical March air was fresh and wind-washed. I was suddenly excited," she wrote. Soon after, the women found the river's channel, although their recollections of how that was accomplished differed. Rawlings claimed that they watched water hyacinths, a floating plant with lovely purple flowers, drifting in the direction of the channel.[9]

> From that instant we were never very long lost. Forever after, where the river sprawled in confusion, we might shut off the motor and study the floating hyacinths until we caught, in one direction, a swifter pulsing, as though we put our hands close and closer to the river's heart. It was very simple. Like all simple facts, it was necessary to discover it for oneself.
>
> We had, in a moment, the feel of the river; a wisdom for its vagaries. When the current took us away that morning, we gave ourselves over to it. There was a tremendous exhilaration, an abandoning of fear.[10]

It is one of her loveliest descriptions, but it didn't happen that way. Smith, a seasoned boater, knew that wind could move hyacinths, disguising the true flow. Instead, she crumpled a handful of dried leaves, submerged her hand, and slowly released the debris, watching it move with the current. The fact that Rawlings had "prettied" up the story didn't bother her a bit. "I always said Marge could describe a magnolia and I could smell it. She was that good," she recalled.[11]

As the women worked their way through the marshy maze, they met different men along the way—one who offered directions and then asked them to send a postcard at journey's end so he wouldn't worry; a lone fisherman who offered a fish which they declined; and a ferryman who corrected them on their true location. But nothing was going to dampen their spirits, especially since men early on had protested, then encouraged their river plans:

"Two women alone? The river runs through some of the wildest country in Florida. You'll be lost in the false channels. No one ever goes as far as the head of the river." Then, passionately betraying themselves, "It will be splendid. What if you do get lost? Don't let any one talk you out of it."[12]

As they moved out of Puzzle Lake and into Lake Harney, a broad river expanse, and then into a more recognizable river flow, the women's anxiety eased. They bought shad and roe from a net fisherman and found a quicker current along a riverbank covered with palms, live oaks, and small trees. "Toward sunset we swung under the western bank at one of those spots a traveler recognizes instinctively as, for the moment, home," Rawlings wrote. They overnighted in a deserted cabin "gray and smooth as only cypress weathers." It was missing windows and a door, but there was a roof, a place for their beds, and, soon, a fire. They ate the fish and roe, along with "French-fried potatoes" and Rawlings's cobbled-together tartar sauce. A hot bath out of buckets, full bellies, and a rising moon made for an exquisite, relaxing evening.[13]

If I could have, to hold forever, one brief place and time of beauty, I think I might choose the night on that high lonely bank above the St. John's River. . . . Suddenly the soft night turned silver. The moon was rising. We lay on our cots a long time wakeful because of the beauty. The moon shone through the doorway and windows and the light was patterned with the shadows of Spanish moss waving from the live oaks. There was a deserted grove somewhere behind the cabin, and the incredible sweetness of orange bloom drifted across us.[14]

Breakfast was a duck that Smith shot and Rawlings roasted in the pot. They luxuriated in sunlight all morning, finally heading to the boat around noon only to discover it filled with water from caulking leaks. But Smith knew just what to do, tearing a shirt into strips that they forced into the cracks with pocket knives. Rawlings "begged to stay another night," but Smith was adamant that they move on; their next camp was downriver underneath an "upturned tree root." Supper was swamp cabbage, cut from a young palmetto, cooked with white bacon and accompanied by Rawlings's baked corn sticks. Smith, with a giggle, later recalled seeing Rawlings, dressed in flowery pajamas, being spooked by an unexpected nest of water moccasins as she attempted to relieve herself.[15]

The next day the women motored across the expanse of Lake Monroe to the public docks at the city of Sanford, "the outpost of large-vessel traffic" on the river. They were quite a sight—tired and unwashed. "Dess strapped around her waist the leather belt that held her bowie knife at one hip and her revolver at the other, and felt better prepared for Sanford than if we had been clean," Rawlings wrote. Next to them was "an immaculate pleasure yacht from Long Island Sound." The well-dressed owner eyed the women, but Smith showed no embarrassment, asking him if it was safe to come into town to get gasoline for the boat. The man replied that it was Sunday, but he'd be happy to send his "man" to get them fuel. Here begins one of the funniest of the women's adventures, told by Rawlings:

> There was a sound inside the yacht. There simmered up the companionway a woman, magnificent in pink spectator sports costume. The crew jumped almost to attention and escorted her down the yacht's gangplank.
>
> The woman snapped over her shoulders, "I must have the car at once. I cannot be late to church for this nonsense."
>
> Our white man turned rosy and made a comradely gesture to us.
>
> He leaned over and whispered, "The car will be back in just a moment. If you don't mind waiting—-. Please wait."
>
> "O.K., fellow," Dess said.
>
> The pink spectator sports swept into a limousine. In a few minutes the car had returned. We were driven in style to a filling station and our tins filled with gasoline. We bought the New York Sunday papers. The yacht crew brought the tins down to us and helped us re-stow our duffle. Dess outlined our trip briefly to the owner. She cranked up and we were off again.
>
> "Good luck!" called the yacht owner. "The very best of good luck!"
>
> He waved after us as far as we could see him, as though reluctant to break a mystic thread. His face was wistful.
>
> "The poor b—," Dess said pityingly and indignantly. "I'll bet he'd give his silk shirt to go down the river with us instead of with Pink Petticoats."[16]

Now the river's flow was distinct. The women camped along the way, picking out dry areas where they would stretch out tarpaulins for shelter and hang mosquito netting for peace of mind. They saw an abundance of wildlife and blooming water plants, casually stopping to fish or swim in the river. They talked to people along the way—a woman pulling in fish lines, another squatting in a shack with a child. They waved to pilots of a lumber steamer and consulted with a former steamship captain, who offered advice on crossing the massive, unpredictable Lake George. Camping the night before tangling with the lake, they encountered three fishermen who "hailed us excitedly. Were we the women who had put in at Fort Christmas nearly a week before? If so, they must know. Word had been sent down the river from other fishermen to watch for us and to report our safety," Rawlings wrote. River folk were looking out for them.[17]

The next day they motored along, hugging the shallow lake's western bank so they were close to shore should a storm whip up. Still, they confronted winds and whitecaps that forced Smith to steer with both arms to keep the path. It took two and a half hours to cross the 11-mile-long lake in the small boat, leaving the women grateful when the river calmed.

Rawlings's description of the remainder of the trip is glossed over, with no specifics about days or camps or activities. Smith said they eased their way north, fishing and camping at their leisure. Near the end of the tale, Rawlings states that one afternoon they turned onto the Ocklawaha River, taking the same path that Harriet Beecher Stowe and so many other writers and tourists had ventured along in the 1800s. Smith's employee met them at Fort McCoy, where they loaded up the boat and headed home. Rawlings admitted she was so wrapped up in the river trip that she was reluctant to return to her regular life, which included an unfinished book and the problematic Charles.

> But when the dry ground was under us, the world no longer fluid, I found a forgotten loveliness in all the things that have nothing to do with men. Beauty is pervasive, and fills, like perfume, more than the object that contains it. Because I had known intimately a river, the earth pulsed under me. The Creek was home. Oleanders were sweet past bearing, and my own shabby fields, weed-tangled, were newly dear. I knew, for a moment, that the only nightmare is the masochistic human mind.[18]

Rawlings told Perkins that she returned with the impression that simple people are filled with kindness and goodness, as evidenced by the river people she had met who were helpful "as none of my sophisticated friends have ever been." On the last day of the trip a great deal about her unfinished manuscript "suddenly straightened itself out in my mind." The resulting book, *Golden Apples,* was published two years later. And by November, Charles was gone for good; Smith believed the river trip convinced Rawlings to divorce him, despite the scandal it made in that era. Rawlings wrote to Perkins describing her marriage as "fourteen years of Hell—of a fourteen-year struggle to adjust myself to, and accept, a most interesting but difficult—impossible—personality. It was a question, finally, of breaking free from the feeling of a vicious hand always at my throat, or of going down in complete physical and mental collapse." Rawlings said she "could have been a *slave* to a man who could be at least a *benevolent* despot—but I feel a terrific relief—I can wake up in the morning conscious of the sunshine, and thinking, 'How wonderful! Nobody is going to give me Hell today.'"[19]

The river trip was a revelation for Rawlings, a voyage that restored her soul and strengthened her resolve to forge ahead. For Smith, who always was curious about "whatever's around the next bend," it was fulfillment of a dream and a tale she would enjoy telling for many years to come. Rawlings would happily remarry a few years later and go on to a celebrated literary career, which included a friendship with African American author Zora Neale Hurston—a delicate but rich relationship during the uncertain days of Jim Crow that informed Rawlings's awakening to the era's racial injustices.

I read "Hyacinth Drift" decades later and caught Dessie's fever, wanting to retrace the women's path. For several years I prodded different female friends to join me. They cast glazed eyes, wondering why this could possibly be a good idea. Then late one night, over cold beers, I broached the idea with Heather McPherson, a friend since our college days at the University of Florida. "I'll do it!" she readily agreed—and she didn't try to back out the next day. Instead, I found myself swept into a vortex of her detailed planning, which rapidly came to include a borrowed boat, extensive maps of the St. Johns River system, and a list of folks to meet along the way. It would be a trip not unlike Rawlings's—one that would steer our lives in new directions, refreshing our careers and leading to new, unanticipated opportunities. It even led to my becoming a college professor and writing this book, a path I never envisioned.

Sixty-one years after Rawlings, we took off to see what the river held in the modern world. In March 1994 I set out on the journey with McPherson, then food editor at the *Orlando Sentinel;* I had worked at the same newspaper but now was a freelance writer. To our great surprise and delight, we discovered that Smith, then known as Dessie Prescott (the surname from the last of her six marriages) was still alive and energetic at age eighty-eight, so we sought her advice, traveling to her home on the Withlacoochee River. While stirring red-eye gravy for breakfast, she talked about her colorful life and her friendship with Rawlings, which had drawn much attention in the years following the author's 1953 death from a cerebral hemorrhage.

"You must learn to use a gun," advised Smith, who became Florida's first professional female hunting and fishing guide and ran a lodge to entertain sportsmen. "It's not the four-legged ones you have to worry about. It's the two-legged kind." Although a gun might come in handy for food, she was more concerned about our safety. "Don't talk too much to people. Don't let them know what you're doing. 'Cause, hell, they could cut you out at another place." But she never tried to talk us out of the trip. Instead of fire-power, we opted for the modern options of cell phones, maps, and aerial photographs.[20]

The women had camped in random sites, but times had changed; the riverfront was more developed with homes and weekend cabins, and land-owners wouldn't take kindly to us showing up on their property. So, we planned our ten-day voyage around fish camps, riverfront hotels, and res-taurants. The 1933 travelers' problems were with wildlife, but our concerns were with human life—trespassing restrictions, heavy recreational boat traffic on some parts of the river, and the threat of late-night river partiers who might be drunk and armed. As it turned out, the people were mostly kind, and, amazingly, we enjoyed similar adventures.

After launching our boat at the same site, we soon were mired in the quandary of Puzzle Lake, worsened by recent storms that had raised water levels and left a vast expanse with no clear path. Channels that looked clear were dead ends, winds turned the boat canopy into an unwanted sail, and soon we ran aground on a sandbar hidden in the coffee-colored waters. A group of beer-sipping good ol' boys, offering no help, watched in amuse-ment as I climbed out of the boat, swearing under my breath, and pushed it into deeper water. Perhaps modern river people weren't so helpful after all.

As it turned out, they were the exception, and we soon agreed with the words of a woman Rawlings had met early on: "The river life's the finest kind of life. You couldn't get you no better life than the river." The March weather was glorious, the wildlife was spectacular—bald eagles, white peli-cans, and more than a few 10-foot alligators, and, once we exited Puzzle Lake, traveling on the boat we dubbed *Dessie* was superb. Our first night we stayed in a trailer owned by a couple, Robert and Deborah Harvey, at Baxter's Point, a jut of land on the east side of the river. They were delightful hosts, wanting to hear all of our plans and offering advice. The next day, after prevailing through more groundings, we stopped at a marina for gas and spotted Robert waving to us, glad that we were safe and sound. The river folk were looking out for us.[21]

At Sanford we pulled into the harbor basin and watched a passing paddlewheel riverboat filled with diners ready for a cruise. We laughingly remembered the women's encounter with the yachtsman. Along the way we had more encounters with people who not only loved the river but were familiar with Rawlings's writings. And sometimes our encounters seemed magical, as if her spirit was along for the ride.

Needing a walk after one long day of motoring, I happened across a sign for the Volusia Museum near the town of Astor. Lillian Dillard Gibson was running the little operation in a small building behind her riverfront home and, as it turned out, had her own connection to Rawlings. Her father, Barney Dillard, had housed the author at his home and told her tales of bear hunts—some recounted in *The Yearling*. In Gibson's cherished copy of the book was this inscription from Rawlings: "For my good friend Barney Dillard who will recognize some of his memories in this book." Late that night McPherson and I ventured out with a state-licensed alligator trapper on waters where William Bartram had his close encounter with the reptiles in 1774. As the guide's light beam scanned the water, hundreds of shining orange reptilian eyes stared back, and I appreciated Bartram's fear.

The river was no longer the solitary trek that Rawlings and Smith experienced. It was filled with spring break vacationers, kayakers, and boats that ranged from multiroom houseboats to open-air pontoon boats to buzzing Jet Skis to the most offensive of all—hair-raising, ear-pounding airboats.

Our final river days revealed even greater changes to the river. The twisting, jungle-like Ocklawaha River from its juncture to the St. Johns at Welaka resembled the women's original return path. However, it now was blocked partway by a dam built in the 1960s as part of an eventually abandoned project to build a barge canal across the state. To navigate back into the women's path, we rerouted through the ghostly canal's remaining locks and barriers and then carefully picked our way across the reservoir created by the dam. As McPherson guided the slow putt-putting boat, I hung over the front edge, looking for any floating logs that might damage our propeller. There were plenty to dodge, and not another boat was visible despite flawless weather.

Ever since the dam's creation there has been a push by environmental activists, led by the Florida Defenders of the Environment (FDE), to remove it and restore the Ocklawaha to its former beauty, which includes many springs that quit flowing because of water pressure caused by the reservoir. Opposition comes from the fishing industry and chamber of commerce types, who argue that the reservoir is important for tourism, especially bass tournaments. As one hotel owner admitted, "It was a mistake when they made it but now that it's here we should keep it." River activists, who call the structure "Dam Shame," argue that it prevents the migration of ten fish species, that bass fishing is better in the undisturbed Ocklawaha route, and that endangered manatees have been killed in the lock gates. They say that it's time for the damn dam to go.

After our sluggish navigation through the reservoir, we arrived at our take-out spot, where our families and a smiling Dessie Smith Prescott awaited. "Did you catch any fish?" were the first words out of her mouth. We nodded and smiled.

Three months later, McPherson and I wrote about our river adventure in a Sunday magazine article for the *Orlando Sentinel*. We also wrote a separate article about Smith because, well, she had plenty to tell about her vibrant life. Five years later she was inducted into the Florida Women's Hall of Fame.

We were pleased with the articles but startled with the positive responses from readers who confessed that they loved the river and Rawlings and "had always wanted to take that trip." I gave directions and advice to many people, unsure of whether they ever succeeded. The articles had struck deep chords with many Floridians, some new to the state but many of them natives who loved the state's beauty. As Anne E. Rowe notes in *The Idea of Florida in the American Literary Imagination,* the success of *Cross Creek* reflects its appeal "to anyone who has longed for the idyllic, pastoral escape from humdrum life."[22]

It is a quality many Floridians crave amid an exploding population. We have exceeded 22 million residents, a number that swells by more than 1,000 per day, leading to urban sprawl that consumes many of the state's natural features. Although Floridians consistently rank the need for growth management as a high priority, few feel that local and state leaders are seriously trying to save the state from being paved over, creating what author Carl Hiaasen has likened in South Florida to "Newark with palm trees." One-third of those polled several years ago stated they would "tell a loved one or friend not to move to the once-vaunted Sunshine State, and one in five is seriously considering moving elsewhere." Ironically, as Rowe notes, "Perhaps in no other state have the conflicting goals of growth and preservation from destruction of the very natural resources that have attracted people been so apparent as they are in Florida." We are loving and trampling Eden to death.[23]

The 1000 Friends of Florida, a nonprofit group working to encourage better growth, estimates that the state will have almost 34 million residents by 2070. A 2017 special report created by the group along with the Florida Department of Agriculture and the University of Florida's GeoPlan Center warns that growth of such magnitude will have big impacts on rural lands, now disappearing at the rate of 10 acres per hour, and water resources. The solution? Support policies that "encourage more compact development, protect sensitive natural lands and significantly increase water conservation."[24]

These are issues I have long discussed with environmentalists, including the late Bill Belleville, an award-winning Sanford writer who applied his passion and talent to bringing attention to natural areas in Florida. When I joined him and several others at Equinox Documentaries, a nonprofit organization, our goal was to develop film projects that would bring that message to the public. The written word is a wonderful way to reach and inform, but you can't beat a video to show the true beauty and value of natural resources.

Early on, the Equinox board decided to bring "Hyacinth Drift" to film, blending the Rawlings narrative with Belleville's vast knowledge of the river assembled in his natural history *River of Lakes: A Journey on Florida's St. Johns River*. The river's health, once compromised by the dumping of raw sewage and industrial waste from communities, now is harmed by pollution born of development and water runoff. But its biggest threat may be the thirsty cities along its route that eye it as a future water source.

We named the project *In Marjorie's Wake* and planned it to be an hour-long, bug-free jaunt that might convert viewers into advocates. Upon learning that Smith, ninety-five, was in declining health, we hastily assembled a small film crew in 2001 and headed to her home. Perched on a stool on her backyard dock, Smith spent two hours recalling her life and friendship with Rawlings. She talked about the origins of the river trip, repeated some of Rawlings's stories, and told a few anecdotes that didn't make the book. Smith had the whole crew in stitches, and her interview was the seed that launched the production. Sadly, she died seven months later.

The next five years involved the mechanics and details of developing a film. Most financing came from individuals, groups, and foundations with Florida roots. Rawlings retains great popularity, and her books are still widely read despite the fact that many academics have dismissed her as a "regional" or "youth" author. Every year, the Marjorie Kinnan Rawlings Society, with members from as far away as Japan, holds a well-attended annual meeting where her works and life are avidly discussed. In 2008, the US Postal Service distributed a stamp featuring a portrait of Rawlings, recognition of her enduring popularity and talent.

There is also a new generation of Rawlings aficionados. In 2017, three young women created *The Marjorie,* a Florida-based reporting nonprofit that "promotes a great understanding of issues related to women and the environment," said cofounder Anna Hamilton. "Our name owes to the work of Marjorie Kinnan Rawlings, Marjorie Harris Carr, and Marjory Stoneman Douglas, three kickass Florida women who stood up for what they believe in and made important strides for Florida's wild lands." Carr, a FDE founder, led efforts to stop the barge canal that damaged and dammed the Ocklawaha River. Douglas was an important writer and activist who worked to protect and restore Florida's Everglades. "Partly as tribute to them and partly as continuation of their efforts, *The Marjorie* publishes in-depth, original reporting on environmental subjects that are often overlooked and under-represented," wrote Hamilton, adding:

> Today I turn to the work of Marjorie Kinnan Rawlings when I feel sad about the state of things and need a pep talk. The ethical questions she posed more than seventy years ago are perhaps more relevant than ever, with the onslaught of the climate crisis, worsening urban sprawl, the compounding of mass extinctions, and the chokehold of micro-plastics in our oceans—choose your own adventure. It's meditative for me to look back at *Cross Creek,* the last chapter in particular, and think on her question, "Who owns Cross Creek?" We can scale this up or down, and extend it to our own regions and homes: Who owns our lands and resources? What is our responsibility to them? How can we best care for them and ourselves? For me, this question is loaded with urgency, as we collectively imagine new ways of thinking about, and being in, the world as we witness the consequences of our extractive, exploitative societies.[25]

Amid the film's planning and fundraising, the producers decided that I should be *in* it. Since I had made the trip (and, importantly, owned and could operate a boat), I would be the "eyes" of experience, sharing my love

218 · Tracing Florida Journeys

and knowledge of Rawlings. Jennifer Chase, a Jacksonville musician and educator, was chosen for her artistic sensibilities and because she had never traveled the river. We were not reenacting the Rawlings–Smith friendship trip but, rather, revisiting their path to discover what had changed or remained the same.

Once again, I was out on the water, accompanied by an entourage of male producers, sound crew, and camera operators. We shot most of the film in one week in October 2006 and, as before, we found some amazing parallels to Rawlings's trip. We made wrong turns and got stuck in Puzzle Lake, but this time we camped two nights along the way (with permits) and enjoyed a week of enchantment. We met and interviewed artists and writers inspired by the Florida landscape and discovered that almost everyone along the way—from deer hunters to game wardens to restaurateurs—were Rawlings fans. Our cameras captured mystical sunrises, a black bear on the river's bank, an otter swimming under the boat—a treasure trove of wildlife.

There was comfort in the river's generous beauty and times when there were no other humans, only the song of wind in the trees and vast expanses of marsh and forests. It was hard to believe that the traffic snarls and strip malls of "civilization" were less than an hour away. Rawlings wrote that she and her neighbors in the rural hamlet of Cross Creek needed "a certain remoteness from urban confusion." In this day and age, that may apply to all Floridians. At the confluence of the Ocklawaha River, I released some of Dessie Smith's ashes into her beloved waterway as Chase sang "Amazing Grace" and tossed flowers into the current. She was there with us, I am sure.[26]

A few weeks later we finished filming at Rawlings's home in Cross Creek, now the Marjorie Kinnan Rawlings Historic State Park, designated a National Historic Landmark in 2007. The Cracker-style wooden house looks much as it did when she lived in it, and a manual typewriter sits on the screened porch atop a desk that Charles built. It is a remarkable place where one can read from Cross Creek and see many of the landmarks she described.

Steven Noll, a University of Florida history professor, regularly assigns Rawlings's works to his classes and takes them to the park. Cross Creek offers, he wrote, "subtle (and not so subtle) understandings of the Florida landscape and ecology—there are parts of the book that give a great feel for the science of ecology without using science at all." Importantly, the book serves as a "window into a lost world of Cracker Florida but also as a mod-

Rawlings's wooden farmhouse is now a state park regularly visited by fans and by those seeking the aesthetic of Florida from a century ago. Courtesy of Bruce Hunt.

ern voice for living in harmony with nature and not using it as a commodity to be exploited."[27]

Our forty-four hours of film were edited to fifty-five minutes before the documentary, entitled *In Marjorie's Wake*, aired on PBS stations across the nation in 2007. It was a monthslong, painstaking process for the producers, who kept the focus on reaching Floridians to show them the beauty of the state to instill activism to save it. Groups and educators continue to air the film today, available through many libraries, and its message is even more important today.

This was all exciting stuff, beyond my imaginings when I convinced McPherson to join me. But it was just part of our voyage with Rawlings. When McPherson returned from the river trip, she used Rawlings as her muse for her journalism work, which came to include a popular weekly newspaper column, and for life.

"It readjusted my lens," McPherson later reflected. "Being able to exhale over those days was like a spa for my mind and soul. My husband even laughs when I am overworked and tense and says, 'I think you need to get back to the river.' Water has an organic calming effect on many people—but it is essential for me. Even though we had some navigation challenges early on, Mother Nature has a way of amping up your intuition. That ability to figure things out on your own is essential in life. No Google Maps, no way to google a possible solution. Just follow your instincts and build on what you have learned. Be calm and the current for all things in life will reveal itself. I think in many ways it revived my career—Marge became my muse and helped me discover my own compass. I thought I was pretty fearless, but on the river I learned to head full-speed around the next bend."[28]

After the magazine articles appeared, I was asked to start teaching an environmental literature course as an adjunct professor at Rollins College, a liberal arts school in Winter Park. One course led to another, and, finally, with the encouragement of my Rollins colleagues, I went back to the University of Florida—a very late-life student—to get my PhD in history. My topic: the role of women in Florida's modern conservation and environmental movements. It was a treasure trove: women created parks, planted trees, cleaned up cities, and advocated to save birds and wildlife before and after they had the right to vote. My rewritten dissertation was published in 2015 as *Saving Florida: Women's Fight for the Environment in the Twentieth Century.* The book's chapter 5 is all about Florida's "Three Marjories"—Rawlings, Carr, and Douglas. Since then, I have given many talks around the state about the environmental women and the Marjories. I also served a three-year stint as executive director of the Marjorie Kinnan Rawlings Society. Best of all, I now am an associate professor in Rollins's environmental studies department, where I frequently incorporate these women into my classes and lead field trips to Cross Creek and the Ocklawaha River. The day I hung a poster for the society, featuring a scene from *The Yearling,* in my newly painted office was one of the proudest of my life.

In the meandering way of rivers and life, Rawlings and "Hyacinth Drift" have been central to my life for many years. They inspired me in my new academic career but also in teaching her works that may encourage others, especially future activists, to appreciate and protect the state's beauty. Perhaps they will find a way do all of this while living out Rawlings's vision: "It seems to me that the earth may be borrowed but not bought. It may be used, but not owned. It gives itself in response to love and tending, offers its seasonal flowering and fruiting. But we are tenants and not possessors, lovers and not masters."[29]

To see the home where Marjorie Kinnan Rawlings lived and wrote, visit the
Marjorie Kinnan Rawlings Historic State Park.

Marjorie Kinnan Rawlings Historic State Park

18700 South County Road 325
Cross Creek, Florida 32640
(352) 466-3672
floridastateparks.org/parks-and-trails/marjorie-kinnan-rawlings-historic
-state-park

Directions: From US 441 outside Micanopy, proceed east on CR 346 approximately 5 miles to CR 325. The entrance to Marjorie Kinnan Rawlings
Historic State Park is 4 miles south, on the west side of CR 325.

Perhaps what is most remarkable about Cross Creek, both the surrounding
community and the house at Marjorie Kinnan Rawlings Historic State Park
in particular, is how little it has changed since the early mid-twentieth century when she lived and wrote here. To be sure, the roads are better paved,
and there are more people living in the surrounding area, but not *too*
many more. It is quiet, even a bit isolated. Traffic is sparse and sometimes
nonexistent. Vast woodland acreage still predominates, and it is still populated with the wildlife that she wrote about: deer, raccoons, and even black
bears. The lakes, along with the creeks connecting them, are still home to a
variety of waterfowl. Devotees of Rawlings's writing will recall her descriptions of her home and experience a palpable familiarity when visiting the
park. The house has been carefully maintained and kept as original as possible, including its eccentricities ("sloping floor has proved no friend to the
aged, the absent-minded, and the inebriated").
Hours: Open daily 9:00 a.m.–5:00 p.m. (closed Christmas Day and Thanksgiving Day). The house is closed in August and September for maintenance.
Guided tours are offered from October to July, Thursday to Sunday: $3 for
adults; $2 for children 6–12; under 5 free. Parking is $3.

Rawlings and her husband Norton Baskin are buried next to each other at
the Antioch Cemetery in nearby Island Grove. To find her grave, drive east
on CR 325 to Island Grove, about 3.8 miles, cross US 301, and continue east
on Southeast 219th Avenue. At Southeast 225th Drive, an unpaved road,
turn left and proceed for 2 miles before turning right on Southeast 189th
Avenue and you will reach the cemetery. Walk about 40 paces to a small
building, turn left, and go 45 more steps to the west to find their flat grave
markers—hers is often adorned with pencils and deer toys.

The Yearling

14531 East County Road 325
Cross Creek, Florida 32640
(352) 466-3999
yearlingrestaurant.net

Just down the road from the park is The Yearling restaurant. Although it didn't exist during Rawlings's lifetime, it does offer Rawlings's memorabilia and southern cooking, and there are cabin rentals on-site.

Final Thoughts

If you have never seen the sun setting in those latitudes, I would recom-
mend to you to make a voyage for the purpose, for I much doubt if,
in any other portion of the world, the departure of the orb of day is
accompanied with such gorgeous appearances. Look at the great red
disk, increased to triple its ordinary dimensions! Now it has partially
sunk beneath the distant line of waters, and with its still remaining half
irradiates the whole heavens with a flood of golden light, purpling the
far off clouds that hover over the western horizon. A blaze of refulgent
glory streams through the portals of the west, and the masses of vapour
assume the semblance of mountains of molten gold. But the sun has
now disappeared, and from the east slowly advances the grey curtain
which nigh draws over the world.

John James Audubon, *Ornithological Biography*

I think about these words of John James Audubon as I watch a glowing
sun dripping into the turquoise water in Key West, Florida. He was ecstatic
about how the light in this part of the world departed below the horizon,
flashing brilliant colors across the sky and clouds. Tonight, I join others
who nightly cheer this event, which is never the same, depending on the
clouds and weather. They are the kind of people I want to be with—those
who find joy in unmistakable beauty and celebrate it with enthusiasm. And
I feel a connection with Audubon, who also appreciated the natural artistry
of our planet.

It is a fitting way to end my journey across Florida, which extended over
three years, coincided with a pandemic, and encompassed countless miles
on land, river, and sea. I followed the literary ghosts and trails of some of
my favorite authors—hiking along John Muir's path, boating in Marjorie
Kinnan Rawlings's wake, and gazing at vistas that stirred William Bartram's
soul. I laughed out loud at some of Zora Neale Hurston's stories and then

soberly considered the working conditions of the camps she visited. And I sighed with amazement at the descriptions of the wild, serpentine Ocklawaha River offered by Harriet Beecher Stowe.

The authors highlighted in these chapters have vastly different definitions of "Florida," which reflect their aspirations and expectations. While many visitors were seeking beauty and recreation, others had motives that greatly skewed their impressions. Hernando de Soto's company looked at rivers as impediments in the hunt for wealth. Jonathan Dickinson felt hardship and danger in pristine coastal beaches. The ill-informed Ingraham expedition eventually gave up its railroad surveying efforts in the face of the mucky reality of Everglades sawgrass.

Revisiting their travels and writings offers the opportunity to understand their culture and views, as different as they may be from my modern thinking. While much of the landscape has been altered, my explorations have given me new insights into Florida's colorful, rich history. I can listen to an alligator roar or the scream of a limpkin or the splashing of a jumping mullet (with eyes mostly closed) and imagine how the world seemed to each of these authors. Their stories reveal how much the peninsula has changed but also how some areas remain mysterious and almost impenetrable. I celebrate the places that have been preserved so that I can share some of their insight and delight—just like this kaleidoscopic sunset in Key West.

My greatest wish is that this book inspires you to journey into the heart of Florida. Perhaps a walk in a swamp or a hike through a forest, accompanied by the words of these travelers, will propel you into new adventures. Hopefully a new connection to the state's wondrous beauty will guide you along a path that includes appreciation of this amazing place and the desire to preserve it.

Acknowledgments

It has been twenty years since I began researching this book. It went on the back burner while life took me on a meandering journey that unexpectedly resulted in a career in academia. I was thrilled to revive it with the support of so many people who deserve my love and thanks.

Bruce Hunt, my friend since high school and an accomplished author and photographer, joined me on most of the research trips for these chapters, sharing meals and long drives. He shot hundreds of images that may never be published, but they are all beautiful. His curiosity, artistic vision, and good nature—as well as his sidebars with information about visiting these sites—are essential to this book. Mary Lou Janson, another high school and college pal and journalist, was a terrific navigator, accompanying me to obscure sites she hadn't planned on seeing, including a cemetery, out-of-the-way historical markers, and a tree preserve. I'm also grateful to the folks who literally walked or boated with me on pathways described in this book: Clay Henderson, who piloted us up the St. Johns River to William Bartram's "Battle Lagoon"; Lars Andersen, who hiked in Paynes Prairie despite the humidity and shirt-piercing mosquitoes; Dr. Jerry and Linda Lorenz, who took us by water to Indian Key and Lignumvitae Key and trudged around them offering their insights; Dr. Keith Ashley and Paul Dunn, who joined me at the Mount Royal mound to ponder its mystery and archaeological treasures; Karen Chadwick, who cruised down the winding Ocklawaha River, pointing to historic sites; hiking friends Jill and Bob Bendick, Karen Coleman, Mark Hammond, and Dr. Patrice Kohl, who braved a cold, breezy day to retrace John Muir's path through Gainesville; Nancy Pepper, who joined me to watch nesting terns on Dry Tortugas; Kim den Beste, who hiked with me on Audubon's trail; Rae Ann Wessel, who sauntered along the Fort Myers waterfront, pointing out the likely starting spot for the Ingraham Everglades expedition; and Elizabeth Friedmann, who shared her fascination with Stephen Crane's shipwreck while touring the lighthouse that was his beacon to shore. Undying appreciation goes to those who lent me manuscripts and/or read portions of this book for accuracy: Dr. Jerald T. Milanich, Dr. Paul E. Hoffman, Dr. Bruce Means, Clay Henderson, Dr. Jerry Lorenz, Dr. Thomas Van Lent, and Frances Nevill. I also appreciate the coaching and information offered by Dr. Paul Gray, N. Y. Nathiri, James "Zach" Zacharias, Merald Clark, Dean DeBolt, John Bass, and Mike Owen, who know great stories about early Florida travelers. I enjoyed listening to every one of them.

It isn't easy to complete a manuscript, especially one that requires interviews and travel during a pandemic. This was only possible through the encouragement and patience of my wonderful editor, Sian Hunter, of the University Press of Florida.

Thanks also to copy editor Susan Murray, proofreader Tana Silva, and indexer Mary Ann Lieser.

And, of course, to my husband, Michael, and sons, Blake and Preston, who have listened to these stories for more than two decades and willingly detoured to a few spots during driving and boating trips to appease my enthusiasm. What a journey!

Notes

Chapter 1. Hernando de Soto

1 Jerald T. Milanich, WebEx interview by the author, January 6, 2020.

2 Jerald T. Milanich and Charles Hudson, *Hernando de Soto and the Indians of Florida* (Gainesville: University Press of Florida, 1993), 21–22.

3 Milanich and Hudson, *Hernando de Soto,* 22–23; Gentleman of Elvas, *True Relation of the Hardships Suffered by Governor Hernando De Soto & Certain Portuguese Gentlemen during the Discovery of the Province of Florida, Now Newly Set Forth by a Gentleman of Elvas,* in *The De Soto Chronicles: The Expedition of Hernando de Soto to North American in 1539-1543,* vol. 1, ed. Lawrence A. Clayton, Vernon James Knight Jr., and Edward C. Moor (Tuscaloosa: University of Alabama Press, 1993), 48.

4 James Alexander Robinson, preface to *True Relation of the Hardships Suffered by Governor Hernando De Soto & Certain Portuguese Gentlemen during the Discovery of the Province of Florida, Now Newly Set Forth by a Gentleman of Elvas,* in *The De Soto Chronicles,* vol. 1, ed. Clayton, Knight, and Moore, 29.

5 Garcilaso de la Vega, *La Florida by the Inca: History of the Adelantado Hernando De Soto, Governor and Captain-General of the Kingdom of La Florida, and of Other Heroic Gentlemen, Spaniards and Indians; Written by the Inca Garcilaso De La Vega, Captain of His Majesty, a Native of the Great City of El Cuzco, Capital of the Kingdoms and Provinces of El Peru,* in *The De Soto Chronicles,* vol. 2, ed. Clayton, Knight, and Moore, 447–48.

6 Milanich and Hudson, *Hernando de Soto,* 27–34.

7 Milanich and Hudson, *Hernando de Soto,* 35. The Vatican has taken steps in recent years to repudiate doctrines that supported colonial seizure and exploitation of Indigenous people (see Elisabetta Povoledo, "Vatican Repudiates 'Doctrine of Discovery,' Used to Justify Colonization," *New York Times,* March 31, 2023, A-7).

8 Elvas, *True Relation of the Hardships,* 57; Charles Hudson, *Knights of Spain, Warriors of the Sun: Hernando de Soto and the South's Ancient Chiefdoms* (Athens: University of Georgia Press, 1997), 67–68.

9 Hudson, *Knights of Spain,* 65–67.

10 Elvas, *True Relation of the Hardships,* 57.

11 Elvas, *True Relation of the Hardships,* 57.

12 Elvas, *True Relation of the Hardships,* 58.

13 Elvas, *True Relation of the Hardships,* 59.

14 Elvas, *True Relation of the Hardships,* 59.

15 Elvas, *True Relation of the Hardships,* 60.

16 Ken Clarke, "Juan Ortiz's Story a Lot Like 'Pocahontas,'" *Orlando Sentinel,* June 27, 1995, https://www.orlandosentinel.com/news/os-xpm-1995-06-27-9506270110 -story.html.

17 Elvas, *True Relation of the Hardships,* 62.

18 Rodrigo Rangel, *Account of the Northern Conquest and Discovery of Hernando De Soto,* in *The De Soto Chronicles,* vol. 1, ed. Clayton, Knight, and Moore, 255.

19 Elvas, *True Relation of the Hardships,* 63–65.

20 Elvas, *True Relation of the Hardships,* 64–65.

21 Rangel, *Account of the Northern Conquest,* 256–57.

22 Paul E. Hoffman, email to author, January 15, 2021.

23 Elvas, *True Relation of the Hardships,* 71–72; Rangel, *Account of the Northern Conquest,* 267–68.

24 Elvas, *True Relation of the Hardships,* 74.

25 De la Vega, *La Florida by the Inca,* 253; Hudson, *Knights of Spain,* 138.

26 Elvas, *True Relation of the Hardships,* 74.

27 Elvas, *True Relation of the Hardships,* 74, 136–38.

28 Milanich and Hudson, *Hernando de Soto,* 233.

29 Milanich and Hudson, *Hernando de Soto,* 236.

30 Milanich and Hudson, *Hernando de Soto,* 237, 241, 243, 250.

31 Michael Gannon, "First European Contacts," in *The History of Florida,* ed. Gannon (Gainesville: University Press of Florida, 1996), 33–34.

32 Milanich and Hudson, *Hernando de Soto,* 254.

33 Milanich and Hudson, *Hernando de Soto,* 5.

34 Milanich and Hudson, *Hernando de Soto,* 4–5.

35 Milanich, interview.

36 David E. Whisnant and Anne Mitchell Whisnant, *Small Park, Large Issues: De Soto National Memorial and the Commemoration of a Difficult History* (Atlanta, GA: National Park Service, 2007), 14.

37 Mark Young and Giuseppe Sabella, "Ready, Set, Fun! Fans of De Soto Grand Parade Line Manatee Avenue," *Sarasota Herald-Tribune,* April 26, 2021, 1-A, 4-A, https:// www.heraldtribune.com/story/entertainment/events/2021/04/08/de-soto-grand -parade-announces-return-bradenton/7145042002/; "Photos: De Soto Heritage Festival Ball 2021," Sarasota *Herald-Tribune,* April 25, 2021, https://www.heraldtribune .com/picture-gallery/news/2021/04/25/photos-de-soto-heritage-festival-ball-2021/ 7374761002/.

38 "The Conquistadors," Punta Gorda Historic Mural Society website, https:// puntagordamurals.org/murals/the-conquistadors/.

39 Elvas, *True Relation of the Hardships,* 64–65.

40 Elvas, *True Relation of the Hardships,* 64–65.

41 Milanich and Hudson, *Hernando de Soto,* 91–110.

42 Milanich and Hudson, *Hernando de Soto,* 100–102, 107.

43 "Hernando de Soto 1539–1540 Winter Encampment at Anhaica Apalachee," Florida Division of Historical Resources website, https://dos.myflorida.com/historical/archaeology/projects/hernando-de-soto-1539-1540-winter-encampment-at-anhaica-apalachee/.

Chapter 2. Jonathan Dickinson

1 Jonathan Dickinson, *Jonathan Dickinson's Journal or God's Protecting Providence, Being the Narrative of a Journey from Port Royal in Jamaica to Philadelphia between August 23, 1696 and April 1, 1697* (Port Salerno, FL: Florida Classics Library, 1985), 5–6.

2 Dickinson, *Journal,* 2.

3 Jason Daniels, "Atlantic Contingency: Jonathan Dickinson and the Anglo-Atlantic World, 1655–1725" (PhD diss., University of Warwick, March 2013), 45–47.

4 Daniels, "Atlantic Contingency," 15–16.

5 Dickinson, *Journal,* 6–7.

6 Dickinson, *Journal,* 7.

7 Dickinson, *Journal,* 7–8; Daniels, "Atlantic Contingency," 123.

8 Dickinson, *Journal,* 8.

9 Dickinson, *Journal,* 8–11.

10 Dickinson, *Journal,* 11.

11 Dickinson, *Journal,* 11–13.

12 Jerald T. Milanich, *Florida Indians and the Invasion from Europe* (Gainesville: Library Press@UF, 2017), 56–57.

13 Dickinson, *Journal,* 14; Leonard W. Labaree, introduction to *Jonathan Dickinson's Journal,* 1985 ed., n.p.

14 Dickinson, *Journal,* 17–18; Milanich, *Florida Indians and the Invasion from Europe,* 59.

15 Dickinson, *Journal,* 21–22.

16 Dickinson, *Journal,* 22–23.

17 Dickinson, *Journal,* 25; Milanich, *Florida Indians and the Invasion from Europe,* 59–60.

18 Dickinson, *Journal,* 25.

19 Dickinson, *Journal,* 27.

20 Amy Turner Bushnell, "Escape of the Nickaleers: European-Indian Relations on the Wild Coast of Florida in 1696, from Jonathan Dickinson's Journal," in *Coastal Encounters: The Transformation of the Gulf South in the Eighteenth Century,* ed. Richmond F. Brown (Omaha: University of Nebraska Press, 2007), 56.

21 Dickinson, *Journal,* 27–29.

22 Dickinson, *Journal,* 29.

23 Milanich, *Florida Indians and the Invasion from Europe,* 65–66.

24 Dickinson, *Journal,* 34–36.

25 Dickinson, *Journal,* 36.

26 Dickinson, *Journal,* 36–37.

27 Dickinson, *Journal*, 40–41.
28 Dickinson, *Journal*, 41–43.
29 Dickinson, *Journal*, 51–53.
30 Dickinson, *Journal*, 56, 61.
31 Dickinson, *Journal*, 65, 76–78.
32 Robert Barrow to His Wife, in appendix B of Dickinson, *Journal*, 1985 ed., 89–92.
33 Author unknown, in appendix A, Jonathan Dickinson, *Journal* (New Haven, CT: Yale University Press, 1945), 129–31; Nicole Eustace, *Covered with Night: A Story of Murder and Indigenous Justice in Early America* (New York: Liveright, 2021), 75, 79.
34 Daniels, "Atlantic Contingency," 205.
35 Daniels, "Atlantic Contingency," 205n1.
36 Author unknown, in appendix A of Dickinson, *Journal*, 1945 ed., 115, 117.
37 Labaree, introduction to *Jonathan Dickinson's Journal*, 1985 ed., n.p.
38 Labaree, introduction to *Jonathan Dickinson's Journal*, 1985 ed., n.p.
39 Eric Gary Anderson, "Red Crosscurrents: Performative Spaces and Indian Cultural Authority in the Florida Atlantic Captivity Narrative of Jonathan Dickinson," *Mississippi Quarterly* 65, no. 1 (Winter 2012): 21.
40 Daniels, "Atlantic Contingency," 107, 109.
41 Bushnell, "Escape of the Nickaleers," 31.
42 Kevin McCarthy, *Florida Lighthouses* (Gainesville: University of Florida Press, 1990), 33, 35.
43 Steve Mentz, telephone interview by the author, June 29, 2020.
44 Steve Mentz, "Shipwrecked in 1696," July 11, 2012, https://stevementz.com/?s=1696.
45 George Blythe, telephone interview by the author, April 24, 2020.
46 Blythe, interview.
47 Blythe, interview.

Chapter 3. William Bartram

1 William Bartram, *Travels of William Bartram*, ed. Mark Van Doren (1928; New York: Dover, 1955), 183; "Declaration of Independence: Transcription," US Archives website, https://www.archives.gov/founding-docs/declaration-transcript.
2 Bartram, *Travels*, 15.
3 Bartram, *Travels*, 21–22.
4 Thomas P. Slaughter, *The Natures of John and William Bartram* (New York: Knopf, 1996), xv.
5 Thomas Hallock, introduction to *Travels on the St. Johns River: John Bartram and William Bartram*, ed. Hallock and Richard Franz (Gainesville: University Press of Florida, 2017), 4.
6 Edmund Berkeley and Dorothy Smith Berkeley, *The Life and Travels of John Bartram from Lake Ontario to the River St. John* (Tallahassee: University Presses of Florida, 1982), 148, 250–54.
7 Henry Laurens to John Bartram, August 9, 1766, in *Travels on the St. Johns River: John Bartram and William Bartram*, ed. Thomas Hallock and Richard Franz (Gainesville: University Press of Florida, 2017), 118–21.

8 Berkeley and Berkeley, *Life and Travels,* 285.

9 Brad Sanders, *Guide to William Bartram's Travels: Following the Trail of America's First Great Naturalist* (Athens, GA: Fevertree, 2002), 4.

10 Bartram, *Travels,* 75–77, 82.

11 Bartram, *Travels,* 86, 93.

12 Bartram, *Travels,* 88–89, 91, 94, 95; "The Last Carolina Parakeet," Audubon Society website, https://johnjames.audubon.org/last-carolina-parakeet.

13 Bartram, *Travels,* 95–96.

14 Bartram, *Travels,* 101–2; Keith H. Ashley, "Archeological Overview of Mt. Royal," *Florida Anthropologist* 58, no. 3–4, (2005): 265–68.

15 Bartram, *Travels,* 103–4.

16 Bartram, *Travels,* 107.

17 Bartram, *Travels,* 149–51.

18 Bartram, *Travels,* 110: Lars Andersen, *Paynes Prairie: The Great Savanna: A History and Guide,* 2nd ed. (Sarasota, FL: Pineapple, 2004), 50.

19 Bartram, *Travels,* 113.

20 Helen G. Cruickshank, *William Bartram in Florida 1774: The Adventures of the Naturalist, Explorer, Artist* (Florida Federation of Garden Clubs, 1986), 41–42.

21 Bartram, *Travels,* 113–15.

22 Bartram, *Travels,* 115–17.

23 Bartram, *Travels,* 117–18.

24 Bartram, *Travels,* 119.

25 Kathryn E. Holland Braund, "The Real Worlds of William Bartram's *Travels,*" in *Bartram's Living Legacy: The Travels and the Nature of the South,* ed. Dorinda G. Dallmeyer (Macon, GA: Mercer University Press, 2010), 450; Jason Herbert, "'We Have Always Been Cow People': Alachua Seminole Identity and Autonomy, 1750–1776," *Florida Historical Quarterly* 100, no. 1 (Summer 2021): 52–55.

26 Bartram, *Travels,* 153–63.

27 Andersen, *Paynes Prairie,* 48–50; Braund, "The Real Worlds," 451.

28 Bartram, *Travels,* 162–63.

29 Bartram, *Travels,* 165.

30 Andersen, *Paynes Prairie,* 53–54; "Red Wolf," Florida Fish and Wildlife Conservation Commission website, https://myfwc.com/wildlifehabitats/profiles/mammals/land/red-wolf/.

31 Bartram, "The Real Worlds," 167; Herbert, "We Have Always Been Cow People," 53.

32 "The Selection of Tallahassee as the Capital," *Florida Historical Society* 1, no. 2 (July 1908): 28–29, http://www.jstor.com/stable/30138214.

33 Slaughter, *The Natures,* xv–xvi, 174, 223.

34 Slaughter, *The Natures,* xv–xvi; Samuel Taylor Coleridge, "Kubla Khan," Poets.org website, https://poets.org/poem/kubla-khan.

35 Charlotte M. Porter, "Bartram's Legacy: Nature Advocacy," in *Fields of Vision: Essays on the Travels of William Bartram,* ed. Kathryn E. Holland Braund and Porter (Tuscaloosa: University of Alabama Press, 2020), 221.

36 Charlotte M. Porter, "An Eighteenth-Century Florida Child: William Bartram," in

Paradise Lost? The Environmental History of Florida, ed. Jack E. Davis and Raymond Arsenault (Gainesville: University Press of Florida, 2005), 58, 60.

37 Slaughter, *The Natures,* xvii, 230, 247, 249; Sanders, *Guide,* 5–6.

38 Sanders, *Guide,* xii, 5.

39 Dorinda G. Dallmeyer, preface to *Bartram's Living Legacy: The Travels and the Nature of the South,* ed. Dallmeyer (Macon, GA: Mercer University Press, 2010), x.

40 Mary Ann Wilcox Anderson, interview by the author, Mount Royal, Florida, June 25, 2019.

41 Keith H. Ashley, interview by the author, Mount Royal, Florida, June 25, 2019.

42 Ashley, interview.

43 Clay Henderson, interview by the author, March 12, 2019, at DeLand, Florida.

44 Henderson, interview.

45 Henderson, interview.

46 Henderson, interview.

47 Lars Andersen, interview by the author, July 18, 2019, Paynes Prairie State Preserve.

48 Andersen, interview.

49 Eric Breitenbach, WebEx interview by the author, April 21, 2021.

50 Breitenbach, interview.

51 *Cultivating the Wild: William Bartram's Travels,* PBS website, https://www.pbs.org/video/cultivating-the-wild-arsdvf/.

Chapter 4. John James Audubon

1 Kathryn Hall Proby, *Audubon in Florida* (Coral Gables, FL: University of Miami Press, 1974), 31. Proby's book contains numerous letters and essays written by Audubon.

2 Gregory Nobles, *John James Audubon: The Nature of the American Woodsman* (Philadelphia: University of Pennsylvania Press, 2017), 4.

3 William Souder, *Under a Wild Sky: John James Audubon and the Making of the Birds of America* (New York: North Point, 2004), 18–21, 78.

4 Proby, *Audubon in Florida,* 14.

5 Proby, *Audubon in Florida,* 15.

6 Proby, *Audubon in Florida,* 18–19.

7 Proby, *Audubon in Florida,* 20.

8 Proby, *Audubon in Florida,* 20.

9 Souder, *Under a Wild Sky,* 272.

10 Proby, *Audubon in Florida,* 21–22.

11 Souder, *Under a Wild Sky,* 272–73; "Manager's Message," Bulow Plantation Ruins Historic State Park website, https://www.floridastateparks.org/learn/managers-message-62; "History of Bulowville," Bulow Plantation Ruins Historic State Park website, at https://www.floridastateparks.org/index.php/learn/history-bulowville. There are many variations in the spelling of Bulow's plantation.

12 Proby, *Audubon in Florida,* 22–23.

13 Proby, *Audubon in Florida,* 23–25.

14 Proby, *Audubon in Florida,* 309–12.

15 Proby, *Audubon in Florida,* 312–13.

16 Proby, *Audubon in Florida,* 315.

17 Proby, *Audubon in Florida,* 316.

18 Souder, *Under a Wild Sky,* 276.

19 Proby, *Audubon in Florida,* 327–28.

20 Proby, *Audubon in Florida,* 39–41, 328–30.

21 Proby, *Audubon in Florida,* 332.

22 Proby, *Audubon in Florida,* 241, 334.

23 Proby, *Audubon in Florida,* 334–35.

24 Proby, *Audubon in Florida,* 335–36.

25 Jerry Wilkinson, "History of Indian Key," http://www.keyshistory.org/indiankey.html.

26 Jerry Wilkinson, "History of Key West," http://www.keyshistory.org/keywest.html; Jerry Wilkinson, "History of Wrecking," http://www.keyshistory.org/wrecking.html.

27 Proby, *Audubon in Florida,* 41–43.

28 Proby, *Audubon in Florida,* 45–47.

29 Zac Zacharias, interview by the author, Daytona Beach, Florida, December 19, 2019.

30 Zacharias, interview.

31 "A Plantation in Early Florida: Mala Compra," Flagler County Historical Society website, https://flaglercountyhistoricalsociety.com/a-plantation-in-early-florida/.

32 Neil Rasnick, interview by the author, Washington Oaks Gardens State Park, July 1, 2020.

33 Oscar Brock, "Florida's Oldest Canoes Recovered in West Volusia," West Volusia Historical Society website, https://www.delandhouse.com/article_fl_oldest_canoes; "Many Layers of History at De Leon Springs," De Leon Springs State Park website, https://www.floridastateparks.org/learn/many-layers-history-de-leon-springs; "Springs at De Leon," De Leon Springs State Park website, https://www.floridastateparks.org/learn/springs-de-leon.

34 Rick Kilby, *Finding the Fountain of Youth: Ponce de León and Florida's Magical Waters* (Gainesville: University Press of Florida, 2013), 17, 72, 75.

35 Proby, *Audubon in Florida,* 66–67.

36 Carol MacDonald, interview by the author, Lake Woodruff National Wildlife Refuge, September 1, 2020.

37 Jerry Lorenz, interview by the author, Tavernier, Florida, February 17, 2020.

38 Proby, *Audubon in Florida,* 256–61; Lorenz, interview.

39 Lorenz, interview; Rene Ebersole, "Color Guard," *Audubon* 115, no. 3 (May–June 2013): 46.

40 Lorenz, interview.

41 Lorenz, interview; Proby, *Audubon in Florida,* 332.

42 "4 Priceless Portfolios Recovered," *Patterson (NJ) News,* June 13, 1977, Newspapers.com; Rebecca Rego Barry, "A Rare Copy of 'Birds of America' Heads to Auction to Benefit Conservation," Audubon.org website, https://www.audubon.org/news/a-rare-copy-audubons-birds-america-heads-auction-benefit-conservation.

43 Charles Lee, "My First Audubon Trip Hasn't Ended Yet . . . ," in *The Wilder Heart of Florida: More Writers Inspired by Florida Nature,* ed. Jack E. Davis and Leslie K. Poole (Gainesville: University of Florida Press, 2021), 34, 37.

44 Proby, *Audubon in Florida,* 281–82.

Chapter 5. John Muir

1 James B. Hunt, *Restless Fires: Young John Muir's Thousand-Mile Walk to the Gulf in 1867–68* (Macon, GA: Mercer University Press, 2012), 49.

2 "Kindred and Related Spirits: The Letters of John Muir and Jeanne C. Carr," Sierra Club website, http://vault.sierraclub.org/john_muir_exhibit/bibliographic _resources/press_releases/kindred_related_spirits.as.

3 Hunt, *Restless Fires,* 52.

4 Donald Worster, *A Passion for Nature: The Life of John Muir* (Oxford: Oxford University Press, 2008), 115.

5 John Muir, *A Thousand-Mile Walk to the Gulf* (Boston: Houghton Mifflin, 1998), 17–18; Worster, *A Passion for Nature,* 120–21; William Frederic Bade, "Introduction," Sierra Club website, https://vault.sierraclub.org/john_muir_exhibit/writings/ a_thousand_mile_walk_to_the_gulf/introduction.aspx.

6 Muir, *Thousand-Mile Walk,* 18.

7 Muir, *Thousand-Mile Walk,* 16, 19.

8 Muir, *Thousand-Mile Walk,* 22–29.

9 Muir, *Thousand-Mile Walk,* 64–71.

10 Worster, *Passion for Nature,* 132.

11 Muir, *Thousand-Mile Walk,* 78–82, 85.

12 Muir, *Thousand-Mile Walk,* 87–88.

13 Muir, *Thousand-Mile Walk,* 89.

14 Hunt, *Restless Fires,* 125.

15 Muir, *Thousand-Mile Walk,* 89–90.

16 Gregg Turner, *A Short History of Florida Railroads* (Charleston, SC: Arcadia, 2003), 31, 33–34.

17 Turner, *Short History of Florida Railroads,* 34–35, 40–41.

18 Muir, *Thousand-Mile Walk,* 93.

19 Muir, *Thousand-Mile Walk,* 95–96, 98–99.

20 Hunt, *Restless Fires,* 127.

21 Muir, *Thousand-Mile Walk,* 107, 111 121–22.

22 Muir, *Thousand-Mile Walk,* 123–25.

23 Kevin McCarthy, *Cedar Key Florida: A History* (Charleston, SC: History Press, 2007), 18, 20, 27.

24 Muir, *Thousand-Mile Walk,* 125–29.

25 Muir, *Thousand-Mile Walk,* 129–30.

26 Muir, *Thousand-Mile Walk,* 140.

27 Muir, *Thousand-Mile Walk,* 144–45, 169–70.

28 Robert Bendick, interview by author, Winter Park, Florida, September 21, 2019.

29 Bendick, interview.

30 John Muir to his sisters Sarah and Annie, November 28, 1898, https://oac.cdlib
.org/ark:/13030/kt196nd6tm/?order=5&brand=calisphere; Kittie Hodgson to John
Muir, May 10, 1907, https://oac.cdlib.org/ark:/13030/kt538nf079/?order=3&brand
=oac4.

31 Bruce Means, telephone interview by the author, November 18, 2019.

32 D. Bruce Means, "Walking Out Loud," unpublished manuscript in possession of
author, 9, 11, 95 (D. Bruce Means © 7/28/14, 10/8/2015, 5/26/17).

33 Means, interview; Means, "Walking Out Loud," 133, 137.

34 Means, interview.

35 Merald Clark, interview by the author, October 14, 2019, Gainesville, FL.

36 Clark, interview.

37 Paul Thibault, telephone interview by author, October 25, 2019.

38 Thibault, interview.

Chapter 6. Harriet Beecher Stowe

1 Charles Edward Stowe, *The Life of Harriet Beecher Stowe* (Boston: Houghton, Mifflin, 1889), 400–401.

2 Joan D. Hedrick, *Harriet Beecher Stowe: A Life* (New York: Oxford University Press, 1994), 329–30.

3 Charles Edward Stowe, *Life of Harriet Beecher Stowe,* 401–2; Hedrick, *Harriet Beecher Stowe,* 306–7.

4 Mary Graff, *Mandarin on the St. Johns* (Gainesville, FL: Regent, 1978), 1, 4–5, 14.

5 Charles Edward Stowe, *Life of Harriet Beecher Stowe,* 402.

6 Charles Edward Stowe, *Life of Harriet Beecher Stowe,* 403.

7 Charles Edward Stowe, *Life of Harriet Beecher Stowe,* 403–4.

8 Silvia Sunshine, *Petals Plucked from Sunny Climes,* facsimile of 1880 edition (Gainesville: University Presses of Florida, 1976), 39.

9 Hedrick, *Harriet Beecher Stowe,* 340–41; Charles Edward Stowe, 404–5, 413.

10 Charles Edward Stowe, *Life of Harriet Beecher Stowe,* 416, 468–69.

11 Hedrick, *Harriet Beecher Stowe,* 370–71.

12 John T. Foster Jr. and Sarah Whitmer Foster, *Beechers, Stowes, and Yankee Strangers: The Transformation of Florida* (Gainesville: University Press of Florida, 1999), 9, 17.

13 Edward A. Mueller, *Ocklawaha River Steamboats* (Jacksonville, FL: Mendelson Printing, 1983), 7–8.

14 Harriet Beecher Stowe, *Palmetto Leaves,* facsimile of 1873 edition (Gainesville: University Press of Florida, 1999), 247, 249–50, 260.

15 Stowe, *Palmetto Leaves,* 259–61.

16 Harriet Beecher Stowe, "Up the Okalawaha: A Sail into Fairy-Land," in *The Wilder Heart of Florida: More Writers Inspired by Florida Nature,* ed. Jack E. Davis and Leslie K. Poole (Gainesville: University of Florida Press, 2021), 95.

17 Bob Bass, *When Steamboats Reigned in Florida* (Gainesville: University Press of Florida, 2008), 80, 82.

18 Bass, *When Steamboats Reigned,* 82, 85.

19 Bass, *When Steamboats Reigned,* 92.

20 Stowe, "Up the Okalawaha," 95.
21 Stowe, "Up the Okalawaha," 96–96.
22 Stowe, "Up the Okalawaha," 98.
23 Stowe, "Up the Okalawaha," 100.
24 Stowe, "Up the Okalawaha," 101.
25 Sidney Lanier, *Florida: Its Scenery, Climate, and History,* Bicentennial Floridiana Facsimile Series (Gainesville: University of Florida Press, 1973), 18, 20.
26 Kirk Munroe, "A Trip over 'Crooked Water,'" *Harper's Weekly* 27, no. 1372 (April 7, 1883): 1, 219.
27 Sunshine, *Petals Plucked from Sunny Climes,* 69–70.
28 Steven Noll and David Tegeder, *Ditch of Dreams: The Cross Florida Barge Canal and the Struggle for Florida's Future* (Gainesville: University Press of Florida, 2009), 266.
29 Karen Chadwick, interview by author on Ocklawaha River, January 11, 2019.
30 Charles Edward Stowe, *Life of Harriet Beecher Stowe,* 417.
31 Graff, *Mandarin on the St. Johns,* 94–98.
32 Rev. Joe Gibbes, interview by the author, Mandarin, Florida, January 10, 2019.
33 Anne Morrow, interview by the author, Mandarin, Florida, January 10, 2019.
34 Sandy Arpen, interview by the author, Mandarin, Florida, January 10, 2019.

Chapter 7. Middle/West Florida Travelers

1 Michael Gannon, *Florida: A Short History, Revised Edition* (Gainesville: University Press of Florida, 2003), 17–18.
2 John Mack Faragher, *Daniel Boone: The Life and Legend of an American Pioneer* (New York: Henry Holt, 1992), 64.
3 Faragher, *Daniel Boone,* 64–65.
4 Faragher, *Daniel Boone,* 65.
5 William Bartram, *Travels of William Bartram,* ed. Mark Van Doren (New York: Dover, 1955), 330–31.
6 Bartram, *Travels,* 331.
7 Bartram, *Travels,* 332.
8 Bartram, *Travels,* 332.
9 Bartram, *Travels,* 333.
10 Charlton W. Tebeau, *A History of Florida* (Coral Gables, FL: University of Miami Press, 1971), 103.
11 Tebeau, *History of Florida,* 103–5.
12 Gannon, *Florida: A Short History, Revised Edition,* 27.
13 Tebeau, *History of Florida,* 114.
14 David Crockett, *The Autobiography of David Crockett,* Modern Student's Library (New York: Charles Scribner's Sons, 1923), 69–70.
15 Tebeau, *History of Florida,* 117.
16 Tebeau, *History of Florida,* 119.
17 James Parton, *The Life of Andrew Jackson* (Boston: Ticknor and Fields, 1866), 597, available at https://books.google.com.
18 Parton, *Life of Andrew Jackson,* 598.

19 Parton, *Life of Andrew Jackson,* 604.

20 Parton, *Life of Andrew Jackson,* 605.

21 Parton, *Life of Andrew Jackson,* 606.

22 Parton, *Life of Andrew Jackson,* 612.

23 Herbert J. Domherty Jr., "The Governorship of Andrew Jackson," *Florida Historical Quarterly* 33, no. 1 (July 1953): 22–24.

24 "About Us," Perfect Plain Brewing Company website, https://www.perfectplain .com/about/.

25 Gannon, *Florida: A Short History, Revised Edition,* 28–29.

26 John Lee Williams, "The Selection of Tallahassee as the Capital," *Florida Historical Society* 1, no. 2 (July 1908): 26–27, http://www.jstor.com/stable/30138214.

27 Williams, "The Selection of Tallahassee as the Capital," 28–33.

28 Williams, "The Selection of Tallahassee as the Capital," 34–35.

29 Williams, "The Selection of Tallahassee as the Capital," 38–39.

30 Williams, "The Selection of Tallahassee as the Capital," 39.

31 Williams, "The Selection of Tallahassee as the Capital," 42–44.

32 Williams, "The Selection of Tallahassee as the Capital," 19–21.

33 Williams, "The Selection of Tallahassee as the Capital," 22–23.

34 Gannon, *Florida: A Short History, Revised Edition,* 28–30.

35 Jerrell H. Shofner, introduction to Sidney Lanier's *Florida: Its Scenery, Climate, and History* (Gainesville: University of Florida Press, 1976), xiii.

36 Sidney Lanier, Florida: *Its Scenery, Climate, and History* (Gainesville: University of Florida Press, 1976), 104–5.

37 Lanier, *Florida: Its Scenery, Climate, and History,* 107–8.

38 Lanier, *Florida: Its Scenery, Climate, and History,* 108.

39 Lanier, *Florida: Its Scenery, Climate, and History,* 111.

40 Lanier, *Florida: Its Scenery, Climate, and History,* 111–12.

41 Lanier, *Florida: Its Scenery, Climate, and History,* 113–15.

42 Lanier, *Florida: Its Scenery, Climate, and History,* 115.

43 Lanier, *Florida: Its Scenery, Climate, and History,* 117, 149.

44 George Catlin, *Letters and Notes on the Manners, Customs, and Condition of the North American Indians,* vol. 2 (Philadelphia: Willis P. Hazard, 1857), 448.

45 Catlin, *Letters and Notes,* 449.

46 Catlin, *Letters and Notes,* 449–50.

47 Catlin, *Letters and Notes,* 450.

48 Catlin, *Letters and Notes,* 451.

49 John James Audubon, *Audubon on Louisiana: Selected Writings of John James Audubon,* ed. Ben Forkner (Baton Rouge: Louisiana State University Press, 2018), 288.

50 Audubon, *Audubon on Louisiana,* 286, 288–89.

51 Caroline Fraser, *Prairie Fires: The American Dreams of Laura Ingalls Wilder* (New York: Metropolitan, 2017), 160.

52 W. D. Chipley, *Facts about Florida* (Louisville, KY: Courier-Journal Press, 188?), 3, 18, 43, State Library and Archives of Florida, https://archive.org/details/ factsaboutflorid00chip/page/n13/mode/2up; Fraser, *Prairie Fires,* 161.

53 Fraser, *Prairie Fires,* 158–61.

54 Rose Wilder Lane, "Innocence," *Harper's Magazine* 144 (April 1922): 578–79.

55 Lane, "Innocence," 583–84.

56 Fraser, *Prairie Fires,* 162–63.

57 Alene M. Warnock, *Laura Ingalls Wilder: The Westville Florida Years* (Mansfield, MO: The Laura Ingalls Wilder Home Association, 1979), 3–4, 24.

58 John Bass, telephone interview by the author, September 11, 2020.

59 Bass, interview.

Chapter 8. Ingraham Everglades Expedition

1 Marjory Stoneman Douglas, *The Everglades: River of Grass* (1947; repr., Sarasota, FL: Pineapple, 1988), 288.

2 Jacob Rhett Motte, *Journey into Wilderness: An Army Surgeon's Account of Life in Camp and Field during the Creek and Seminole Wars 1836–1838* (Gainesville: University of Florida Press, 1963), 144, 232.

3 Buffalo Tiger and Harry A. Kersey Jr., *Buffalo Tiger: A Life in the Everglades* (Lincoln: University of Nebraska Press, 2002), 35.

4 Motte, *Journey into Wilderness,* 143.

5 John T. Sprague, *The Origin, Progress, and Conclusion of the Florida War,* facsimile of 1848 edition (Gainesville: University of Florida Press, 1964), 389, https://ufdc.ufl .edu/UF00026717/00001/4j.

6 Jack E. Davis, *An Everglades Providence: Marjory Stoneman Douglas and the American Environmental Century* (Athens: University of Georgia Press, 2009), 62–63.

7 "North to South through the Everglades in 1883, Vol. II," ed. Mary K. Wintringham, *Tequesta* 24 (1964): 59–60.

8 "North to South through the Everglades," 33–34.

9 "North to South through the Everglades," 64–65.

10 Alonzo Church, "A Dash through the Everglades: being a full and accurate account of the strange things seen by a party crossing that place with a very interesting account of their adventures and a record of the great hominy eating done on that journey, all by an observer," March 12, 1892, 1, https://ufdc.ufl.edu/AA00007670/ 00001.

11 James E. Ingraham, "James Ingraham Diary of an Exploration Trip through the Everglades," 4–5, https://ufdc.ufl.edu/UF00095319/00001.

12 Ingraham, "James Ingraham Diary," 7, 9.

13 Walter R. Moses, "Record of Everglades Exploring Expedition, Written as a Journal or Travel Log, Dating from Mar. 14, 1892 to Apr. 16, 1892. Includes List of Expedition Members, Daily Temperatures, and Detailed Accounts of the Entire Trip; Document Property of Sydney Chase and Transcribed by Secretary Wallace R. Moses," 22, https://ufdc.ufl.edu/AA00007669/00001.

14 Church, "A Dash through the Everglades," 9–10.

15 Ingraham, "James Ingraham Diary," 9, 11.

16 Moses, "Record of Everglades Exploring Expedition," 17, 26–27.

17 Church, "A Dash through the Everglades," 15.

18 Church, "A Dash through the Everglades," 15–16.

19 Church, "A Dash through the Everglades," 16.

20 Douglas, *The Everglades,* 292.

21 Douglas, *The Everglades,* 292–93; Hugh L. Willoughby, *Across the Everglades: A Canoe Journey of Exploration by Hugh L. Willoughby,* 2nd paperbound ed. (Port Salerno, FL: Florida Classics Library, 2009), 64.

22 Willoughby, *Across the Everglades,* 115.

23 Willoughby, *Across the Everglades,* 116, 131.

24 Willoughby, *Across the Everglades,* 13.

25 Douglas, *The Everglades,* 286.

26 Douglas, *The Everglades,* 312–13.

27 "A Changing Florida," Seminole Tribe of Florida website, https://www.semtribe .com/stof/history/a-changing-florida.

28 Michael Grunwald, *The Swamp: The Everglades, Florida, and the Politics of Paradise* (New York: Simon & Schuster, 2006), 196.

29 John Kunkel Small, *From Eden to Sahara: Florida's Tragedy* (Sanford, FL: Seminole Soil and Water Conservation District, 2004), 62.

30 Marjory Stoneman Douglas, *Voice of the River,* with John Rothchild (Sarasota, FL: Pineapple, 1987), 135–36, 190–91.

31 Grunwald, *The Swamp,* 221.

32 Patsy West, *The Enduring Seminoles: From Alligator Wrestling to Ecotourism* (Gainesville: University Press of Florida, 1998), 5.

33 Davis, *An Everglades Providence,* 590.

34 Grunwald, *The Swamp,* 302; Davis, *An Everglades Providence,* 596–97.

35 Grunwald, *The Swamp,* 3–4.

36 Tom Van Lent, Zoom interview by the author, May 28, 2020.

37 Van Lent, interview.

38 Van Lent, interview.

39 Paul Gray, telephone interview by the author, July 7, 2020.

40 Gray, interview.

41 Rae Ann Wessel, interview by the author, Fort Myers, Florida, July 24, 2020.

42 Wessel, interview.

43 Wessel, interview.

44 Mike Owen, telephone interview by the author, August 13, 2020.

45 Owen, interview.

Chapter 9. Stephen Crane

1 Willa Cather, "When I Knew Stephen Crane," http://www.online-literature.com/ willa-cather/4311/.

2 Paul Sorrentino, *Stephen Crane: A Life of Fire* (Cambridge, MA: Belknap Press of Harvard University Press, 2014), 165–66.

3 Sorrentino, *Stephen Crane,* 213.

4 Lillian Gilkes, *Cora Crane: A Biography of Mrs. Stephen Crane* (Bloomington: Indiana University Press, 1960), 22–25; Sorrentino, *Stephen Crane,* 217–18.

5 T. Frederick Davis, *History of Jacksonville, Florida and Vicinity, 1513–1924,* facsimile of 1925 edition (Gainesville: University of Florida Press, 1964), xv–xvi, 202–3.

6 Sorrentino, *Stephen Crane,* 217–19; Gilkes, *Cora Crane,* 25; Elizabeth Friedmann, email to author, June 23, 2022.

7 Sorrentino, *Stephen Crane,* 207.

8 Kimberly Lane Eslinger. "'. . . and all the men knew the colors of the sea . . .': Historical and Archeological Investigation of the SS *Commodore*'s Remains, Ponce Inlet, Florida" (master's thesis, East Carolina University, August 2005), 34.

9 Sorrentino, *Stephen Crane,* 211.

10 Eslinger, ". . . and all the men knew," 38.

11 Stephen Crane, "Filibustering: The Center of the Industry Found in Jacksonville, Fla," April 28, 1897, reprinted in *Prairie Schooner* 43, no. 3 (Fall 1969): 290.

12 Napoleon Bonaparte Broward, "Napoleon Bonaparte Broward: Candidate for Governor," 8, https://journals.flvc.org.

13 R. W. Stallman, *Stephen Crane: A Biography* (New York: George Braziller, 1968), 244.

14 Sandra Henderson Thurlow, "Lonely Vigils: Houses of Refuge on Florida's East Coast, 1876–1915," *Florida Historical Quarterly* 76, no. 2 (Fall 1997): 152, 159–61, 169–70; information display at Ponce de Leon Inlet Lighthouse Museum, Ponce Inlet, Florida.

15 Kevin M. McCarthy, *Florida Lighthouses* (Gainesville: University of Florida Press, 1990), 2, 25–27; Jill Martin, "Ponce Inlet Lighthouse: Tallest in Florida," https://www.visitflorida.com/travel-ideas/articles/arts-history-tallest-light-house-in-florida-ponce-inlet-lighthouse/; information display at Ponce de Leon Inlet Lighthouse Museum, Ponce Inlet, Florida.

16 Stephen Crane, "There was a man who lived a life of fire," Famous Poems and Poems website, http://famouspoetsandpoems.com/poets/stephen_crane/poems/13411.

17 Eslinger, ". . . and all the men knew," 60.

18 Stephen Crane, "Stephen Crane's Own Story," *New York Post,* January 7, 1897, Ponce Inlet Lighthouse website, https://www.ponceinlet.org/z/-vf.0.0.0.165.635055CA53C8E6A60879CEB33FA56617818CFB6797FD70EE16A7B1F4970614E5.

19 Crane, "Stephen Crane's Own Story."

20 Crane, "Stephen Crane's Own Story."

21 Crane, "Stephen Crane's Own Story"; Sorrentino, *Stephen Crane,* 222.

22 Crane, "Stephen Crane's Own Story."

23 Stephen Crane, "The Open Boat," https://americanenglish.state.gov/files/ae/resource_files/the-open-boat.pdf.

24 Crane, "The Open Boat."

25 Crane, "The Open Boat."

26 Crane, "The Open Boat"; Stallman, *Stephen Crane: A Biography,* 251.

27 Crane, "The Open Boat."

28 Crane, "The Open Boat."

29 Crane, "The Open Boat."

30 Gilkes, *Cora Crane,* 58–61; Sorrentino, *Stephen Crane,* 223–25; Stallman, *Stephen*

Crane: A Biography, 254; Cora Taylor to Stephen Crane, telegram, January 3, 1897, in Stephen Crane, *Letters,* ed. R. W. Stallman and Lillian Gilkes (New York: New York University Press, 1960), 137n183.

31 Sorrentino, *Stephen Crane,* 224–25.

32 Stallman, *Stephen Crane: A Biography,* 275, 287–90; Gilkes, *Cora Crane,* 87–88.

33 Stallman, *Stephen Crane: A Biography,* 350–51; Sorrentino, *Stephen Crane,* 367–68; Gilkes, *Cora Crane,* 111–12.

34 William L Alden, "London Literary Letter," *New York Times,* July 7, 1900, 21, Newspapers.com.

35 Gilkes, *Cora Crane,* 313–15, 331–40, 352–57; Friedmann, email.

36 Elizabeth Friedmann, interview by the author, Ponce Inlet, Florida, August 6, 2018.

37 Friedmann, interview.

38 Friedmann, interview.

39 Friedmann, interview; Friedmann, email.

40 Crane, "The Open Boat."

Chapter 10. Zora Neale Hurston

1 Zora Neale Hurston, *Mules and Men* (New York: HarperCollins Amistad, 1990), 1.

2 Hurston, *Mules and Men,* 2.

3 Valerie Boyd, *Wrapped in Rainbows: The Life of Zora Neale Hurston* (New York: Scribner, 2003), 17, 19, 21–22.

4 Zora Neale Hurston, *Dust Tracks on a Road: An Autobiography,* 2nd ed. (Urbana: University of Illinois Press, 1984), 18.

5 Hurston, *Dust Tracks,* 61–64.

6 Hurston, *Dust Tracks,* 20–21, 86–89.

7 Hurston, *Dust Tracks,* 89, 100–105. For a complete look at Hurston's life, see Boyd, *Wrapped in Rainbows.*

8 Hurston, *Dust Tracks,* 168–69.

9 Hurston, *Dust Tracks,* 169–71; Boyd, *Wrapped in Rainbows,* 114–15, 142–44; Hurston, *Mules and Men,* 4.

10 Hurston, *Mules and Men,* 8.

11 Hurston, *Mules and Men,* 8.

12 Hurston, *Mules and Men,* 13–17.

13 Hurston, *Mules and Men,* 19–20.

14 Hurston, *Mules and Men,* 20–21.

15 Hurston, *Mules and Men,* 31–34, 55–56.

16 Hurston, *Mules and Men,* 56.

17 Hurston, *Mules and Men,* 2–3.

18 Hurston, *Mules and Men,* 57.

19 Boyd, *Wrapped in Rainbows,* 146–47, 154–59, 162.

20 Hurston, *Dust Tracks,* 36, 177.

21 Hurston, *Mules and Men,* 59–61, 63–64.

22 Tiffany Ruby Patterson, *Zora Neale Hurston: A History of Southern Life* (Philadelphia: Temple University Press, 2005), 130.

23 Patterson, *Zora Neale Hurston,* 128, 132.

24 Hurston, *Mules and Men,* 61, 65.

25 Hurston, *Mules and Men,* 65.

26 Hurston, *Mules and Men,* 65–66.

27 Hurston, *Mules and Men,* 66–67.

28 Hurston, *Dust Tracks,* 186–88.

29 Hurston, *Dust Tracks,* 188–89.

30 Hurston, *Mules and Men,* 175, 178–79.

31 Hurston, *Mules and Men,* 179.

32 Boyd, *Wrapped in Rainbows,* 373–74, 377, 438.

33 Boyd, *Wrapped in Rainbows,* 314.

34 Boyd, *Wrapped in Rainbows,* 313.

35 Boyd, *Wrapped in Rainbows,* 314.

36 Stetson Kennedy, "Florida Folklife and the WPA, An Introduction," 12, from Zora Neale Hurston and the WPA in Florida: Documents and Audio, Florida Memory State Library and Archives of Florida, https://www.floridamemory.com/learn/class room/learning-units/zora-neale-hurston/documents/stetsonkennedy/.

37 Zora Neale Hurston, *Go Gator and Muddy the Water: Writings by Zora Neale Hurston from the Federal Writers' Project,* ed. Pamela Bordelon (New York: Norton, 1999), 69.

38 Kennedy, "Florida Folklife and the WPA," 13.

39 Boyd, *Wrapped in Rainbows,* 322–23.

40 Kennedy, "Florida Folklife and the WPA," 17.

41 "Taylor County & Perry, Florida History," https://sites.google.com/site/taylorcounty history/home/9b-turpentine-stills-in-taylor-county/aycock-lindsey.

42 Josh Goodman, email to the author, January 4, 2021.

43 Boyd, *Wrapped in Rainbows,* 323.

44 Pamela Bordelon, "Biographical Essay," in *Go Gator and Muddy the Water: Writings by Zora Neale Hurston from the Federal Writers' Project* (New York: Norton, 1999), 39.

45 Zora Neale Hurston, "Turpentine Camp—Cross City," 15–16, from Zora Neale Hurston and the WPA in Florida: Documents and Audio, Florida Memory State Library and Archives of Florida, https://www.floridamemory.com/learn/classroom/ learning-units/zora-neale-hurston/documents/essay/.

46 Hurston, "Turpentine Camp," 16–17.

47 Hurston, "Turpentine Camp," 17.

48 Patterson, *Zora Neale Hurston,* 57–58.

49 Robert N. Lauriault, "From Can't to Can't: The North Florida Turpentine Camp 1900–1950," *Florida Historical Quarterly* 67, no. 3 (January 1989): 316.

50 Jerrell H. Shofner, "Postscript to the Martin Tabert Case: Peonage as Usual in the Florid Turpentine Camps," *Florida Historical Quarterly* 60, no. 2 (October 1981): 162.

51 Shofner, "Postscript to the Martin Tabert Case," 167.

52 Kennedy, "Florida Folklife and the WPA," 19.

53 Boyd, *Wrapped in Rainbows,* 323.

54 Henry Louis Gates, "Afterword. Zora Neale Hurston: 'A Negro Way of Saying,'" in *Zora Neale Hurston, Mules and Men* (New York: HarperCollins Amistad, 1990), 287–88, 296.

55 "The History of Putnam Lodge," Putnam Lodge website accessed June 27, 2022, at http://www.putnamlodge.com/history.php.

56 N. Y. Nathiri, Webex interview by the author, October 1, 2020.

57 N. Y. Nathiri, "Discovery," in *Zora! Zora Neale Hurston: A Woman and Her Community,* ed. Nathiri (Orlando: The Orlando Sentinel, Sentinel Communications Company, 1991), 7.

58 Nathiri, "Discovery," 7.

59 Wanda Randolph, interview by the author, Eatonville, Florida, January 11, 2021.

60 Randolph, interview.

61 Nathiri, interview.

62 Boyd, *Wrapped in Rainbows,* 438.

Chapter 11. Marjorie Kinnan Rawlings

1 Marjorie Kinnan Rawlings, *Cross Creek* (Jacksonville, FL: South Moon, 1992), 342.

2 Rawlings, *Cross Creek,* 342.

3 Rawlings, *Cross Creek,* 343.

4 Rawlings, *Cross Creek,* 344.

5 Marjorie Kinnan Rawlings to Maxwell E. Perkins, March 3, 1933, in *Max & Marjorie: The Correspondence between Maxwell E. Perkins and Marjorie Kinnan Rawlings,* ed. Rodger L. Tarr (Gainesville: University Press of Florida, 1999), 95.

6 Maxwell E. Perkins to Marjorie Kinnan Rawlings, March 6, 1933, in *Max & Marjorie,* 96.

7 Rawlings, *Cross Creek,* 345.

8 Rawlings, *Cross Creek,* 345–47.

9 Rawlings, *Cross Creek,* 347.

10 Rawlings, *Cross Creek,* 347.

11 Dessie Smith Prescott, interview by the author, near Crystal River, Florida, September 23, 2001.

12 Rawlings, *Cross Creek,* 343, 345, 348.

13 Rawlings, *Cross Creek,* 350.

14 Rawlings, *Cross Creek,* 350.

15 Rawlings, *Cross Creek,* 351; Prescott, interview.

16 Rawlings, *Cross Creek,* 352–54.

17 Rawlings, *Cross Creek,* 354–56.

18 Rawlings, *Cross Creek,* 357–58.

19 Marjorie Kinnan Rawlings to Maxwell E. Perkins, March 18, 1933, in *Max & Marjorie,* 99–101; Marjorie Kinnan Rawlings to Maxwell E. Perkins, November 11, 1933, in *Max & Marjorie,* 130–31.

20 Prescott, interview.

21 Rawlings, *Cross Creek,* 344.

22 Anne E. Rowe, *The Idea of Florida in the American Literary Imagination* (Gainesville: University Press of Florida, 1992), 112.

23 Carl Hiaasen, *Tourist Season* (New York: G. P. Putnam's Sons, 1986), 24; Rowe, *The Idea of Florida,* 138.

24 "Special Report: What Is Your Vision for Florida's Future?," 17, 1000 Friends of Florida website, https://1000friendsofflorida.org/florida2070/wp-content/uploads/2017/08/FOF-1080-Newsletter-Spring-2017-v12-web.pdf.

25 Anna Hamilton, email to author, November 15, 2019.

26 Rawlings, *Cross Creek,* 3.

27 Steven G. Noll, email to the author, May 16, 2020.

28 Heather McPherson, email to the author, September 23, 2019.

29 Rawlings, *Cross Creek,* 368.

Index

Leslie Kemp Poole, a fourth-generation Floridian, is associate professor of environmental studies at Rollins College. She is the author of *Saving Florida: Women's Fight for the Environment in the Twentieth Century* and coeditor of *The Wilder Heart of Florida: More Writers Inspired by Florida Nature.*